ANCIENT SCRIPTS &
MODERN EXPERIENCE ON
THE ENGLISH STAGE
1500–1700

ANCIENT SCRIPTS & MODERN EXPERIENCE ON THE ENGLISH STAGE 1500–1700

by Bruce R. Smith

PRINCETON

Princeton University Press

MCM·LXXXVIII

For my parents,
Francis Ray Smith & Birdie Mae Reed Smith

CONTENTS

LIST OF ILLUSTRATIONS

(ix)

ACKNOWLEDGMENTS

THOUGH ONLY one person's name appears on the title page, this book, like the theatrical productions it studies, owes its existence to the cooperation of a great many people. Alan Dessen was full of encouragement and good advice when I submitted the firstlings of the project, an essay on court productions of Plautus and Terence, to *Renaissance Drama* more than a decade ago. The suggestion that I develop my research on Roman comedy into a full-scale study of classical scripts onstage came from David Bevington in a seminar sponsored by the Folger Institute of Renaissance and Eighteenth-Century Studies. His sharp eye for details and sure sense of direction were invaluable in the early and middle stages of my research and writing. Further help in finding a sense of the whole amid so many separate facts came from the careful readings that Maurice Charney and Samuel Schoenbaum gave the manuscript toward the end of the project. Certain parts of the book benefited also from the attentions of Gordon Davis and Elias Mengel.

For advice on my translations from Greek and Latin I am grateful to my colleagues in classics at Georgetown, Edward Bodnar, s.j., Joseph O'Connor, and Victoria Pedrick. Thérèse-Anne Druart of the Georgetown Philosophy Department helped me with translation from sixteenth-century Dutch. Another Georgetown colleague, O. B. Hardison, Jr., put me in contact with John R. Elliott, Jr., and Alan H. Nelson, editors of the Oxford and Cambridge volumes in the *Records of Early English Drama* series, each of whom generously shared his research with me in advance of its publication. Rare books and manuscripts in the keeping of the British Library, the Bodleian Library, the library of All Souls College Oxford, Trinity College Library Cambridge, the Folger Library, the special collections department of the Georgetown University Library, and the Rare Books Division of the Library of Congress were made all the more pleasurable to take in hand by the courtesy and efficiency of the staffs of those institutions.

Robert Brown, Literature Editor of Princeton University Press, has been a gentle guide through the technical intricacies of publishing. For permission to include material that was published in a somewhat different form in *Renaissance Drama*, (N.S. 6 and 9), I am grateful to Northwestern University Press.

Financial support for my research and writing came from the American Council of Learned Societies, which awarded me a fellowship in 1979–1980, and from Georgetown University, which supported the project with two Summer Research Grants and released time from teaching duties on two occasions. In making these awards the ACLS and Georgetown offered encouragement that was far more than monetary.

Reading Renaissance editions of the classics, constantly turning from the original text to the accumulated centuries of commentary printed alongside, one realizes how much any reconstruction of the past is a group, not an individual, venture. Certainly that is the case with this book. For the generosity, patience, and knowledge of all the people named here I am grateful.

B.R.S.

Ferrara
May 1987

ANCIENT SCRIPTS &
MODERN EXPERIENCE ON
THE ENGLISH STAGE
1500–1700

In p[r]imis one longe cloke of reade clothe of tissue faced
w[i]th grene sasenett.
It[e]m one other cloke of blewe velvett w[i]th golden flowers
that [M]ardocheus wore on.
It[e]m two read sey clockes spanishe fassion garded and faced
w[i]th yellow seye.
It[e]m one cloke of yellowe cotton [gar] w[i]th a rownd cape
garded w[i]th blew bokeram.
It[e]m Gnatoes clocke spanishe fassion of read cotto[n] w[i]th
iii gardes of [y]ellow cotton.
. . .
It[e]m a cote for [M]iles w[i]th a longe St. Andrewes crosse
before and behinde.

—from "A trew Inventorie made the 8[th] daye of
Marche A[nn]o D[omi]ni 1562 . . . of all the
players apparell belonginge to the chestes
in the m[aste]rs uttre chambre,"
ST. JOHN'S COLLEGE, CAMBRIDGE

PROLOGUE

ONE DAY in the mid-1480s, students of Pomponius Laetus's academy mounted a five-foot-high platform in a square in Rome and proceeded to act out Seneca's *Hippolytus*. It was the first time that a "tragedy" had been publicly performed in well over a thousand years. In that fact Pomponius took pride, not only as a scholar who wanted to revive classical drama but as a Roman citizen who wanted to restore his city to its ancient glory. Remembering the event in print a year or so later, Sulpicius Verulanus pointed out that Rome had not seen an enactment of a tragedy for centuries (*iam multis saeculis*); in the present age (*hoc aevo*) he and Pomponius Laetus had been the first to inspire their students by teaching them to act out the very plays that their ancient Roman forebears saw.[1] In having their students declaim Latin scripts, Sulpicius and Pomponius were following the precept and the example of Cicero and Quintilian, whose treatises on how to educate Roman orators were being examined anew for advice on how to educate Renaissance statesmen.

Among the scholars in Pomponius's circle was William Lily, who brought back some of the Italian master's educational methods when he returned to England and became headmaster of St. Paul's School in 1512. Inspired by the direct contacts of men like Lily and Grocyn, as well as by the indirect influence of books on humanist education, Cambridge dons began as early as 1510–1511 to include comedies by Terence as part of the colleges' Christmas festivities. For classical tragedy, it is only spotty documentation, surely, that makes Westminster School's production of Seneca's *Hippolytus* in the mid-1540s the first recorded performance in England. By midcentury, in England no less than in Italy, the plays of

---

1. Sulpicius's description of the occasion occurs in his letter to Cardinal Raphaele Riario prefaced to Vitruvius, *De architectura* (Rome, 1486), repr. in Beriah Botfield, ed., *Prefaces to the First Editions of the Greek and Roman Classics and of the Sacred Scriptures* (London, 1861), pp. 177–79.

Plautus and Terence, of Seneca and Euripides, were challenging the prominence that had belonged for centuries to saints' plays, morality plays, and cycles that dramatized the great events of the Bible. All over Europe, Pomponius's production of Seneca's *Hippolytus* marked a new epoch in drama.

It marks, indeed, the emergence of our own assumption that comedy and tragedy are somehow present in the very nature of human experience. However natural the division may seem to us, "comic" and "tragic," unlike the taboo and the sacred, are not categories of experience that we find in cultures all over the world. We tend to think of them as an opposition implicit in the very scheme of things, but they are one of the specific legacies from Greece and Rome that distinguishes our civilization from the civilizations of the East. Though "comic" and "tragic" survived during the Middle Ages as ways of labeling stories with happy endings and unhappy endings, it was not until the sixteenth and seventeenth centuries, fifteen hundred years after Sophocles, Euripides, Plautus, and Terence had last been performed in the theaters of the Roman Empire, that tragedy and comedy regained their ancient importance as ways of giving dramatic coherence to human events. This time, however, the structures of comedy and tragedy were brought to bear on the experience of two different cultures. It was not only the experience of classical antiquity that was given form and meaning on the stage but the accumulated experience of European Christianity during the intervening centuries.

We can sense the convergence of two cultures, perhaps the clash of two cultures, in the prologue that Sulpicius provided for a repeat performance of *Hippolytus* before Pope Innocent VIII in the Castel Sant'Angelo. Sulpicius felt obliged not only to define tragedy but to justify it to his audience, to tell them not only what they were about to see but how they should respond to it. Today, explains the speaker of the prologue, it is a "tragedy" that will be performed—a kind of play that recounts the misfortunes of heroes: "Something new will appear before you, a grave and pitiable happening that will cause every onlooker to leave the playing-place instructed and cautioned."[2] In these words we may be hearing not so much a pedagogue's pedantry as a producer's perplexity about what the audience will make of his play. Fear of moral criticism is barely disguised in the prologue's confident voice: for the Pope and his colleagues, serious drama was religious drama. What sense would they make, then, of Phaedra's incestuous lust? How would they reconcile Hippolytus's exemplary chastity with the horrible fact of his death?

Putting on a classical play, as Pomponius and Sulpicius seem to have realized, was not quite like digging up an ancient statue and placing it in one's garden. A play, after all, is not an object but an *event*. It is a plan for human interaction. It is people talking to people. As such I take it in this book. These pages chart the rediscovery of tragedy and comedy, not in the books of humanist scholars, but on the stages of England's schools, colleges, inns of court, and royal court, and finally in the public theaters of sixteenth- and seventeenth-century London. The story of how classical plays were excavated out of the dust of monastic libraries and were printed, studied, and imitated makes up a chapter in the history of European dramaturgy that is familiar already. Historians have usually laid out the plot of that chapter in terms of narrative material, poetic style, and formal structure: classical drama reappeared about 1500, they tell us, and quickly imposed its character types and plot motifs, its styles of speech, and its structure of scenes and acts on the vagaries of medieval drama.[3] Instructed

---

2. My quotation from Sulpicius's prologue is translated from Wilhelm Creiznach, *Geschichte des neueren Dramas* (Halle, 1901), 2: 370–71, who offers a full account of Pomponius's dramatic activities. Cf. also 2: 1–7.

3. The informing principle of major histories of European drama like Creiznach's, this view is also implicit in standard histories of English drama like F. P. Wilson, *The English Drama, 1485–1585* (Oxford, 1969), pp. 102–50, and John Loftis et al., eds., *The* Revels *History of Drama in English*, Vol. 2 (1500–1576) (London, 1980): 215–32. R. Warwick Bond's long introductory essay to *Early Plays from the Italian* (Oxford, 1911), pp. xv–cxviii, states the case for classical influences on modern comedy. On tragedy, see John W. Cunliffe, *The Influence of Seneca on Elizabethan Tragedy* (London, 1893); H. B. Charlton, *The Senecan Tradition in Renaissance Tragedy* (1921; repr. Man-

by classical example, sixteenth- and seventeenth-century play-wrights learned to separate "comic" characters and "comic" plots from the "tragic" characters and "tragic" plots that jostle so indecorously in medieval drama. Modern playwrights were then in a position to distinguish the "lower" and "higher" styles appropriate to these opposed kinds of materials and to order the jumbled episodes of medieval drama into a rational five-act structure. The history of European drama from 1500 to 1700 becomes, in this view, a testament to the steadily increasing influence of "classical" norms, even in conservative England, which finally joined the rest of Europe when neo-classical taste belatedly arrived along with restored monarchy in 1660. Art triumphed over Nature, neoclassical Reason over medieval whim. Looked at in this way, certain plays loom large as landmarks, often out of all proportion to their acclaim at the time or to their critical estimation since: *Gorboduc* as the first "regular" English tragedy and *Ralph Roister Doister* as the first "regular" English comedy enjoy a textbook fame that far outstrips their success as scripts for the stage.

Influence in the arts is seldom so simple as this essentially nineteenth-century idea of Progress would have it. Instead of a *progressive* model, this book proposes a *dynamic* model in which "influence" works both ways. Sixteenth- and seven-teenth-century playwrights, actors, and audiences may have given classical comedy and classical tragedy increasing sover-eignty over how characters speak and how events fall out, but playwrights, actors, and audiences alike were disposed to understand ancient drama in their own anachronistic terms, even when supposedly "classical" ideas held sway after the Restoration. "Influence" is perhaps a less apt term for this state of affairs than "confluence." Since the Renaissance itself, critics have been pointing out the marks that ancient drama has left on modern; this book looks at the matter from the opposite direction as well and considers the marks that modern drama has left on ancient, particularly on the first

chester, 1946); and F. L. Lucas, *Seneca and Elizabethan Tragedy* (Cambridge, 1922).

stage productions of Greek and Latin scripts in modern times. In these physical confrontations between classical heroes and modern Englishmen, we can observe how each party had to accommodate itself to the other, how the protagonists of Greek and Roman drama were compelled to fit in with the staging traditions and moral assumptions of the Middle Ages, and how, at the same time, modern audiences were challenged to revise their customary ways of looking at plays and to explore two new structures of thought and feeling—"comic" and "tragic"—until those two categories reestablished their dominion over the entire dramatic universe in Restoration neoclassicism. From 1500 to 1700, we can trace in the interplay between things classical and things medieval our own understanding of comedy and tragedy as two fundamental ways in which human imagination sizes up the world.

As a phenomenon unique in dramatic history, Greek tragedy positively demands that we see it in its original social context. Sharply focused on indomitable heroes, the scripts of Aeschylus, Sophocles, and Euripides address a conflict between individuals and the theological/legal/social order in which individuals must live—a conflict that may be universal but one that seems to have been crucial in fifth-century Athens.[4] A not dissimilar conflict energizes ancient comedy. The scripts of Aristophanes, Plautus, and Terence give free play to satiric and romantic impulses that run counter to the restraints of everyday social existence. When we look at drama in such a way, we are doing to scripts what structural anthropologists do to other kinds of data about human society: we are studying how man as a social creature organizes and systemizes his experience. It is a structuralist model adapted from anthropologists like Claude Lévi-Strauss and Victor Turner that informs my attempt to bring to imaginative life the information we have about Greek and Roman drama on the Renaissance stage. Particularly important here is Victor Turner's

4. See, for example, Jean-Pierre Vernant, "Greek Tragedy: Problems of Interpretation," in *The Structuralist Controversy*, ed. Richard Macksey and Eugenio Donato (Baltimore, 1972), pp. 273–89.

insistence that in complex societies drama functions as a way
of working through conflicts. As "time out" from everyday
existence, drama lets us countenance ideas and feelings that
may challenge social consensus; it finds ways of dealing with
those ideas and feelings, either by discrediting them in the
course of the play or by changing the terms of consensus in
the end.[5] Even if a dramatic performance merely confirms an
audience's prejudices, no one ever leaves the theater the same
as he arrived. Watching the spectacle of a mother seducing her
stepson, listening to the rhetoric of sexual passion will cause
Pope Innocent and his colleagues to leave the playing-place
"instructed" and "cautioned." Or so Sulpicius assures them.

It should come as no surprise that conflict marks Renais-
sance revivals of classical drama when conflict marked the
contexts in which those revivals were staged. The first three
chapters of this book set in place three structures—critical,
spatial, and social—in which sixteenth- and seventeenth-cen-
tury Englishmen watched the productions of classical comedy
reconstructed in Chapter Four and the productions of classical
tragedy reconstructed in Chapter Five. Each of these three
structures has its own organizing principles; each its own
terms of conflict. Cicero, Horace, and Aristotle disposed
modern actors and audiences to think about the nature of
drama in radically different ways; the various spaces in which
plays were mounted gave viewers, physically and psycholog-
ically, a choice of perspectives on what they saw; the different
social contexts in which audiences came together determined
just how open or closed the dialogue might be between voices
of dissent and voices of authority. Chapters One, Two, and
Three describe three increasingly narrower contexts for
viewing the performances discussed in Chapters Four and
Five: the philosophical assumptions that Englishmen brought
to drama were the same all over Renaissance Europe; the
physical contexts in which they positioned themselves were
similar to those elsewhere in Europe but incorporated certain

5. Victor Turner, *From Ritual to Theatre: The Human Seriousness of Play*
(New York, 1982), especially pp. 60–70.

distinctively English features; the social contexts in which they came together, though not without their counterparts elsewhere, were peculiarly English.

Individually each of these three contexts has already attracted scholars' attention: Anne Righter has traced how scripts for the Elizabethan stage, Shakespeare's in particular, reflect changing ideas about just what a play is; Richard Southern, Glynne Wickham, John Orrell, and others have reconstructed the variety of physical arrangements that related sixteenth- and seventeenth-century actors to sixteenth- and seventeenth-century spectators; Alfred Harbage, M. C. Bradbrook, Ann Jennalie Cook, and John Loftis have taken census of the different audiences who assembled in public theaters and in private.[6] In the first three chapters, I have brought together these ideas about play, place, and patrons, sought out some of the classical and Renaissance texts that stand behind them, and attempted to isolate the oppositions between ancient and modern ideas that made each context so volatile between 1500 and 1700. Whether in the households of sixteenth-century schools and colleges, or in the Elizabethan public theater, or in the playhouses of Restoration London, these tensions were never really resolved. What we observe in all three contexts is not a linear progress of classical ideas overtaking medieval ideas but a dynamic between ancient ideas and modern.

Those tensions are, I believe, the very reason that classical comedy and classical tragedy, once reintroduced to the stage, became something more than antiquarian curiosities and took hold of modern imagination. If tragedy and comedy flour-

6. On philosophical contexts, see Anne Righter, *Shakespeare and the Idea of the Play* (London, 1962). On physical contexts, Richard Southern, *The Staging of Plays Before Shakespeare* (London, 1973); Glynne Wickham, *Early English Stages 1300–1660*, 3 vols. (London, 1959–1981); and Richard Southern, *Changeable Scenery* (London, 1952). On social contexts, Alfred Harbage, *Shakespeare and the Rival Traditions* (New York, 1952); M. C. Bradbrook, *The Rise of the Common Player* (Cambridge, Mass., 1962); Ann Jennalie Cook, *The Privileged Playgoers of Shakespeare's London, 1576–1642* (Princeton, 1981); and John Loftis, "The Social and Literary Context," in *The* Revels *History of Drama in English*, Vol. 5, ed. John Loftis et al. (London, 1976): 1–40.

ished as dramatic kinds in the sixteenth and seventeenth centuries, it was because they fulfilled philosophical, social, and aesthetic needs that morality plays, saints' plays, and Biblical drama could no longer satisfy. Comedy and tragedy came to assume the same function they had served in ancient times: they engaged issues that mattered in how the audience lived their lives. It was the matter of historical and cultural distance that let classical drama speak to the contradictions in Renaissance experience in ways that traditional religious drama no longer could. To hold this particular mirror up to nature was to see an image different from one's own. It invited the viewer to examine his assumptions and find his cultural bearings. That explains, perhaps, why comedy and tragedy as dramatic types have proved so adaptable to the rapid cultural changes of the past five hundred years and have showed such staying power since Pomponius Laetus sent his students out into a square in Rome and introduced a medieval public audience to Seneca's *Hippolytus*.

The oppositions between ancient and modern ideas outlined in the first three chapters guide my attempt in Chapters Four and Five to describe all the documented occasions on which Greek and Roman plays were staged in England between 1500 and 1700. The information we have about these productions is generally of three sorts: the scripts as they were adapted for acting, eyewitness accounts of performances, and financial records. With a few exceptions, the occasions that I have studied derive not from a fresh search of manuscript sources but from the performances cataloged in Alfred Harbage and S. Schoenbaum's *Annals of English Drama 975–1700*, second edition (1964, with supplements 1966 and 1970); *Records of Early English Drama: Cambridge* (1988); and *Records of Early English Drama: Oxford* (1988).[7] I have, however, looked at the manuscript of every unprinted adaptation of classical drama that these sources record, as well as at important manuscript

7. Alfred Harbage and S. Schoenbaum, *Annals of English Drama 975–1700*, 2d ed. (Philadelphia, 1964); Alan H. Nelson, ed., *Records of Early English Drama: Cambridge* (Toronto, 1988). John R. Elliott, Jr., ed., *Records of Early English Drama: Oxford* (Toronto, forthcoming).

records like the journal of Alexander Nowell, headmaster at Westminster School in the 1540s.

In studying the actual stage productions that are the subject of this book, I have distinguished three kinds of evidence and have ranked that evidence in a descending hierarchy of importance. For the most part I concentrate on classical plays that are known actually to have been performed in England, including plays that bill themselves as adaptations of classical originals. When our understanding of these stage productions is likely to be enhanced, I have broadened the focus to include English translations and adaptations contemporary with the staged scripts but not intended for performance. On occasion I have broadened the focus further still to notice how classical scripts were produced on the continent. Largely outside my range of interest are original plays that are simply *influenced* by classical scripts. With a few exceptions like Gascoigne and Kinwelmershe's *Jocasta*, Shakespeare's *The Comedy of Errors*, and Heywood's *The English Traveler* and *The Captives*, my survey is limited to adaptations of particular classical plays that actually call themselves adaptations. Restricting the number of plays in this way does not, however, constrict the scope of their significance. The oppositions and tensions that make these twenty productions so interesting are the same oppositions and tensions we can observe in the stage successes of Marlowe, Jonson, Shakespeare, Chapman, Marston, and Middleton. They are, indeed, the very oppositions and tensions that keep comedy and tragedy alive today. If studying these productions prompts a reader to think more searchingly about comedy and tragedy in the twentieth-century theater, this book will have served its purpose.

I · Critical Contexts

And here, who soever hath bene diligent to read advisedlie over, *Terence, Seneca, Virgil, Horace,* or els *Aristophanes, Sophocles, Homer,* and *Pindar,* and shall diligently marke the difference they use, in proprietie of wordes, in forme of sentence, in handlyng of their matter, he shall easelie perceive, what is fitte and *decorum* in everie one, to the trew use of perfite Imitation. Whan *M. Watson* in S. Johns College at Cambridge wrote his excellent Tragedie of *Absalon, M. Cheke,* he and I, for that part of trew Imitation, had many pleasant talkes togither, in comparing the preceptes of *Aristotle* and *Horace de Arte Poetica,* with the examples of *Euripides, Sophocles, and Seneca.* Few men, in writyng of Tragedies in our dayes, have shot at this marke.[1]

SETTLED COMFORTABLY in their Cambridge rooms in the early 1540s, Roger Ascham and his colleagues brought together seven different historical periods, three different civilizations, and two very different ideas about the nature of drama. Homer (eighth century B.C.), Pindar (518–438 B.C.), Sophocles (c. 496–406 B.C.), and Aristophanes (c. 450–c. 385 B.C.) speak for at least three separate periods in Greek civilization; Terence (c. 195–159 B.C.), Virgil (70–19 B.C.), Horace (65–8 B.C.), and Seneca (4 B.C.–A.D. 65), for at least three separate periods in Roman civilization. Seen from the distant perspective of sixteenth-century Englishmen, these ancient playwrights merged into a chorus who spoke with a single voice. For Ascham and his colleagues, "true imitation" was a straightforward matter of copying ancient models.

"The precepts of Aristotle" are not, however, the same as "the precepts of Horace." By *mimēsis* Aristotle meant something altogether different from Horace's *imitatio.* Mimēsis in Aristotle's analytical view is the very basis of all the human arts, which differ from each other in the particular objects they imitate, in the means they use to produce that imitation, and in the mode (narrative or dramatic in the case of poetry)

1. Roger Ascham, *The Scholemaster* (1570), ed. William Aldis Wright (Cambridge, 1904), p. 284.

in which the imitation is carried out. Imitatio in Horace's practical view is the more limited matter of studying good examples to perfect one's own style. The difference between Aristotle and Horace on this single matter of imitation reflects fundamental differences in how they understand what goes on when actors speak and move and audiences watch and listen. Aristotle and Horace assume, that is to say, different ideas about the ontology of drama. Everything in Aristotle conduces to make us view the play as an object: the clear visual bias of mimēsis itself (Aristotle's illustrations are all painted or sculpted images), the distinctions among the "objects" (*hetera*, "other things") that the various arts imitate, the very definition of *poiesis* as "a made thing." Horace's bias, on the other hand, is not visual but verbal, and the remarks on drama that make up one-third of his *Ars poetica* follow Cicero and Quintilian in conceiving of the play as a rhetorical event, an act of communication between speaker and listener. The difference between Horace and Aristotle is the difference between going to "hear" a play and going to "see" one.[2]

The rhetorical idea of poetry in general and drama in particular remained current in the Middle Ages. Aristotle's *Poetics*, by contrast, did not arrive in Europe until the middle of the fifteenth century, the very last of the philosopher's works to be recovered from antiquity. Giorgio Valla had published a Latin translation in 1498, and the Greek text had appeared from the Aldine press in 1508, but it was not until the publication of Francesco Robortello's commentary in 1548, several years after Ascham's Cambridge symposium, that Aristotle's *Poetics* began to be widely known and discussed—and then only because Robortello managed to translate Aristotle's ideas into critical terms that Renaissance scholars already knew from Latin writers. It is an open question, indeed, whether Watson, Cheke, and Ascham knew the *Poetics* firsthand at all,

---

2. Anne Righter, *Shakespeare and the Idea of the Play* (London, 1962), traces this distinction through the speeches and stage directions of sixteenth-century English scripts.

or only through references in other books.[3] Scholars like Ascham may have rediscovered Greek drama, but they read it—literally and figuratively—in Latin terms. It was within this philosophical context, with its two opposed ideas about the very nature of drama, that scholars, actors, and audiences studied, performed, and watched the scripts of Sophocles, Aristophanes, Euripedes, Plautus, Terence, and Seneca. As the balance between Aristotle's ideas and the ideas of Cicero, Quintilian, and Horace shifted within that context, so too did audiences' perceptions about why tragic heroes die and how the happy endings of comedy come about. To understand why comedy and tragedy were reclaimed for modern audiences in just the forms they were, we must consider first the general view of classical theater that Cicero, Quintilian, and Horace offered to Renaissance readers, then the challenge to this system presented by Aristotle's *Poetics*, and finally the ways in which the Romans and the Greeks were brought to common terms. In that compromise, comedy and tragedy took on the adaptability to changing experience that has given them vitality down to our own day.

I

To sixteenth-century scholars, Cicero stood forth as the readiest guide to ancient drama for three reasons: he spoke a language they knew well, he had a great deal to say, and he confirmed what they already thought about drama. As a guide to Roman civilization, Cicero offered himself to Renaissance readers as a kind of Will Durant or Kenneth Clark. He was the dictator of prose style, the authority on humanistic education,

3. On the reception of Aristotle's *Poetics* in sixteenth-century Italy, see Bernard Weinberg, *A History of Literary Criticism in the Italian Renaissance* (Chicago, 1961), 1: 349–634, 2: 635–714. Weinberg sketches the main outlines of his two-volume study in "From Aristotle to Pseudo-Aristotle," in *Aristotle's "Poetics" and English Literature: A Collection of Critical Essays*, ed. Elder Olson, (Chicago, 1965), pp. 192–200. Marvin T. Herrick traces the same pattern of Horatian interpretation of the *Poetics* and carries the story down to 1700 in *The Poetics of Aristotle in England* (New Haven, 1930), pp. 8–79. See also Joan C. Grace, *Tragic Theory in the Critical Works of Thomas Rymer, John Dennis, and John Dryden* (Rutherford, N.J., 1975), pp. 13–32.

the perfect exemplar of the Renaissance ideal of a private con-
templative man who gives himself up to the service of the
state. Animated by the force of Cicero's own example and
filled with detailed instructions, Cicero's rhetorical treatises,
particularly his *De oratore*, offered a program for training
Roman orators that humanists turned into a program for
training Renaissance statesmen.

Not surprising in a man whose powers of self-dramatiza-
tion were great both in speaking and in writing, Cicero was
fascinated by plays, players, and playing. Though he never
addresses himself to the theater exclusively as better known
authorities like Vitruvius do, when he does mention scripts
and performances, he writes about them with an immediacy
that no other classical writer, Greek or Roman, can match.
One of Cicero's favorite comparisons is between the art of the
actor and the art of the orator. Indeed, Plutarch claims that
Cicero studied the one to perfect the other:

for his gesture and pronunciation, having the self same defects of
nature at the beginning, which Demosthenes had: to reform them,
he carefully studied to counterfeit Roscius, an excellent comediant,
and Aesop also a player of tragedies. Of this Aesop men write, that
he playing one day Atreus' part upon a stage (who determined with
himself how he might be revenged of his brother Thyestes) a servant
by chance having occasion to run sodainly by him, he forgetting him-
self, striving to show the vehement passion and fury of this king,
gave him such a blow on his head with the sceptre in his hand, that
he slew him dead in the place. Even so Cicero's words were of so
great force to persuade, by means of his grace and pronunciation.[4]

If Plutarch is right about the power of the actor's example,
Cicero later had the opportunity of returning Roscius the
favor when he defended the great comedian from a charge of
breach of contract with a business partner. In his *Saturnalia*
Macrobius tells a similar story about Cicero and the players.

---

4. Plutarch, Life of Cicero, trans. Thomas North (1579) in *The Lives of the
Noble Grecians and Romans* (1579), ed. Paul Turner (Carbondale, Ill., 1963), 2:
72. Cicero's references to the stage are cataloged in F. W. Wright, *Cicero and
the Theatre* (Northampton, Mass., 1931).

Such warm friends were Roscius and Cicero, says Macrobius, that they used to match themselves against each other to see which of them could express the same idea in the greater number of ways. Roscius had such a high opinion of his own skill, Macrobius relates, that he wrote a book comparing the art of the public speaker with the art of the actor.[5]

Behind the dozens of theatrical instances and anecdotes in Cicero's treatises, speeches, and letters is the assumption that plays are rhetorical events: occasions when speakers harangue an audience. It was a notion of drama that Cicero's Renaissance readers entertained already. In morality plays and the Biblical cycles, characters speak directly to the audience with just the face-to-face immediacy that Cicero describes. In his treatises on rhetoric Cicero points out the artful devices that orators can use to sway listeners and cites examples of those devices from plays in performance. Speechmaking and play-acting, he implies, use the same skills. Drama provides models both for how a speaker should work up arguments, as outlined in De inventione, and how he should put those arguments across, as developed in De oratore. In the latter treatise Cicero takes as an example the opening exposition in Terence's Andria and proposes it as a model for how speechmakers should lay out an argument. Simo, the hardheaded old father who has marriage plans for his son that, as usual, work at cross-purposes to true love, takes his slave Sosia aside and untangles the past, present, and future complications of the plot: "Thou shalt heare all the matter from the beginning, so shalt thou understand both my sonnes life and my intent, as also what I would have thee to doe in this behalfe." Cicero commends the neatness of this partition and points out how in the speech that follows each of the three divisions is taken up one by one: first the son's past philanderings, then the father's present plans, finally the strategem he hopes to try with Sosia's help. "Just as he turned his attention first to each point as it arose, and after dispatching them all stopped

5. Macrobius, The Saturnalia, 3.14.12, trans. P. V. Davies (New York and London, 1969), p. 233.

speaking, so I favour turning our attention to each topic and when all have been dispatched, winding up the speech."[6] Economical in his dramaturgy, Terence was a model for how to lay out an argument; elegant in his style, he was a model for how to put that argument across to an audience. In *De oratore* Cicero cites this same set of speeches from *Andria* when he is discussing the art of narration. Terence knows just how to fill out the narrative with clarifying detail, just when to punctuate it with interruptions from Sosia.[7]

Filled with acts of violence and fraught with ethical questions, tragedies were even better suited than comedies for this kind of logical and rhetorical analysis. And among the traditional subjects of Greek and Latin tragedy, none raised more complex issues than Orestes. Cicero considers his case at some length in *De inventione*. Once you have determined whether a case is simple or complex, explains Cicero, once you have determined whether it turns on a written document or rather involves general reasoning, "then you must see what the question in the case is [*quaestio*], and the excuse or reason [*ratio*], the point for the judge's decision [*iudicatio*] and the foundation or supporting argument [*firmamentum*]. All of these should develop out of the determination of the issue." The case of Orestes touches each of these considerations:

For instance, to make my meaning clear, let me dwell on a simple and well-known example: If Orestes be accused of murdering his mother, unless he say, "I was justified; for she had killed my father," he has no defence. If this excuse were taken away, the whole debate would be taken away, too. Therefore the excuse in this case is that she killed Agamemnon. The point for the judge's decision [iudicatio] is that which arises from the denial and assertion of the reason or excuse. Suppose, for example, that the excuse has been set up which we mentioned a little while ago. "For she," he says, "had killed my

6. *Andria*, 49–54, trans. Richard Bernard in *Terence in English* (Cambridge, 1598), fol. A5; Cicero, *De inventione*, 1.23.33, trans. H. M. Hubbell, Loeb Library (London, 1949), p. 69. Future references to *De inventione* are cited in the text.

7. *De oratore*, 2.80.326–29, trans. H. Rackham, Loeb Library (London, 1942), 1: 444–45.

father." "But," the opponent will say, "your mother ought not to have been killed by you, her son; her act could have been punished without your committing a crime." From this narrowing or limitation of the excuse the chief dispute arises, which we call iudicatio or point for the judge's decision. It is as follows: "Was it right for Orestes to kill his mother because she had killed Orestes' father?" The *foundation* is the strongest argument of the defence, and the one most relevant to the point for the judge's decision; for example, if Orestes should choose to say that his mother had shown such disposition towards his father, himself, and his sisters, the kingdom, the good name of the clan and household that her own children were of all people in the world most bound to exact the penalty from her.

(1.13.18–14.19)

A far cry, this, from Aeschylus's *Eumenides!* As a lawyer, Cicero assumes that Orestes' predicament is reducible to a clear-cut issue. All one has to do is to go to work on the facts with the proper logical apparatus. Though Cicero is not talking here about a particular Orestes play, his attitude describes a way of responding to tragic heroes. Tragedy, he implies, is a matter of presenting arguments. The task for an intelligent reader or observer is to act as a judge: to consider the facts, to pass a verdict, to pronounce an iudicatio. An audience listens to a tragedy as a jury listens to testimony. This assumption about the rhetorical nature of drama has, as we shall see, enormous consequences for comedy and tragedy as they were put back onstage in the sixteenth century.

Cicero's trial of Orestes shows how naturally drama-as-rhetorical-event implies a moral program, a case to be demonstrated. This assumption, too, was shared by Cicero's Renaissance readers. The theatrical citations in Cicero's philosophical works must have sounded not very different from morality plays. Tragedies, obviously enough, were filled with eminently citable *sententiae*; but comedies, too, were grist for the moral mills turned by the interlocutors in Cicero's philosophical dialogues. In Book Three of the *Tusculan Disputations*, for example, M— and A— turn to consider the variety of ways in which man can alleviate distress. Foresight is one of these:

Therefore, herein trulye is little doubte, that all such thinges as are counted evell, are then moste greevous, when they fall sodaynelye. Wherfore, although this thinge onely doth not cause sorow, yet neverthelesse because the setlyng and preparynge of the minde, is of great force to assage the gryefe, let everye man forethynke such, inasmuch as they may happen to a man. And Trulye, it is a great poynt of wysedome, for a man to looke for all such casualties, as customably happen to men, not to mervayle at any thynge when it doth chaunce, and not to doubt but anye mischyefe whyche is not chaunced maye well ynoughe happen.

M— ("I doe gladly brynge in my talke the verses of our poetes," he has declared earlier) remembers an instructive speech in Terence's *Phormio*:

Wherefore let everye man in hys prosperitye,
Muse with himselfe, by what means he may beare adversitye.
Some peryll, losse, or cruell exyle, when he returneth home.
His childes offence, or his wives death, let him aye thinke upon.
And these as commen let him take besydes some straunger payne,
If some good chaunce befall to him, let him take that as gayne.

Inasmuche as Terence hath spoken this so wyselye, whyche he borowed of philosophye, shall not we out of whose store it was taken, bothe saye the same better, and also thinke it more constantlye?[8]

"Saye the same better" indeed a philosopher might. What M— has done is to wrench the speech completely out of dramatic context. Quoted in the quiet of M—'s Tusculan garden, it sounds like sober advice; declaimed on the stage in Rome, it is framed with comic irony. The speaker is the cantankerous old father Demipho, just returned to Athens to discover his son Antipho married to a commoner and his slave Geta in cahoots with the lovers. An audience's sympathies, one would think, are with the lovers, not with the father; Demipho, long-suffering as he is, figures as a blustering blocking-figure. His advice that every man should "Muse with himselfe, by

8. Cicero, *Tusculan Disputations*, 3.14.30–15.31, trans. John Dolman as *Those fyve questions, which Marke Tullye Cicero disputed in his manor of Tusculanum* (London, 1561), fols. 07–07ᵛ.

what means he may beare adversitye" is hardly the message
we carry away from the theater. (Antipho's new wife, as it
turns out, is Demipho's long-lost niece, and all ends felici-
tously.)

M— has on the same literalistic blinders when he quotes
from Terence's *Eunuchus* later on in the *Tusculan Disputations*.
The scene he cites is the very opening of the play. Thais, a
courtesan whose wit and charm are one of the comedy's chief
delights, has asked her nobly born lover Phaedria to leave
town for two days so she can enjoy the company of his rival,
the braggart soldier Thraso. Phaedria is beside himself ("What
then shall I doe? shall I not goe? what not now when I am so
kindly called?") and receives gentle but mocking counsel from
his slave Parmeno: "O master, its not in your power to rule
that by advise, which is void of good counsell, neither
observes any meane. For in love are these many vices[:] inju-
ries, suspicions, enmitie, truce, warre, and peace againe out of
hande. If you should require to make these incertainties certen
by reason, you should do no more, then if you endeavor with
reason to runne madde."9 These are the lines that come to
mind when in Book Four M— is discussing with A— the var-
ious disorders of the spirit. Among mankind's distresses, love
is the chief, and M— quotes Parmeno's catalog of love's vices
("injuries, suspicions, enmitie, truce, warre, and peace againe
out of hande") to prove the point. The general conclusion to
be drawn, says M—, is that love is not a "natural" feeling and
is better avoided. If audiences of Terence's *Eunuchus* had heard
Parmeno's speech in the same spirit as M—, there would
hardly have been any reason for going on with the play and
spoiling the moral effect by discovering that the lovers get to
enjoy their desires, after all.

For all their familiarity with playscripts, for all their ready
store of quotations, the interlocutors in Cicero's philosophical
dialogues have an amazing capacity for ignoring dramatic
contexts and missing the comic point. If Demipho congratu-
lates himself on expecting the worst, if Parmeno teases his

9. Terence, *Eunuchus*, 59–63, trans. Bernard, fol. HIᵛ.

master Phaedria about his dizzy passion, if Phaedria himself cannot find a logical way out of jealousy, if Phormio applies his wit to saving young lovers from grumpy parents, we are to take their speeches as homilies and their plights as moral lessons. The assumption is that acting is like oratory: plays are intended to demonstrate an argument. Reading Terence's plays as Cicero saw them—or at least as Cicero quoted them in his old age—Renaissance readers would have found a reassuring universality in ancient drama. The milieu of Terence's comedies may have been exotic and Grecian, his characters may have seemed morally dubious, the language they spoke may have been the colloquial Latin of ancient Rome, but the moral lessons they offered seemed as relevant in the sixteenth century as they were in the first century B.C..

In keeping with his notion of drama as a species of oratory, an act of deliberation, Cicero frequently mentions in his letters one particular kind of moral program: it is the political side of plays in performance that inspires Cicero's most detailed observations. This, too, was a feature of drama that Renaissance readers already appreciated. Latin tragedy as Cicero describes it in performance sounds very much like *Respublica* or *Magnificence*. It was during Cicero's lifetime, in 55 B.C., that Rome acquired its first permanent stone theater, and even its physical layout dramatized the close connection between plays and politics. On his eastern campaigns Pompey had been impressed with the magnificent theaters of Greek cities and determined that Rome should have one. Aware that reactionary senators a century before had balked at spending public money on so extravagant a project, Pompey cleverly contrived that the theater include a grandiose portico ("Pompey's porch" it is called in Shakespeare's *Julius Caesar*) to be used as a meeting place for the Senate. The theater itself could be explained away as a kind of annex. Would that Martial had been alive to have written an epigram about it all! Plays (not to mention brutal games and bloody combats) took place side by side with political debate. Comparing the two was hard to avoid. Appropriately, it was in Pompey's portico rather than in the regular Senate House that one of the most dramatic events of the century was staged: the assassination of Julius Caesar.[10]

Over and over in his speeches and letters Cicero alludes to political allegory in stage plays as if it were a common thing. "If you have any news of practical importance," he enjoins Atticus in a particularly gossipy letter about Mark Anthony's machinations, "let me hear it; if not, give me full details as to who were cheered by the people at the mimes, and the epigrams of the actors."[11] *Dicta mimorum* could be potent political propaganda. Actors were adept at giving a sharp new political edge to lines that might be centuries old, and audiences were just as adept at detecting the jab—and howling their approval or their rage. Several such occasions are described by Cicero in some detail.

Pompey himself came in for public criticism in the theater. In July 59, one year after Pompey, Caesar, and Crassus had wrested power to themselves and formed the First Triumvirate, public disaffection was running high. Caesar had just been granted an unprecedented five-year command in Cisalpine Gaul that would give him time enough, distance enough, and troops enough to build up power and seize control of the state on his own. Cicero himself was suspicious; "the popular feeling," he writes to Atticus,

can be seen best in the theatre and at public exhibitions. For at the gladiatorial show both the leader [Pompey?] and his associates were overwhelmed with hisses: at the games in honour of Apollo the actor Diphilus made an impertinent attack on Pompey, "By our misfortunes thou art Great," which was encored again and again. "A time will come when thou wilt rue that might," he declaimed amid the cheers of the whole audience, and so on with the rest. For indeed the verses do look as though they had been written for the occasion by an enemy of Pompey: "If neither law nor custom can constrain," etc. was received with a tremendous uproar and outcry. At Caesar's entry

10. In his life of Pompey, Plutarch says that Pompey modeled the new Roman structure on the theater of Mytilene, but made it larger and more splendid (42.4). Cf. William Beare, *The Roman Stage* (London, 1950), pp. 161–62.

11. Cicero, *Letters to Atticus*, 14.3, trans. E. O. Winstedt, Loeb Library (London, 1925), 3: 221.

the applause dwindled away; but young Curio who followed was applauded as Pompey used to be when the constitution was still sound. Caesar was much annoyed: and it is said a letter flew post haste to Pompey at Capua. They are annoyed with the knights who stood up and clapped Curio, and their hand is against every man's.

Curio was hardly the man to applaud. Crossing the Rubicon nine years later, Caesar was able to buy out his honor for sixty million sesterces. In his version of Pompey's humiliation in the theater, Valerius Maximus makes it appear that the great general was actually present and that Diphilus pointed his finger at him.[12]

Publius Clodius Pulcher was not so lucky. A political opportunist whose stunts had included masquerading as a woman to gain admission to Caesar's house while his wife and other ladies were celebrating the rites of the Bona Dea, Clodius became Caesar's man in Rome while the general was away consolidating his forces in Cisalpine Gaul. He was Cicero's implacable enemy. Nor, to hear Cicero tell it, was he a friend of the people. At a performance of Lucius Afranius's comedy *Simulans* (*The Pretender*)—Cicero delights in the irony of the name—

the whole company, speaking all together in loud tones, bent forward threateningly and looking straight at the foul wretch, loudly chanted the words,

This, Titus, is the sequel, the end of your vicious life!

He sat utterly disconcerted, and the man who used to make his meetings resound with the hoots of a ribald claque was hooted away by the speech of genuine actors.[13]

Cicero is at his biting best in telling this anecdote because the revenge he was exacting was personal. Clodius had been one of the ringleaders who drove Cicero into exile in 58 B.C., and now one year later, just recalled to Rome, Cicero was defending his ally Sextius from a trumped-up charge of having used an armed guard during his tribunate.

12. Ibid., 2.19. Compare Valerius Maximus, 6.2.9.
13. Cicero, *Pro sestio*, 55.118, trans. R. Gardner, Loeb Library (London, 1958), p. 197.

Later in his speech *Pro Sextio*, Cicero recalls in proud detail how he himself was the subject of theatrical propaganda when the Senate had sentenced him to exile. The play being acted was Accius's *Eurysaces*. Singling out the senators in the audience, seated together in the social hierarchy, the great actor Aesopus turned the theater into a courtroom and Accius's tragedy into a lawyer's brief on Cicero's behalf:

For while he uttered the words:

> Who with firm spirit helped the public cause,
> Upheld it, ever stood with the Achivi—

with what force he made it clear that I had stood on your side, as he pointed to your assembled Orders! He was encored by all when he went on to say:

> In wavering affairs did never waver
> His life to offer, nor did spare his head.

What shouts of applause greeted his performance of this passage, when they took no notice of the acting, but applauded the words of the poet, the earnestness of the actor and the hope of my recall!
Our greatest friend, in this our greatest war.

What may have been lacking in Accius the great Aesopus improvised on the spot:

The actor himself added the words
> Endowed with greatest genius
out of friendship for me and perhaps the spectators approved owing to some regret for my absence.

(56)

Scenes like this one demonstrate just how thin the wall was that separated the senators' portico from Pompey's theater. Not surprisingly, the turmoil of events that followed Caesar's assassination in that same portico spilled over onto the stage next door. In two of the speeches that he delivered against Mark Anthony after the event, Cicero recalls the applause in support of Brutus that interrupted Accius's *Tereus* during the Apollinarian games in July 44.

In these four instances—the attack on Pompey by the actor Diphilus, the humiliation of Clodius during Afranius's *Simu-*

lans, Aesopus's defense of Cicero during Accius's *Eurysaces,* and the public applause for Brutus during Accius's *Tereus*— Cicero provides four of the most intimate and immediate accounts of ancient drama in performance to be found anywhere. All four are highly charged with political double meanings. To Cicero's Renaissance readers it must have seemed that political allegory was of the very essence of the Greek and Latin scripts they had inherited from Athens and Rome—and political allegory of a timeless sort. Cicero makes it clear that neither Afranius nor Accius could have originally intended the contemporary applications to which their scripts were put. Politics and play—the sport was in putting the two together. Actors took it as a challenge to their ingenuity; audiences, as a challenge to their perspicacity. As Aesopus showed in *Eurysaces,* an actor might even add lines to sharpen the political point. Following ancient example, Renaissance actors and Renaissance audiences might just as readily find correspondence between ancient playscripts and their own political situation and might just as readily add lines and scenes to drive the point home. Cicero's writings, then, reflect three well-defined interests in the theater—rhetorical, moral, and political—that determine what the great statesman, philosophizer, and orator reports about the Greek and Latin playscripts he read and the performances of them he saw at Rome. Those three concerns, so close to the features of late medieval drama, earned classical plays a prominent place in the curriculum of Renaissance schools—and in the propaganda programs of Renaissance statesmen.

II

Two important intermediaries, Quintilian and Horace, stood between Cicero and Renaissance schoolmasters. Quintilian had taken Cicero's scattered ideas and codified them into the *Institutio oratoria,* a practical manual on how to educate statesmen. Unlike Cicero's clever advocate, able to argue any proposition, even a false one if the ends justify the means, Quintilian's ideal orator is above all a *vir bonus,* a *good* man. Once, Quintilian explains, oratory and philosophy had not been separate pursuits, but when advocacy became a way of making money, speakers forgot all about moral philosophy and left its study to what Quintilian disdains as "weaker intellects." The result has been a disastrous divorce between statesmen and thinkers, between deeds and deliberations. Quintilian's insistence on reuniting the two became the battle cry of militant Renaissance humanists, who wanted, above all, to unite man's wit to know the truth with his will to make it a reality. "Let our ideal orator," they said with Quintilian, "be such as to have a genuine title to the name of philosopher."[14] It remained for Renaissance humanists like Erasmus to Christianize Quintilian's vir bonus, and the educational worth of classical drama was securely established. *De ratione studii* (1511), the blueprint of curriculums and teaching methods that Erasmus drew up for the foundation of St. Paul's School in 1509, takes Terence as a particularly apt example in teaching a teacher how to teach. After introducing an author's life, commenting on his language, and commending his enjoyable usefulness, a teacher finally "should turn to philosophy and skilfully bring out the moral implication of the poets' stories, or employ them as patterns, for example, the story of Pylades and Orestes to show the excellence of friendship; that of Tantalus the curse of avarice."[15] When scripts like Terence's were not just read but acted out, the moral program came to rhetorical life, casting the audience in the role of jurors.

In Horace's *Ars poetica* (17 B.C.; first printed, 1470) Cicero's sensibility and Quintilian's pedagogy became a system of poetics. Thanks to synthesizers like Donatus, the fourth-century grammarian who was St. Jerome's tutor, Horace's ideas if not the *Ars poetica* itself enjoyed wide currency in the Middle Ages. In *De comoedia*, a treatise reprinted in virtually every Renaissance edition of Terence, Donatus offers, for example, an account of the origins and development of ancient drama that is cribbed from *Ars poetica*, 275–94. More than his histor-

14. *Institutio oratoria*, trans. H. E. Butler, Loeb Library (London, 1921), 1.Pr.18–19. See also Cicero, *De oratore*, 3.15.57.

15. Trans. Brian McGregor in *Collected Works of Erasmus*, ed. Craig R. Thompson, Vol. 2 (Toronto, 1978): 682–83. On Roman rhetoric as the basis for humanist education, see T. W. Baldwin, *William Shakespere's Small Latine & Lesse Greeke* (Urbana, Ill., 1944), 1: 75–184, 2: 1–238.

ical information, however, it was Horace's critical principles that earned him a secure place in medieval thought.

> . . . he hath every suffrage, can apply
> Sweet mix'd with sowre, to his Reader, so
> As doctrine, and delight together go.[16]

Qui miscuit utile dulci—Horace's interests in poetry fitted neatly into the place assigned to Rhetoric in the Trivium as codified by Martianus Cappella, midway between useful ideas of Philosophy on the one hand and the detailed study of Grammar, delight in words themselves, on the other.

Indeed, Horace's overriding concern with the relationship between poem and reader, with what the poet should do to achieve such and such an effect, stamps the *Ars poetica* with a definite rhetorical character. The poet becomes a kind of advocate, attempting to sway his reader/audience. Usually it is, in fact, an audience, not readers, that Horace has in mind. Whether the Pisos, to whom he was writing his epistle, were especially interested in plays, or whether drama provided the clearest literary example of rhetorical principles at work, Horace spends fully two-thirds of the *Ars poetica* talking about drama. The rhetorical character of the *Ars poetica* was made explicit by Renaissance commentators. Bodius Ascensius, whose commentary, first published in 1500, was often reprinted with Horace's text in the sixteenth century, is particularly insistent on citing Cicero and Quintilian for explanations, clarifications, and examples of Horace's ideas. By studying Horace through frames of commentary like that of Badius, Renaissance readers found in the *Ars poetica* a full and unified system of poetics conceived totally in the rhetorical terms dictated by Cicero and Quintilian.[17]

---

16. Horace, *Ars poetica*, 343–44, trans. Ben Jonson as "Horace, Of the Art of Poetrie" (rev. version, 1640), in *The Complete Poetry of Ben Jonson*, ed. William B. Hunter, Jr. (New York, 1963), p. 309. Future quotations from the *Ars poetica* are taken from Jonson's translation; line references to the Latin original are cited in the text. An earlier English translation by Thomas Drant had appeared in 1567.

17. Sixteenth-century Italian commentaries on Horace are studied in Weinberg, *History*, 1:71–249.

All three of Cicero's interests in drama are addressed by Horace. If he never acknowledges any specific *ad hominem* allusions, Horace at least grants poetry tremendous political power. A specific instance is the moral stand that the Chorus in tragedy should assume:

> It still must favour good men, and to these
> Be wonne a friend; It must both sway, and bend
> The angry, and love those that feare t'offend.
> Praise the spare diet, wholsome justice, lawes,
> Peace, and the open ports, that peace doth cause.
> Hide faults, pray to the Gods, and wish aloud
> Fortune would love the poore, and leave the proud.   (196–201)

To this moral dogma, we should observe, Horace gives a distinctly political cutting edge in his talk of justice, laws, and peace. Like Quintilian, Horace further requires that the poet himself be a vir bonus. "The very root of writing well, and spring," says Horace in words that echo Quintilian, "Is to be wise . . . ."

To Cicero's third interest in drama, rhetorical technique, Horace makes two important refinements that became critical doctrine in the sixteenth and seventeenth centuries. The first concerns decorum. Since the audience is ultimately the focus of attention in the rhetorical view of drama, it is *their* expectations that must determine both the style of language and the nature of the characters who speak and act in a play. The language, first of all, must suit the status of the characters, elevated for tragedy, lowly for comedy, else

> If now the phrase of him that speakes, shall flow
> In sound, quite from his fortune; both the rout
> And Roman Gentrie, jearing, will laugh out.   (112–13)

The characters themselves should correspond to the audience's expectations about the stock traits typical of different ages and stations in life:

> Heare, what it is the People, and I desire:
> If such a ones applause thou dost require,
> That tarries till the hangings be ta'en downe,

And sits, till the *Epilogue* saies *Clap*, or *Crowne*:
The customes of each age thou must observe,
And give their yeares, and natures, as they swerve,
Fit rites. (153–57)

Horace's insistent focus on the audience as the arbiter of both style and character raises—but does not answer—crucial questions that will concern us in Chapter Three. Who *is* the audience? The public at large? Or cultivated men like Horace himself and the Pisos?

Horace's second refinement in rhetorical technique we have noticed already in Ascham's "true imitation." For success in swaying one's audience, Horace declares, two things are necessary: both *ingenium* (native wit) and *ars* (craft). And the source of ars, as Cicero and Quintilian testify, is imitation of established masters. Coupled with Cicero's citations of classical dramatists, the effect of Horace's advice was to canonize Plautus, Terence, and Seneca in a way Horace himself, so casual in his advice, never does.

Taken together, then, Cicero, Quintilian, and Horace offered Renaissance readers a self-consistent, fully realized system for interpreting playscripts. Fundamental to that system was a sense of those scripts as plans for a rhetorical event, an exchange between an actor speaking *in loco poetae* and using all the devices of persuasion to convince his listeners of a moral argument, often one with political implications. The critical principles that are implied by Cicero, collected by Quintilian, and systematized by Horace we can see graphically in fifteenth- and sixteenth-century editions of the Greek and Roman dramatists. Almost never are we allowed to approach the text by ourselves. First, we must make our way through prefatory treatises that, like the dust jacket of a modern book, advertise the virtues of what we are about to read and, like the introduction to a critical edition, tell us all about such matters as the author's life, the genre he writes in, the metrical arrangements he uses. When we do finally reach the dramatic text, it is framed by running commentaries, ancient and modern, that often overwhelm the few lines of text that can

be squeezed in on a folio page. Lest we miss them in the com-
mentaries, memorable sententiae in the text are marked with
running quotation marks down the left margin. Occasionally
these sententiae are indexed at the back under such headings
as "the infelicity of love," "moderation," "the reward of ava-
rice." So great was the Renaissance love of the sententious that
in some cases readers could dispense with text altogether.
Claiming inspiration from Cicero, who so often quotes from
Euripides, Michael Neandrus put together in *Astrologia Euri-
pidea Graecolatina* (Basel, 1559), an anthology of sententiae
that gives merely a plot summary for each play, followed by a
numbered collection of memorable speeches, both in the
Greek original and in Latin translation, some only a single
line, some as long as a dozen lines or more, each tagged with
a marginal label. Woodcuts, finally, sometimes fill out Renais-
sance editions of the Greek and Roman dramatists and give us
a visual sense of what the fable would be like in a reader's
imagination if not in an actual observer's view of the stage.
(See Figure 1.)

There was competition among printers not only to come up
with *the* definitive text but to gather between two covers the
most inclusive collection of commentaries. A successful edi-
tion in Latin or Greek could command a pan-European
market and go through multiple printings for thirty years or
more. The edition of Terence printed by Benedict Prévost at
Paris in 1552 provides a particularly monumental example. So
many authorities are collected in *P. Terentii Afer poetae lepidis-
simi comoediae* that the great eighteenth-century bibliographer
Thomas F. Dibdin was inspired to dub Prévost's tome "the
folio variorum."[18] In addition to a well edited text the volume
contains

    1. arguments for each play by Melanchthon,
    2. annotations on genre and diction by Erasmus,
    3. textual notes by Antonius Goveanus,

18. Thomas F. Dibdin, *An Introduction to the Knowledge of Rare and Valuable
Editions of the Greek and Latin Classics*, 4th ed. (London, 1827), 2: 470.

4. a treatise on the meters of comic verse by Julius Caesar Scaliger,
5. an essay on comedy by L. Victor Faustus,
6. textual notes by Pietro Bembo,
7. prefatory matter and a running commentary by Donatus,
8. a special interpretation of *Heauton Timorumenos* by Joannes Calphurnius Brixiensis,
9. a commentary on difficult passages and rhetorical niceties by Adrianus Barlandus,
10. a running commentary by Bartolemaeus Latomus, with arguments for individual scenes, notes on the narrative divisions of the fables, and remarks on rhetoric,
11. a running commentary by Petrus Marsus,
12. textual notes by Joannes Rivus,
13. notes on *Andria* and *Eunuchus*,

plus Willichius's commentary at the end and Erasmus's, Goveanus's, and Bembo's commentaries at the beginning, not to mention Melanchthon's arguments and Scaliger's and Faustus's treatises. Each act of every play is illustrated with a woodcut. Taking in hand an edition like this one, we can quite literally look over the shoulder of a Renaissance reader and see how he would take in Terence's text. The philosophical context first sketched in by Cicero and Quintilian and then elaborated by Horace and his Renaissance interpreters appears here as a graphic reality. With such a frame to compose our view, what we must inescapably make out in Terence's text are rhetorical niceties, moral lessons, and political commentary.

The opening lines of Terence's *Eunuchus*, for example, positively demand that audiences laugh, that philologists expound, that moralists cluck their tongues. Phaedria's confusion when Thais asks him to give place for awhile to his rival Thraso earns him Cicero's condemnation for the vehemence of his love in the *Tusculan Disputations* and for his abuse of reason in *De natura deorum*, as well as a citation from Quintilian for his rhetorical questioning, inverted word order, and rhythmic looseness. His servant Parmeno's reply—"in love are these many vices[:] injuries, suspicions, enmitie, truce,

Phormionis

Primus actus

FIGURE I. Terence, *Comoediae*, ed. Jodocus Badius Ascensius
(Lyon: Trechsel, 1493), fols. D8ᵛEI.

warre, and peace againe out of hande"—prompts Cicero in the *Tusculan Disputations*, we recall, to the general conclusion that love is not a natural feeling and should be avoided.

Just such philological noting in the margin, just such rhetorical underlining with a pen, just such moral emphasis with quotation marks we discover in the commentaries collected in Renaissance editions of the play. Donatus's fourth-century gloss sets the pattern. "Here an *exemplum* is offered," says Donatus, "that a man in love is not in control of himself, that it is a wise man who is not in love or is otherwise affected." He goes on to cite parallels from Plautus and Menander for some of Terence's phrases before settling down to some very close observations on Terence's diction. About "Once she shut the dore on me, now she calles me againe" he says, for example, "In both cases he makes an injury out of a word, saying both 'Once she shut the dore on me' rather than 'she would not let me in' and 'now she calles me againe' rather than 'she asks me to return,' which would have been more moderate."

Melanchthon's line on the opening scene of *Eunuchus*, and indeed on the whole play, is even more sternly moral than Cicero's and Donatus's:

Comedies offer us numerous likenesses of life, to wit, what is appropriate in behavior, what is not appropriate, what variety there is in human nature, how all kinds of events happen to come about, how great the power of fortune is, how often counsel deceives us in danger. And this fable in particular has a tremendous variety of characters, counsels, and eventualities. This excellent comedy sets forth an example to shy, mild-mannered youths who think about their honest duty. Here are no honest examples, no honest counsels. For the play represents the loves of a courtesan.

Moral considerations inspire Petrus Marsus to something more than marginal comment:

This scene teaches us to beware the fury of such a love. Its excess is rightly reprehended: it shatters the soul in pieces, and, careening from reason's good judgment, it destroys freedom, which the noble soul strives after in every pursuit. It pulls man down, the divine creature born for glory and great things, so that it almost turns him back into an irrational animal. What could be more ridiculous! Phaedria is an example of a noble youth whose eyes of reason the harlot's wiles have beclouded and blindfolded, so that he can't pull himself out of love's snares, however much he regrets his mistake. Such is the power of this passion.

Latomus manages to combine moral outrage with a calm appreciation of how neatly Terence uses the first scene to lay out the plot. We are reminded of how Cicero in *De inventione* analyzes the opening scene of *Andria*:

The play starts off with the youth's confusion and complaint in such a way that it stretches out into the narration of the plot. It expresses, moreover, the madness of immoderate love and with what difficulty the wise soul tears itself away from such debilitating evil. Then, too, the youth is set against his soldier-rival in the story, thus laying out the argument, which includes the life of a silly, vainglorious man as well as a harlot's depravity.

Adrianus Barlandus, finally, notes allusions to this famous scene elsewhere in classical literature. Most noteworthy of all is Cicero in the *Tusculan Disputations*. Quintilian mentions the opening lines in his discussion of gesture. An actor speaking Phaedria's lines, he says, "will vary the modulations of his voice, together with the movements of hand and head." And Horace in his satires (2.3.258–71) virtually recreates the whole scene as part of a mocking account of love.[19] Though writing nearly sixteen hundred years after Cicero and Quintilian and nearly twelve hundred years after Donatus, these Renaissance commentators bring to Terence's text precisely the same moral, philological, and rhetorical preoccupations.

The rhetorical excellences were even grander, the philological parallels more instructive, the moral lessons more widely applicable when the commentators turned to tragedy. Without mentioning any particular play by name, Cicero and Quintilian, we have seen, were both drawn to the figure of Orestes as the perfect test case for analyzing motives, organizing a defense, and determining guilt. When Renaissance edi-

19. *P. Terentii Afer poetae lepidissimi comoediae* (Paris, 1552), fols. S3ᵛ–S4. My translation.

tors and commentators write about tragedy, they first of all adopt Cicero's forensic stance: why does the tragic hero act as he does? But they go further. When one asks Cicero's judicial questions with Quintilian's moral absolutes in mind, there can be no relativity in the answers: judged against the ideal standard of the vir bonus, are the tragic hero's actions to be defended or condemned? When, finally, the commentators add Erasmus's Christian canons to Quintilian's ethical ideals and Cicero's legal inquisition, the question becomes totally one of moral judgment: are the hero's actions right, or are they wrong? It is before this tribunal of Cicero, Quintilian, and Erasmus that tragic heroes must pass in Renaissance editions of Sophocles, Euripides, and Seneca.

Modern readers are most likely to associate Orestes with Aeschylus's *Oresteia*. But the veteran playwright's difficult Greek, bewildering choruses, and disappointing lack of incident made him a remote and shadowy figure throughout the sixteenth century, praised in passing but not widely read or studied and almost never acted. When Renaissance scholars thought about Orestes, they thought about Euripides. His *Orestes*, as we shall see, is one of the classical plays known to have been staged before Queen Elizabeth I. A less judgmental, idealistic, and morally dogmatic mind than Euripides' is hard to imagine. His version of the aftermath of Orestes' murder of Clytemnestra and Aegisthus wrenches the myth out of the remote times of Aeschylus's trilogy into a contemporary foreground where motives seem confused and ideals are tainted with flesh-and-blood realities. Orestes seems innocent enough at the beginning of the play but suddenly turns bloodthirsty with his decision to murder Helen and take hostage her daughter Hermione. Yet it is hard to denigrate him completely, since the figures of political and moral authority in the play, Menelaus and Tyndareus, are themselves petty, vindictive, and calculating. As the Hellenistic scholiast says, "The whole cast of characters is off-putting, because, except for Pylades, they are all bad and disgraceful."[20] In such a dramatic universe there seems to be no moral center of gravity.

20. Cited by William Arrowsmith in the introduction to his translation of

The Renaissance commentators supply one of their own devising. Melanchthon offers no preface to the play, but the sententiae he marks and the marginal glosses he supplies in his translation imply a definite interpretation. In the great debate between Orestes and Tyndareus (ll. 491ff. and 544ff.), Melanchthon chooses to ignore Tyndareus's vindictive rage and Orestes' genuine grievances and slashes the moral tangle with a single stroke of the sword of truth: "Slaughter cannot be vindicated with yet more slaughter."[21] Melanchthon has inquired into Orestes' case with Cicero's analytic acuity, Quintilian's moral idealism, and Erasmus's Christian conviction and has condemned the hero to well-deserved suffering. In his Latin translation of the play, Caspar Stiblin is even more dogmatic. When we see Orestes' suffering, says Stiblin, "we take thought how grievously God turns against wrong-doers, how mournful are the ends of monstrous emotions, what torture there is, what swords wound the conscience because of divine displeasure." The "God" Stiblin has in mind must be Jehovah, since Apollo drops in at the end of Euripides' play, most incongruously, and explains how it was he who made Orestes murder his parents and now all is forgiven. On this final scene, one of Euripides' most ironic, all the Renaissance commentators keep tactful silence.

In the multiple commentaries that bulk so large in Renaissance editions of Greek and Roman tragedy and comedy, one thing above all impresses a twentieth-century reader: the implication that there is a single authoritative way of viewing classical drama. The frame around the text is an amalgam of what the best readers and scholars have had to say across the centuries, and the astonishing thing is how much in agreement they seem. Hellenistic grammarians, Donatus, fifteenth-century humanists, the most recent sixteenth-century scholars all reinforce each other, at least on major issues. No allowance is made for the historical and philosophical differences that

the play in *Euripides IV*, ed. David Grene and Richmond Lattimore (Chicago, 1958), p. 108.

21. *Euripidis tragoediae* (Basel, 1558), fol. c6ᵛ. My translation.

distance Terence (fl. second century B.C.) from commentators as widely separated as Donatus (fl. A.D. fourth century) and Melanchthon (1497–1560). However different the physical arrangements may have been in Greek and Roman theater buildings, however different the social character of the audience, the philosophical aspects of the plays themselves seemed timeless and perfectly compatible with Renaissance experience. Euripides' anguished malefactors and Terence's lovesick youths and crochety fathers seemed quite at home in a timeless Christian universe that subsumed the particular moments in historical time when Euripides and Terence happened to have lived. It is not surprising, then, how little the critical framework changes in the course of the sixteenth and seventeenth centuries. New manuscripts might yield better texts, more factual knowledge might come to light about the ancient stage, Aeschylus and Aristophanes might come to enjoy the wider readership of Sophocles and Euripides and Plautus and Terence, but the philosophical context implied by the prefaces and commentaries accompanying sixteenth- and seventeenth-century editions of the Greek and Roman playwrights changed hardly at all.

III

By all accounts, the tidy bookracks and tidy minds of Renaissance critics should have been thrown into disarray by Aristotle's newly rediscovered *Poetics*. The single difference between Aristotle's theoretical conception of mimēsis and Horace's practical advice on imitatio, noted already, reflects fundamental differences between the two critics' ideas about the very nature of drama. Horace's rhetorical view is focused on the ways in which performing a play is like giving a speech: like Cicero and Quintilian, Horace never loses sight of the fact that a play consists of characters standing in front of an audience and speaking to them directly. In the physical immediacy of the play-as-rhetorical-event three things stand out: (1) the "message," the philosophical program of the play, (2) the style of the speeches, and (3) the nature of the speakers, i.e., characterization. Aristotle's objective view, on the other hand, is focused on the ways in which a play is like a painting, a piece of sculpture, or other art object. Tragedy is "a process of imitating an action which has serious implications, is complete, and possesses magnitude . . . through a course of pity and fear completing the purification of tragic acts which have those emotional characteristics": Aristotle never loses sight of the fact that a play is a species of poiesis, "a made thing," a piece of fiction with a beginning, middle, and end, just as a painting has a foreground and a background and a statue has a top and a bottom. In this less immediate, more philosophical sense of the play-as-object two things are important: (1) the structure of the art object itself, i.e., how the imitated action is arranged, and (2) the corresponding "structure" of the audience's response, particularly its *emotional* response. Ethical considerations do figure in this response, of course—Aristotle points out that the suffering hero should be neither altogether good nor altogether bad—but for Aristotle these ethical considerations are a means to the end of arousing pity and fear. In Horace's rhetorical view, by contrast, moral issues are an end in themselves.

Aristotle's notion of *katharsis*, with its excitation of the emotions of "pity" (*eleos*) and "fear" (*phobos*), rests upon a basic assumption that tragedy works its effects primarily by emotional, not by rational, means. Perhaps, as Gerald Else has suggested, the entire *Poetics* is to be seen as an answer to Plato's two great objections to poetry: that it imitates appearances, not Ideas, and that it appeals to emotion, not intellect. Tragedy is indeed a form of imitation, Aristotle counters Plato, but it imitates an action, not Ideas; nor does it pretend to make philosophy's appeal to the intellect.[22] The result is a very different view of tragedy from that implied by Cicero, Quintilian, and Horace: as described by Aristotle, tragedy is not reducible to a moral argument that can be proved like a case in court.

From these different views of the ends of tragedy follow

22. This thesis is advanced by Gerald F. Else in his introduction to the *Poetics* (Ann Arbor, 1967), pp. 2–8.

Aristotle's and Horace's very different ideas about characterization. The three terms that Aristotle uses for character are all devoid of any psychological suggestion: *prosōpon* means, literally, "aspect" or, by analogy, "mask"; *prattontes* and *drontes* are the "doers" or "enactors" of the dramatic events.[23] When Aristotle does use the word *ēthos*, less literally a term of histrionic jargon than the other three, he nonetheless restricts it to how a stage-figure acts: " 'character' [ēthos] is that kind of utterance which clearly reveals the bent of a man's moral choice (hence there is no character in that class of utterances in which there is nothing at all that the speaker is choosing or rejecting). . . ."[24] Character exists only as action reveals it. By contrast, Horace's term for character is *mos, mores* ("will," "inclination," "conduct," "morals"), a word that replaces Aristotle's sense of external acting with a strong sense of internal choosing. The profound difference between Greek ēthos and Latin mores is recognized by no less an authority than Quintilian. Emotions, he observes, fall into two classes:

the one is called *pathos* by the Greeks and is rightly and correctly expressed in Latin by *adfectus*; the other is called *ēthos*, a word for which in my opinion Latin has no equivalent: it is however rendered by mores and consequently the branch of philosophy known as *ethics* is styled *moral* philosophy by us. But close consideration of the subject leads me to think that in this connexion it is not so much *mores* in general that is meant as certain particular aspects; for the term *mores* includes every attitude of the mind. The more cautious writers have preferred to give the sense of the term rather than to translate it into Latin.   (6.2.8–9)

That is, mores sums up all the thoughts and emotions of a man; ēthos particularizes the inclinations that converge when a man makes choices. With its insistent focus on the actor who actually stands in front of us and speaks, the rhetorical view

23. John Jones, *On Aristotle and Greek Tragedy* (London, 1962), pp. 29–46.
24. Aristotle, *Poetics*, 1450.b.5ff., trans. Gerald F. Else (Ann Arbor, 1967), pp. 28–29. Future quotations from the *Poetics* are taken from Else's translation; line references to the Greek original are cited in the text.

of drama offers us, not the "mask" or "enactor" of Aristotle's objective view, but a rounded character.

Despite Aristotle's challenging ideas, the desks and minds of sixteenth- and seventeenth-century critics remained neatly ordered. None of the distinctions obvious to us looking back four hundred years later seemed quite so apparent to the Renaissance scholars who took in hand Aristotle's *Poetics* after it was first printed in Giorgio Valla's Latin translation of 1498: they simply interpreted what they read according to the rhetorical model of drama set in place by Cicero, Quintilian, and Horace. In fact, few people took in hand Aristotle's text at all until Francesco Robortello published his commentary in 1548—and thoroughly rhetoricized the *Poetics* to make it accord with Horatian dogma. All over Europe in the sixteenth and seventeenth centuries critics of drama pursued the same logically impossible end: they attempted to accommodate the new ideas of Aristotle with the already familiar ideas of Horace. In "An Execration upon Vulcan," for exmaple, Ben Jonson laments that among the manuscripts claimed by a fire in his library was an English translation of "All the old *Venusine*, in *Poetrie*, / and lighted by the *Stagerite*, could spie" (ll. 89–90).[25] Aristotle, he implies, was Horace's mentor, or perhaps Jonson as translator used the *Poetics* to illustrate the *Ars poetica*. Not only pragmatic poets like Jonson but theoretical systematizers like Thomas Rymer failed to see the ontological differences that separate the play-as-object from the play-as-rhetorical-event. As a result, their criticism is an unstable mixture of Horatian and Aristotelian ingredients.[26] As maddening as it might be for aesthetic philosophers in their books, that

25. *Complete Poetry*, ed. Hunter, p. 190

26. Charles B. Schmitt, *Aristotle and the Renaissance* (Cambridge, Mass., 1983) shows how *all* of Aristotle's writings were similarly assimilated into already existing modes of thought in the fifteenth, sixteenth, and early seventeenth centuries. In his introduction to *Aristotle's "Poetics" and English Literature* (pp. ix–xxviii) Elder Olson demonstrates how assumptions about literature in particular remained primarily Horatian and concludes, "it is hardly too extreme to say that the general development of neoclassical criticism would have remained much the same had the *Poetics* never figured in it" (p. xviii).

ambiguity proved richly suggestive for actors on the stage, as
we shall see in charting the changes in comedy and tragedy
onstage between 1500, when Aristotle was virtually
unknown, and 1700, when in theory at least he reigned
supreme.

In the meantime, we can follow the creative interplay of
Aristotle's and Horace's ideas by considering how five six-
teenth- and seventeenth-century critics of drama address the
two central ideas in Aristotle's scheme: (1) the "mistake"
(*hamartia*) that accounts for the tragic hero's downfall and thus
dictates the shape of the plot, and (2) the emotional "purging"
(katharsis) that the spectators experience as the results of that
mistake become clear. Francesco Robortello (1516–1567),
Daniel Heinsius (1580–1665), Theodore Goulston (1572–
1632), Thomas Rymer (1643–1713), and John Dryden (1631–
1700) represent not only five distinct phases in the amalga-
mation of Aristotle's observations with Horace's dogma but
five distinct approaches to drama in general. Proceeding as a
medieval philosopher might, Robortello sets up his *In librum
Aristotelis de arte poetica explicationes* (1548) as a line-by-line
commentary that takes the *Poetics* as a pre-text and produces
an essentially new treatise—one that is more Horatian than
Aristotelian.[27] Heinsius, by contrast, approaches the *Poetics*
wholisticly: he first made a fresh translation of it into Latin
(published separately in 1610), then isolated the main lines of
Aristotle's argument, and within that outline rearranged the
sketchy and corrupt text of the *Poetics* into a more logical
order and amplified it with his own explanations and with
ideas from Horace. The result was a sixteen-chapter treatise
De tragoediae constitutione ("On the Ordering of Tragedy"),
first published at Leiden in 1611 and reprinted with stylistic
revisions in 1643. As much as an elucidation of Aristotle, *De
tragoediae constitutione* was intended as a how-to-do-it manual
for playwrights, and as such it found its way into the *Discov-
eries* of Ben Jonson and indirectly into the critical pronounce-

27. Robortello's commentary is discussed in detail by Weinberg, *History*,
1: 388–404.

ments of John Milton and John Dryden.[28] More than anyone else, it was Heinsius who first gave seventeenth-century readers a sense of the Aristotelian forest amid the Ciceronian trees. As the first publication of the *Poetics* in England, Theodore Goulston's *Aristotelis de poetica liber, Latine conversus, et analytica methodo illustratus* (London, 1623) illustrates how a successful physician and amateur scholar used the philosophical commonplaces of his own day to construe Aristotle's Greek. Significantly, it was Aristotle's *Rhetoric* that Goulston had turned to first; his Latin translation was published in 1619, four years before his version of the *Poetics* appeared. Famous today for using the neoclassical rules to dismiss *Othello* as "a Bloody Farce, without salt or savour," Thomas Rymer is a lonely and eccentric English representative of a type that congregated at the very center of literary affairs in Cardinal Richelieu's France: the doctrinaire Aristotelian who attacks the supposed faults of modern drama with all the zeal of a convert and all the presumption of a critic who writes no plays himself. Rymer, as we shall see, resembles most of his French mentors in remaining blithely unaware of the Horatian beam in his own eye. Dryden, finally, speaks as a practicing dramatist who picks up useful critical ideas wherever he can find them, without worrying overmuch about how they hang together logically.[29]

For Aristotle, hamartia is a "mistake"—no more, no less. It is not the mistake itself that engages his attention so much as the *results* of that mistake. When he sets out to categorize the different kinds of plots, Aristotle concentrates on the various kinds of outcome, not on the various kinds of mistake. Among the possible outcomes

28. Heinsius's *De tragoediae constitutione* is considered both by Paul R. Sellin, *Daniel Heinsius and Stuart England* (Leiden and London, 1968), pp. 123–46, and Baerbel Becker-Cantarino, *Daniel Heinsius* (Boston, 1978), pp. 143–53. Sellin also traces Heinsius's influence on Jonson (pp. 147–63), Milton (pp. 164–77), and Dryden (pp. 178–99).

29. Dryden's eclecticism is stressed by Edward Pechter, *Dryden's Classical Theory of Literature* (Cambridge, 1975), pp. 11–35; his constant awareness of his seventeenth-century audience, by Grace, *Tragic Theory*, pp. 89–128

it is clear first of all that [1] neither should virtuous men appear undergoing a change from good to bad fortune, for that is not fearful, nor pitiable either, but morally repugnant; nor [2] the wicked from bad fortune to good—that is the most untragic form of all, it has none of the qualities one wants: it is productive neither of ordinary sympathy nor of pity nor of fear—nor again [3] the really wicked man changing from good fortune to bad, for that kind of structure will excite sympathy but neither pity nor fear, since the one [pity] is directed towards the man who does not deserve his misfortune and the other [fear] towards the one who is like the rest of mankind—what is left is the man who falls between these extremes. Such is a man who is neither a paragon of virtue and justice nor undergoes the change to misfortune through any real badness or wickedness but because of some mistake [hamartia]; one of those who stand in great repute and prosperity, like Oedipus and Thyestes: conspicuous men from families of that kind.   (1452.b.30–1453.a.10)

If, as Aristotle insists, plot, not character, is the primary element of tragedy, hamartia could be simply a tactical error, an action done in ignorance, as Oedipus, for example, chooses to pronounce an edict that will exile from Thebes whoever is causing the plague. No moral importance is attached to the mistake.[30] Indeed, Aristotle goes out of his way to specify that the hero is "neither a paragon of virtue and justice nor undergoes the change to misfortune through any real badness or wickedness." In another context he distinguishes the characters of tragedy, "better than we are," from the characters of comedy, "worse than we are" (1448.a.1–15), but morality has less to do with that difference than social status. The word Aristotle uses is *spoudaios*, "worthwhile." *Spoudaioi*, the heroes of tragedy, are "men of consequence"; *phauloi*, the protagonists of comedy, are "worthless people," "men of no consequence."

From medieval drama the playwrights and critics of the Renaissance inherited two patterns for making philosophical

---

30. Gerald F. Else, *Aristotle's Poetics: The Argument* (Cambridge, Mass., 1957); Jones, *On Aristotle*, pp. 18–20; Walter Kaufmann, *Tragedy and Philosophy* (New York, 1968), pp. 70–80.

and aesthetic sense out of calamity: either the protagonist sins and is punished for it, as morality plays would have it, or the protagonist falls through the constant turning of Fortune's wheel, as Boccaccio arranges things in *De casibus virorum illustrium*. The two patterns can be crossed, as when a protagonist like Chaucer's Troilus sins by losing sight of Christian truth and trusts to Fortune instead, but the patterns remain distinct in how they interpret the universe, providential or haphazard, and how they view the hero in relation to the world around him, responsible chooser or passive victim.[31] The *Poetics*, then, posed a real dilemma: if the hero of tragedy is a good man, how are we to account for the mistake that brings him to grief? To the Renaissance way of looking at things, Aristotle must have seemed surprisingly uninterested in the philosophical issues.

Robortello attempts to make sense of this very un-Christian state of affairs by invoking the pattern of morality plays: hamartia as he translates it is a "grave and great fault":

For Aristotle meant . . . that the tragic action is not drawn from the fault of just any man who might be of the people and of unknown origin. Therefore, Aristotle very cleverly posited these two things: first, a grave and great fault [*peccatum grave & magnum*] and then that the hero should fall from happiness to misery. For these things cannot happen at the same time to any body unless he be a man of the highest authority and dignity and placed by fortune in the highest degree of happiness.[32]

Agnus Dei, qui tollis peccata mundi, miserere nobis: far from being a tactical mistake, Robortello's "fault" is a *sin*, an action that demands moral judgment. How can a man not be evil and yet

31. J.M.R. Margeson, *The Origins of English Tragedy* (Oxford, 1967), distinguishes four worldviews in English Renaissance drama: (1) a world ruled by Fortune, (2) a world of faith in universal order and divine justice, (3) a world of skepticism, and (4) "a realm between faith and doubt." The first two are inheritances from the Middle Ages; the third and fourth are Renaissance innovations.

32. Francesco Robortello, *In librum Aristotelis de Arte Poetica explicationes* (1548), facsimile reprint (Munich, 1968), p. 132. All translations from Robortello are my own. Future references are cited in the text.

be guilty of a "peccatum grave & magnum"? Robortello
replies: unlike the hero of a morality play, the hero of a
tragedy sins in ignorance. The consquences, however, remain
the same. To frame the moral question here, Robortello intro-
duces the distinction between voluntary acts and involuntary
acts that Aristotle makes in the *Nicomachean Ethics* (3.1.1–3).
Involuntary acts only, Robortello insists, belong to tragedy:
"The distinguishing of these actions Aristotle says is useful to
legislators, so that they can determine who should be pun-
ished and who should not. For *voluntary* deeds ought to be
atoned for with punishment; *involuntary* deeds often demand
forgiveness, because they are pitiable. It is useful to distin-
guish these matters not only for legislators but also for tragic
poets, so that they can know the action that fits tragedies
best." A bad act voluntarily committed cannot be the subject
of tragedy, because Aristotle specifies that the tragic hero is
basically a good man. "There remains, then, the one action of
those who sin [*peccant*] involuntarily; for these are worthy of
pity and forgiveness. It is this kind of action that the tragic
poets choose and attempt to express and imitate. Therefore,
when Aristotle searches for the man who is the mean between
good and bad, it is this very one that he singles out, who sins
in ignorance and with lack of foresight. For he is not good,
since he has sinned; but neither is he altogether bad, since he
has sinned unwittingly and is sorry that he has sinned" (pp.
131–32).

The result of Robortello's carefully legalistic reasoning is to
make the tragic scenario a great deal more restrictive than it is
with Aristotle: (1) the "sin" has to be something heinous (pec-
catum grave & magnum), (2) the protagonist has to commit
the sin in ignorance, and (3) repentance must follow. Like the
distinction between voluntary and involuntary actions, this
final stipulation comes from the *Nicomachaean Ethics*, in which
Aristotle specifies that an act is involuntary "only when it
causes the agent pain and regret" (3.1.13). Coupled with the
loaded Christian term "peccatum," "pain and regret" assume
with Robortello a moral significance that Aristotle never gave
them. Does, then, calculated evil have no place in tragedy?

What about such thoroughly voluntary sinners as Aegisthus and Clytemnestra? Can there be no innocent victims either? What about Electra and Orestes? Robortello addresses these questions directly and singles out these protagonists particularly. What Aristotle offers, he concludes, is an ideal model; what poets have chosen to do in practice is something else again. Robortello thus leaves a critical door open to admit protagonists other than repentant sinners who have acted in ignorance, but he insists that all comers submit their tragic mistakes to the audience's moral judgment.

One way of understanding hamartia, then, was to relate it to the morality-play pattern of crime and punishment. The second way was to relate it to the rule of Fortune in Boccaccio's *De casibus virorum illustrium*. This is the tactic implicit in Theodore Goulston's Latin translation of the *Poetics*. The hero of tragedy "is changed and falls into Adverse Fortune not because of an evilness of spirit or depravity," Goulston translates, "but because of some human error [*propter Erratum aliquod humanum*]." A marginal note makes the implications even clearer: "He acts unfortunately [*infeliciter*] not out of depravity of spirit but out of a lack of foreknowledge [*praeinscitia*]."[33] With its connotations of *errare* ("to wander, to stray," "to waver"), Goulston's *erratum* is far from the grave sin, the peccatum, that Robortello reads into hamartia. Infeliciter transposes the whole matter out of a providential universe ruled by rewards and punishments into one governed by the chance turnings of Fortune's wheel. Of the two attempts to square the *Poetics* with medieval theology, Goulston's is perhaps the closer to Aristotle's meaning, yet Robortello's commanded the greater following among sixteenth- and seventeenth-century critics.

Thinking in terms of morality plays and *de casibus* narratives, Robortello and Goulston try in different ways to square hamartia with Christian morality. Thinking in terms of the *Iliad* and the *Odyssey*, Daniel Heinsius tries to reconcile

---

33. *Aristotelis de Poetica Liber, Latine conversus, et analytica methodo illustratus* (London, 1623), pp. 11–12. Translations from Goulston's Latin are my own.

hamartia with the seventeenth-century conception of the epic hero as a paragon of virtue. Though Aristotle does recognize in the *Poetics* that epic and tragedy share the same source myths, he takes pains to point out the concentration of plot and the dramatic mode that distinguish tragedy from epic; Heinsius, on the other hand, clearly wants to identify tragedy with the genre that Renaissance poetics ranked at the highest reach of human imagination: "Men say that although Sophocles, a divine man, had Aeschylus to imitate, he nevertheless copied Homer, and that he followed the latter in another form of writing even though he could have followed the first in his very own. Although certain things in the epic are different, yet both the regard for grandeur in expression and the choice of words that has to be made are the same—just as in the action too and its arrangement, there is no great distinction. The passions, moreover, are almost identical."[34] If sixteenth-century critics like Robortello were predisposed to read tragedy in terms of morality plays, seventeenth-century critics like Heinsius were eager to convert it into a species of epic. Aristotle seemed, indeed, to invite such an attempt by describing the tragic hero as spoudaios, "worthwhile," "better than we are." Thinking in Horace's rhetorical terms, Heinsius identifies spoudaios not with social consequence but with moral uprightness: "For Aristotle's position is neither that only people of the best moral character are to be introduced, nor that if others whom all agree to be wicked are introduced, good manners must be given them, but that as many persons of the best moral character as the design permits should be introduced into one and the same play. Indeed, although both sorts are necessary and although decorum rests on the grounds as much of the one as of the other, the good are to be preferred to the extent that they render more benefit when they are viewed" (ch. 14, p. 91). In the epic view, as in the morality-

---

34. Heinsius, *De tragoediae constitutione*, 2d ed. (1643), trans. Paul R. Sellin and John J. McManmon, as *On Plot in Tragedy* (Northridge, Calif., 1971), ch. 17, p. 114. Future references to Sellin and McManmon's translation are cited in the text.

play view, hamartia poses difficulties. The epic hero, at least as he was viewed in the seventeenth century, is an exemplar of virtue, a larger-than-life *vir bonus*. How, then, can he be guilty of a mistake? To answer this dilemma, Heinsius, like Robortello, invokes the *Nicomachean Ethics* and distinguishes involuntary from voluntary acts. Unlike Robortello, however, Heinsius plays down the status of the mistake as "sin": the tragic protagonist, he says, "offends" unintentionally. Though Heinsius conceives the hero himself in Horace's moral terms, he grants hamartia a neutrality closer to what Aristotle intended.

Thoroughgoing Aristotelian though he claims to be, Thomas Rymer follows the sixteenth-century rhetoricians in understanding spoudaios in moral terms; he thus shares Heinsius's conviction that the tragic hero ought to be as good as possible. Modern travesties like Beaumont and Fletcher's *Rollo Duke of Normandy* may titilate the audience with prodigies of evil, Rymer says, but ancient tragedies admit no real malefactors:

> The *Poets* consider'd, that naturally men were affected with *pitty*, when they saw others suffer more than their fault deserv'd; and *vice*, they thought, could never be painted too ugly and frightful; therefore, whether they would move *pitty*, or make *vice* detested, it concern'd them to be somewhat of the severest in the punishments they inflicted. Now, because their hands were tied, that they could not punish beyond such a degree; they were oblig'd to have a strict eye on their Malefactor, that he transgrest not too far, that he committed not *two* crimes, when responsible for *one*: nor, indeed be so far guilty, as by Law to deserve death.[35]

Though Rymer never acknowledges the inspiration of epic, he follows Heinsius in devising a tragic scenario in which the emphasis is less on the hero's mistake than on his grand passions, grand language, and equally grand moral stature.

---

35. Rymer, *The Tragedies of the Last Age Consider'd and Examin'd by the Practice of the Ancients, and by the Common Sense of All Ages* (1678), in *The Critical Works of Thomas Rymer*, ed. Curt A. Zimansky (New Haven, 1956), p. 27. Future references to Rymer's criticism are taken from this edition and are cited in the text.

As we might expect from a man who not only wrote heroic plays like *Aureng-Zebe* but vigorously defended them in print, John Dryden gives this epic view of the tragic hero its most extreme statement. We behold with fear, Dryden says, a misfortune that happens "to persons of the highest quality." "But when we see that the most virtuous, as well as the greatest, are not exempt from such misfortunes, that consideration moves pity in us, and insensibly works us to be helpful to, and tender over, the distressed, which is the noblest and most godlike of moral virtues. Here 'tis observable that it is absolutely necessary to make a man virtuous, if we desire he should be pitied: we lament not, but detest, a wicked man, we are glad when we behold his crimes are punished, and that poetical justice is done upon him."[36] Even in his own time, Dryden notes, Euripides was censured for egregiously wicked characters like Phaedra—one of the very reasons Euripides was more popular than any other tragic dramatist except Seneca when classical playscripts were first brought back to the stage in the sixteenth century. Seventeenth-century taste, at least as Dryden articulates it, adheres to a more idealistic standard. A thinker of good common sense and a dramatist of good business sense, Dryden will not go quite all the way in turning tragic heroes into epic demigods: "Shall we therefore banish all characters of villainy? I confess I am not of that opinion; but it is necessary that the hero of the play be not a villain; that is, the characters which should move our pity ought to have virtuous inclinations, and degrees of moral goodness in them. As for a perfect character of virtue, it never was in nature, and therefore there can be no imitation of it; but there are allays of frailty to be allowed for the chief persons, yet so that the good which is in them shall outweigh the bad, and consequently leave room for punishment on the one side, and pity on the other" (1: 245–46).

Hamartia, then, is "frailty." Aristotle's "mistake," Robor-

36. Dryden, "The Grounds of Criticism in Tragedy," prefaced to *Troilus and Cressida* (1679), in *Of Dramatic Poesy and Other Critical Essays*, ed. George Watson (London, 1962), 1: 245. Future references to Dryden's criticism are taken from this edition and are cited in the text.

tello's "sin," and Goulston's "error" are actions; Dryden's "frailty" is an aspect of character, part of the mores that define the tragic hero. The example of Dryden's own plays demonstrates how often this "frailty" is bound up with the very qualities that make the hero great. With Dryden we discover for the first time the now commonplace idea that hamartia is not so much a mistake in action as a "flaw" in character, a fatal crack in the heroic armor.

The structure of the plot is the first of Aristotle's objective interests in drama; the structure of the audience's response is the second. Eleos and phobos: tragedy works its effect, says Aristotle, by arousing these two strong, basic emotions. "The one [pity] is directed towards the man who does not deserve his misfortune and the other [fear] towards the one who is like the rest of mankind" (1453.a.1–5). For the hero's sufferings we feel compassion; at the reflection that such a fate might just as easily overtake us we feel fear. Aristotle never quite makes the point explicit, but eleos and phobos are fundamentally opposite emotions: the soft, out-flowing quality of compassion runs counter to the hard, inward-turning quality of fear. Indeed, part of the special appeal of tragedy seems to be its capacity to arouse these two visceral, radically opposite emotions and keep them in tension. Holding an objective view of drama, Aristotle describes the audience's response to tragedy as a poise between conflicting emotions. Holding a rhetorical view, Cicero and Horace see drama as single-mindedly devoted to one big effect: to convince the audience of a particular argument and to manipulate the audience's feelings to that end. Viewed rhetorically, a play thus aims at a single, well-focused emotion—like or dislike—not at two emotions, and certainly not at two emotions that are ambiguously in conflict with one another. The sixteenth- and seventeenth-century critics who try to reconcile the *Poetics* with the *Ars poetica* must somehow interpret eleos and phobos so that they work together rather than pull in opposite directions.

The Latin equivalents that Robortello finds for eleos and phobos are just as resonant with Christian overtones as peccatum. For Robortello, eleos is *misericordia*. "Pity" and "compassion," to be sure, are two of the meanings of misericordia, but so, too, is the morally more complicated matter of "mercy." "His mercy [misericordia] is on them that fear Him throughout all generations. He hath showed strength with His arm: He hath scattered the proud in the imagination of their hearts. He hath put down the mighty from their seat: and hath exalted the humble and meek." The mercy celebrated in the Magnificat is *unmerited* pity: from his morally superior position God might justifiably condemn, but he condescends instead to spare "them that fear Him." Fear (*timiditas*) is the very condition for mercy. Both emotions are defined with reference to the moral absolutes by which the hero's hamartia is to be judged.

Robortello's term for phobos is *terror*. Though appropriated from Seneca, terror likewise betrays Christian rather than Greek assumptions. Robortello observes:

This fear, indeed, is nothing else than a kind of fearful conscientiousness [*religio quaedam meticulosa*], by which the souls of men are bound, for true conscientiousness [*vera religio*] is that in which respect towards the Gods is joined together with dutiful conduct in order to secure the greatest blessings for the offspring of those men; for it is right that men should offer gratitude to the immortal Gods with holy sacrifices, remembrances, and a grateful soul. This is the best reverence [*cultus Deorum*], the chastest, the holiest, the fullest of duty and true conscientiousness, that with voice and spotless mind we should venerate the authors of all our happiness, just as we should not be terrified of cruel tyrants. . . . But when tragedy is enacted and recited, fear of the Gods takes possession of our souls and shows that the Gods are always ferocious punishers.   (p. 128)

With mercy we reach out to the undeserving sufferer; with terror we stand back before the wages of sin. In keeping with his Christian convictions as well as with his rhetorical model, Robortello never forgets that the whole end of tragedy is an act of moral judgment. The emotions of compassion and fear that Aristotle describes as the effects of the play-as-object become part of the deliberative process that Robortello assumes in the play-as-rhetorical-event.

Aristotle may have countered Plato by insisting that tragedy

communicates as much by emotion as by intellect, but he pos-
itively invites Platonist intellect to take its revenge when he
chooses the puzzling metaphor of katharsis to describe trage-
dy's emotional effect. "Purgation"? In what sense do eleos and
phobos "purge"? Robortello articulates both of the explana-
tions that have been proposed by ancient and modern critics.
Citing a parallel use of the term "katharsis" in Aristotle's *Pol-
itics*, Robortello first defines the term in its literal, physiolog-
ical sense. Katharsis in this view is a kind of emotional diar-
rhetic: "This clearly pertains to people who are held back from
pity and fear, with great turbulation of the soul, so that it is
lightened and purged pleasurably, just as cursed suppliants
when they use sacred songs to purify the soul" (p. 53).
Tragedy, that is, arouses the powerful emotions of eleos and
phobos so as to "get them out of the system." But Robortello
also recognizes a metaphorical, ethical interpretation of
katharsis that is more compatible with the rhetorical view of
plays in performance. Pity and fear are not just "purged" but
"purified"; they are not just released but articulated and
refined. We feel sorrow at fictional adversity, says Robortello,
so as to face up to real adversity with less sorrow. "Add to this
that often men feel sorrow and fear wrongly, while poets in
the recitations of their tragedies offer the most noble persons
and events for pity, which justly each man—or rather each
wise man—dreads; men learn to recognize what those things
are that justly arouse pity and sorrow and what things justly
inspire fear" (p. 53). Tragedy, that is, purges *in order* to purify:
it trains our emotions and makes us better judges of life.
Goulston, too, has it both ways: by the neat device of sup-
plying two verbs for Aristotle's one, he describes katharsis as
both "purging" (*purgans*) and "purifying" (*expians*) (pp. 11–
12). Once again Aristotle's sense of the play-as-object is sub-
ordinated to Cicero's sense of the play-as-rhetorical-event.
However much they might be distracted by Aristotle's
emphasis on the well-constructed plot, sixteenth- and seven-
teenth-century critics never ceased to heed Horace's still small
voice:

> . . . he hath every suffrage, can apply
> Sweet mix'd with sowre, to his Reader, so
> As doctrine, and delight together go.

Heinsius seems to go out of his way to avoid such a patently Christian term as Robortello's peccatum, yet the misericordia and horror that figure in his translation of Aristotle's definition are not without their moral overtones, particularly when we consider the distinctly moral end that Heinsius sets for katharsis. His ingenious explanation of the term falls somewhere between the purgation that Aristotle implies and the purification that Robortello reads into it: "Since this Muse is primarily engaged in arousing the passions, Aristotle therefore thinks its end is to temper these very passions and put them back into order. The passions proper to it are two: pity [misericordia] and horror [horror]. As it arouses these in the soul, so, as they gradually rise, it reduces them to the right measure and forces them into order" (ch. 2, p. 11). Thus, in Heinsius's own example, a doctor learns to temper the horror and pity that would naturally overwhelm a man when he first sees a soldier wounded in battle. "This is what the things exhibited in the theater must answer to, because it is a kind of training hall for our passions which (since they are not only useful in life but even necessary) must there be readied and perfected" (ch. 2, p. 12). With Heinsius as with Robortello, katharsis is the efficient cause of tragedy; instructing while delighting, the final cause.

Even Rymer shares this assumption that tragedy works its effects not just emotionally but intellectually. Like a forensic oration, a play in performance attempts to sway the audience's judgment, to convince them of a moral argument. Horace and the Latins, claims Rymer, reckoned "as the *Greeks* had done" that "the *End of Poetry* was as well to be profitable, as to be pleasant" (p. 96). The tragic poet in particular "cannot please but must also profit; 'tis the Physick of the mind that he makes palatable" (p. 75). Just how this "Physick" works Rymer explains in his hilariously intemperate dismissal of *Othello*. Whether carried away by his own fury or quietly influenced

by Heinsius, Rymer fails to make any precise distinction
between katharsis as purging and katharsis as purification.
True tragedy, he implies, does both; *Othello*, he splutters,
does neither.

On two occasions, in the Preface to *Troilus and Cressida* and
in *A Parallel of Poetry and Painting*, Dryden cites with approval
René Le Bossu's account of how a poet goes about his work:
"For the moral (as Bossu observes) is the first business of the
poet, as being the groundwork of his instruction. This being
formed, he contrives such a design, or fable, as may be most
suitable to the moral. After this he begins to think of the per-
sons whom he is to employ in carrying on his design; and
gives them the manners which are most proper to their several
characters. The thoughts and words are the last parts, which
give beauty and colouring to the piece." Homer began the
Iliad, we are to imagine, with the moral that "union preserves
a commonwealth"—the very moral with which Dryden con-
fesses he himself began *The Conquest of Granada*—and Sopho-
cles cast about and landed the story of Oedipus as a way of
demonstrating that "no man is to be accounted happy before
his death" (2: 186, 1: 248). Unfortunately, neither the preface
to *Troilus and Cressida* nor *A Parallel* is cast in the dialogue
form of *An Essay of Dramatic Poesy*, so no fictional interlocutor
can step up and voice the objections that a cynical reader must
inevitably be thinking here. However unlikely Bossu's prop-
osition may be—one particularly doubts the part about *The
Conquest of Granada*—Dryden could hardly find a more
forceful way of indicating that it is Horace, not Aristotle, who
better helped him rationalize his work as a dramatist. It is not
surprising, then, that Dryden should find katharsis too lim-
ited as an end for tragedy. "Other ends as suitable to the nature
of tragedy may be found in the English, which were not in the
Greek," he lists as the second of his two objections in his copy
of Rymer's *Tragedies of the Last Age*. Moral instruction, cer-
tainly, is among the other ends that Dryden sets for tragedy,
but so too are emotions other than pity and fear. In *An Essay
of Dramatic Poesy*, Eugenius cites Aristotle, but it is Dryden
himself who stands behind the assertation that "The end of

tragedies or serious plays . . . is to beget admiration, compassion, or concernment" (1: 46). Accepting "compassion" as pathos and "concernment" as a gentlemanly form of eleos, we are left with "admiration" as the distinctly un-Aristotelian member in this triad of emotions. Mentioned in neither the *Poetics* nor the *Ars poetica*, "admiration" nonetheless figures prominently in critical statements about tragedy from sixteenth-century writers like Minturno, Scaliger, and Sidney.[37] They use the term for just the reason that Dryden does: tragedy and epic present the same kinds of stories and, to the Renaissance view at least, the same kinds of heroes. For the tragic hero's undeserved suffering we feel "commiseration"; at the thought that a similar punishment might be visited on us we feel "concernment"; before the sheer monumentality of the hero we stand back in "admiration." "Commiseration" and "concernment" attach to the hero as an "enactor" of the play-as-object; "admiration," to the hero as a moral spokesman in the play-as-rhetorical-event.

Even though seventeenth-century critics like Heinsius, Rymer, and Dryden share the rhetorical prejudices of sixteenth-century critics like Robortello, Minturno, and Scaliger, they bring to classical playscripts a better articulated knowledge of classical history. That sense of historical relativity produced two far-reaching effects: it led to a critical reassessment of classical drama, and it made seventeenth-century dramatists acutely aware of the differences that separated their own plays from the classical scripts they admired.

The increased sophistication of classical scholarship in the seventeenth century encouraged critics to think about tragedy—and comedy too, for that matter—as something more than the undifferentiated whole it had seemed in the sixteenth century. Unlike Robortello, Heinsius appreciates the qualitative differences that separate Latin tragedy from Greek tragedy, not to mention the stylistic differences that separate Aeschylus from Sophocles from Euripides:

37. Herrick, *Poetics of Aristotle*, pp. 27–28, traces "admiration" as a term in sixteenth- and seventeenth-century criticism.

just as Latin speech reached its full development during the reign of Caesar Augustus, so too did tragedy, which was tumbled by many storms up to the time of Accius and Pacuvius, brought to full perfection (as we indeed think) by Varius, and thereafter (when it had taken on its stylistic hues from Ovid, who wrote a *Medea*) barely arrived at Seneca safe and sound—in the rest of the late poets it has scarcely a spark of life left. It is not only far inferior to the middle-stage but is much less deserving of praise than the beginning, since many in Augustus' age also had no hesitation in preferring Accius to the rest.

(ch. 16, p. 115)

Heinsius's adulation of Varius is safe from critical dispute, since only the most fragmentary fragments of his plays survive in other authors' quotations. Altogether new here is Heinsius's sense of Latin tragedy as a *developing* phenomenon with a beginning, a middle stage, and a period of decadence.

Altogether new here, too, is Heinsius's denigration of Seneca. Turning what Aristotle says about plot into a practical standard of criticism, Heinsius finishes *De tragoediae constitutione* by showing what a jumble of high-sounding speeches the scripts attributed to Seneca are, not to mention the neo-Latin plays that imitate Seneca's loose plotting and stylistic excesses. Wielding Aristotle's standard of structural elegance, Heinsius goes on to attack Euripides, too, and topple him from the position of undisputed popularity he had enjoyed since classical plays first began to be printed and acted in the fifteenth century. In that place of eminence Heinsius sets Sophocles. It was not so much Euripides' free plotting as his evil characters that prompted Dryden, as we have seen already, to prefer the plays of Sophocles. Evil characters, clearly enough, are unfit for epic "admiration." About Seneca, too, Dryden adheres to seventeenth-century taste. In his adaptation of Sophocles' *Oedipus*, says Dryden, Corneille "miserably failed in the character of his hero: if he desired that Oedipus should be pitied, he should have made him a better man. . . . Seneca, on the other side, as if there were no such thing as nature to be minded in a play, is always running after pompous expression, pointed sentences, and philosophical notions more proper for the study than the stage. The Frenchman followed a wrong scent; and the Roman was absolutely at cold hunting"(1: 233). In such pronouncements we witness the triumph of neoclassical order over Renaissance copiousness. How Dryden improved on Seneca, Corneille, and Sophocles himself we shall observe when we study the Dorset Garden performances of Dryden and Lee's *Oedipus*.

If seventeenth-century critics were newly aware of the differences that separated classical playwrights from each other, seventeenth-century dramatists were just as aware of the differences that separated classical playwrights from themselves. The Battle of Ancients and Moderns could be declared only when the Moderns were self-conscious enough about their own identity to proclaim independence. Oblivious to the vast historical and cultural differences that separated them from the Greek and Roman past, sixteenth-century scholars like Ascham would not even have understood the grounds for declaring war. Even Sophocles needed changing to accord with the very different circumstances of seventeenth-century England. Dryden observes in his objections to Rymer: "tho' nature . . . is the same in all places, and reason too the same, yet the climate, the age, the dispositions of the people to whom a poet writes may be so different that what pleased the Greeks would not satisfy an English audience" (1: 214). Such a historical sense of the audience differs in several ways from the senses of the audience that dramatists held in the sixteenth century, as we shall see in Chapter Three. Dryden's acute awareness of the people who pay to watch his plays, his calculation of their prejudices and expectations, is just one of the ways in which his view of drama is rhetorical rather than objective. Aristotle may claim that tragedy does not even have to be performed to work its effect; Dryden knows that the truth of tragedy is to be found in the boxes—and in the box office.

On the theater front, at least, the Battle of Ancients and Moderns was fought between antagonists with two different senses of history and two different assumptions about what a play is: the Ancients were convinced that Aristotle and Horace had found out rules that were good for all times, all places, and all audiences; the Moderns had a Ciceronian sense of the historical present in which a play was actually being performed. The conflict set in opposition two different views of drama: an objective view and a rhetorical view. As there were no victors in the Battle of Ancients and Moderns at large, so in the skirmish on the seventeenth-century stage neither the play-as-object nor the play-as-rhetorical-event ever held the field completely.

Our usual way of viewing history would lead us to expect "progress" from 1500 to 1700, that is to say, a gradual move from the medieval rhetorical view of plays in performance to a neoclassical objective view. What we discover instead is constant interplay between the two. There is fundamental uncertainty about just what a play *is*, rhetorical event or aesthetic object. That uncertainty may have made dramatic criticism the less tidy, but it made comedy and tragedy onstage the more adaptable to changing experience. The same creative interplay between opposites we find also in the physical spaces in which sixteenth- and seventeenth-century audiences watched Roman citizens cavort and mythic heroes die.

II · *Spatial Contexts*

What crye and noyse caused the tragedye playd in the hous of myn host and my frend Marcus potumus [*sic*] whan Thoas there pr[e]sent sought Orestes and ensearched so narowly / that he cam to the place / where he founde tweyne of the whiche he knewe that he [i.e., Orestes] was one. Pylades his felawe there / whiche toke upon hym thenne the name of Orestes of full will & purpoos to dye for hym / And the said Pylades[,] Orestes felawe[,] thene constantly sayeng[,] ["]yet am I he, whiche ye have sought and not Pylades,["] how glad the peple were whan they sawe this played and feyned ye knowe wel[.] And how moche more glad[,] trowethe[,] / they wolde have ben. yf they had seen it doon in very dede.[1]

WHEN JOHN TIPTOFT, Earl of Worcester, sat down in the 1480s to translate this theatrical anecdote from Cicero's *De amicitia*, he imagined the event taking place, not in one of the vast public theaters of Cicero's distant Rome, but in one of the makeshift playing places Tiptoft knew firsthand in late-fif-teenth-century England. Nowhere in Europe in Tiptoft's time was there any such thing as a public theater, and so, under-standably, he transferred the playing of this "tragedye" of *Orestes* to the usual venue for dramatized romance in the Middle Ages, the great hall of a nobleman's house, a monas-tery, or a college. The spectators that Cicero places clapping their unanimous approval in the huge semicircle of seats (*tota cavea*) that fronted the Roman stage are in Tiptoft's version gathered around an open playing area ("the place," the *platea* of medieval stage directions). Nothing in Cicero's brief Latin plot summary suggests Tiptoft's image of King Thoas roaming about "the place" in pretended search until he hap-pens on Pylades and Orestes, who may have been standing there in pretended "unfindableness" all the while.

Tiptoft's essentially medieval vision of what *Orestes* was like in performance is preserved by both of the later Renaissance

1. Cicero, *De amicitia*, 7.24, trans. John Tiptoft, Earl of Worcester, as *Tullis de amicitia in Englysh* (London, 1481), fol. A8.

men who translated *De amicitia* into English. Ignoring Cic-
ero's cavea, or perhaps not understanding the technical
meaning of the term, John Harington of Stepney (1550) posi-
tions the spectators around a central playing space: Cicero's
stantes, most likely rising from their seats in the cavea as they
start to applaud, become in Harington's translation "the
herers that stode aboute." As late as 1577, Thomas Newton is
still imagining the event as an entertainment in a great hall
when he refers to Pacuvius's *Orestes* as a "newe Enterlude."
Cicero's stantes are, once again, "the standers by."[2]

Implicit in the diction of Tiptoft, Harington, and Newton
alike is an understanding of the logistics of acting plays and
watching plays that differs markedly from the physical cir-
cumstances in which plays like Pacuvius's *Orestes* were in fact
acted and watched in ancient Rome. How could they have
imagined it otherwise? Lacking any firsthand acquaintance
with actual ruins, English translators of Cicero's story, like
English producers of classical scripts, had access in print to
only the most impressionistic and fragmentary information
about ancient theater buildings. From Pliny and Cassiodorus,
readers could piece together a picture of structures fabulous in
size and splendor. When producers of plays and designers of
buildings wanted more practical information, they could turn
to Vitruvius and Pollux, but the details they discovered there
contradicted medieval staging conventions in several funda-
mental ways. A great deal turns on the obvious disparity in
size. Where Cicero's theater seated thousands, the great hall
of a college, monastery, or nobleman's house accommodated
only hundreds, if not just scores. The Roman theater was an
outdoor affair; Tiptoft, Harington, and Newton gather actors
and audience together under the roof of a great hall. The
geometry of Vitruvius's design is predicated on a circle; medi-
eval great halls were rectangular. Where Vitruvius and Pollux
describe a permanent architectural ensemble, Renaissance
actors and audiences were used to a makeshift playing area,

2. John Harington, *The booke of freendeship of Marcus Tullie Cicero* (1550),
ed. Ruth Hughey in *John Harington of Stepney: Tudor Gentleman: His Life and
Works* (Columbus, Ohio, 1971), p. 151; Thomas Newton, *Fouure Severall
Treatises of M. Tullius Cicero* (London, 1577), fols. B3ᵛ–B4.

adapted to the possibilities at hand. Medieval performers made their entrances and exits out of a simple booth or from "mansions" grouped around "the place"—or even out of the crowd and into the round with nothing at all to back them up. The Roman theater positioned the players in front of a façade that dominated the entire theater; doors in this permanent façade gave actors their entrances and exits. Hence the fundamental difference between what ancient audiences and modern audiences imagined the playing space to be. Where medieval actors and audiences thought of "the place" as any place the action required—or even as no particular place at all—the Roman theater endowed the doorways of the façade and the playing area in front of it with a definite fictional identity.[3] Vitruvius's cryptic remarks about painted panels in this façade invited Renaissance designers to indulge their delight in illusionistic perspective.

All of these details add up to two fundamentally different senses of architectural—and psychological—space. Where medieval spectators and players informally shared the same physical space in castle hall, market square, city street, or cathedral nave, the Roman theater assigned them to architecturally separate spaces. Where medieval onlookers were used to an easy give-and-take with the players, encouraged by the space they shared in common, the Roman theater set them so far apart that theater architects like Vitruvius had to give special attention to sightlines and acoustics. The differences between medieval and Roman ideas of the theater amount to a difference between an organic, intuitive sense of space and a constructed, rational sense of space.[4] The informality and pragmatism of medieval staging stand in sharp contrast to

3. On the direct relationship between actors and audience in medieval staging arrangements, see Richard Southern, *The Medieval Theatre in the Round* (London, 1957), and Anne Righter, *Shakespeare and the Idea of the Play* (London, 1962), pp. 13–42. Greek and Roman staging arrangements are surveyed in Cesare Molinari, *Teatro*, trans. Colin Hamer as *Theatre through the Ages* (London, 1975), pp. 57–72. See also Bamber Gascoigne, *World Theatre* (London, 1968), pp. 67–95 (medieval) and pp. 23–46 (classical).

4. Rudolph Wittkower, *Architectural Principles in the Age of Humanism* (1952; repr. New York, 1971), pp. 101–54.

Vitruvius's geometrical ground plan and his "scientific" working out of sightlines and acoustics. Each of these two different senses of space sets the viewer in a different relationship to what he sees. Standing about "the place" in the middle of a great hall or a city square, the viewer of medieval drama is simply a part of the space around him; his relationship to that space is immediate and wholistic. Seated in Vitruvius's cavea, the viewer of classical drama is positioned on a geometrical grid that forces him to "place himself" with respect to what he sees; his relationship to the space around him is detached, self-aware.

We can experience these disparate effects firsthand by comparing what it is like to stand in the great hall at Hampton Court, the scene for a production of Plautus's *Menaechmi* in 1526, with what it must have been like to to sit in Sir Christopher Wren's Drury Lane Theater, the scene for Seneca's *Thyestes* as adapted by John Crowne in 1680, for Terence's *Eunuchus* as adapted by Sir Charles Sedley in 1687, and for Plautus's *Amphitruon* as adapted by John Dryden in 1690. We encounter not just two different styles of decoration—gothic at Hampton Court and classical at Drury Lane—but two very different ways of structuring space. (See Figures 2 and 3.) The colonnade of the Drury Lane design divides the side walls into a geometric grid of rectangles, each with its recessed arch. We would experience the auditorium as one large rectangular block made up of smaller rectangular blocks. Behind a proscenium arch midway on the gently raked stage, seven pairs of sliding panels, each smaller and slightly closer than the one before it, are provided to give perspective depth to the scenes painted on the panels. Tiers of seats in the auditorium are raked at carefully calculated angles to enhance the illusionistic effect. In such a space we as spectators take our place in an elaborate geometrical scheme. We are invited if not compelled to experience the theatrical space rationally—and therefore to be conscious of ourselves in relationship to it. The great hall at Hampton Court invites no such self-reflection. The roof beams may be placed at regular intervals, but they start high up the walls, curve upwards, and lead the eye toward the cen-

FIGURE 2. Great Hall, Hampton Court Palace (1514–1520).

FIGURE 3. Sir Christopher Wren design for a theater, likely Drury Lane (c. 1672).

tral arches, creating a sense of one whole open space beneath. With nothing to set us apart, we intuitively feel part of that whole.

These differences in the physical relationship between audience and actors have, as we shall see when we begin to reconstruct particular productions, subtle but decisive consequences for comedy and tragedy as they emerged from the printed page and found their way onto the stage—and into the emotional and intellectual experience of sixteenth- and seventeenth-century Englishmen. Just as early-sixteenth-century scholars perceived no temporal, philosophical distance between themselves and the ancient scripts, so early-sixteenth-century audiences felt no physical, psychological distance between themselves and the actors speaking a few feet away. The organic space of medieval great halls was a perfect setting for the play-as-rhetorical-event. By the time critics like Heinsius began to advance Aristotle's conception of the play-as-object, audiences were beginning to find themselves in the geometric spaces of neoclassical theaters. Again, physical context and philosophical context matched perfectly. In size, in shape, in the identity of the playing area, in the psychological sense of space, in the critical relationship between actors and audience, the history of sixteenth- and seventeenth-century theater design shows us a series of attempts to reconcile medieval and classical ideas of staging.

I

Just as Renaissance scholars looked to Cicero and Horace, not to Aristotle, for guidance in how to read Greek and Latin plays alike, so their sources of practical information about the ancient stage were primarily Roman, not Greek. Only Pollux, whose *Onomasticon* was twice printed in Greek in the sixteenth century (Venice, 1502, and Florence, 1520) and once in Latin translation (Basel, 1541), offered much information on Greek theaters, and even then the structural features and acting conventions that Pollux defines belong to Hellenistic theaters of the first century, half a millennium after Sophocles. Indeed, most of the information available in Latin authors like Pliny,

Livy, Vitruvius, Donatus, and Isidore of Seville postdates the scripts that Renaissance scholars studied.

The general impression of ancient theater buildings that these authors communicated was worthy of Mandeville's *Travels*. That impression had little to do, however, with the theaters in which the surviving scripts had actually been performed. As in Renaissance England, in classical Greece and Rome great plays had preceded great playing-places. Even Plautus and Terence were originally acted in temporary wooden theaters, a full century before Rome acquired its first permanent stone theater under Pompey. The theaters Vitruvius, Pollux, and the others conjured up for Renaissance readers were the gargantuan structures of the Roman Empire, the end products of centuries of adaptation, experimentation, and elaboration. Oblivious to this evolution through time, Renaissance scholars put together a composite picture of the ancient theater that collapsed eight hundred years of theatrical history into a single idealized moment.

Pompey's theater was the most renowned. Describing the structure in a famous letter of his *Variarum liber* (first printed, Augsburg, 1472; reprinted in collected works, Paris, 1579), Cassiodorus gave Renaissance viewers a nostalgic vantage point for looking back on a grandeur that seemed impossible to recapture:

O Time, what do you not undo! What fastness do you not shake in pieces! We might sooner expect mountains to fall than the theater's solidity to be shaken: the massive pile was made out of rough stones, so that it seems to be a thing of nature, despite the human artifice. Perhaps we would not even have detected that if we had not chanced to notice the hidden junctures that bring those caverns of suspended stones together in beautiful shapes, so that we might sooner think the crypts to be high mountains than that this was something made by man. The ancients built this place holding so many people to create a stupendous spectacle seeming to hold dominion over the entire world.[5]

5. Cassiodorus, *Variarum*, 4.51, in Migne, *Patrologiae Latinae*, 69 (Paris, 1848), cols. 642–44, my translation.

Earlier Latin authors corroborated Cassiodorus's epic vision. On one occasion, Pliny reports, Pompey's theater had been completely covered in gold by Nero (33.54). Even more richly furnished was a prodigious theater erected by Marcus Scaurus:

the stage had three lofts one above another, wherein were three hundred and threescore columnes of marble; (a straunge and admirable sight in that citie, which in times past could not endure six small pillars of marble, hewed out of the quarrey in mount Hymettus, in the house of a more honourable personage, without a great reproch and rebuke given unto him for it;) the base or nethermost part of the stage, was all of marble; the middle of glasse (an excessive superfluitie, never heard of before or after;) as for the uppermost, the bourds, plankes, and floores were guilded; the columnes beneath, were (as I have said before) fortie foot high, wanting twaine: and between these columnes (as I have shewed before) there stood of statues and images in brasse to the number of three thousand. The Theatre it selfe was able to receive fourescore thousand persons to sit well, and at ease. Whereas the compasse of *Pompeies* Amphitheatre (notwithstanding the cittie of Rome so much enlarged, and more peopled in his time) was devised for to containe no greater number than fortie thousand seats at large.[6]

Not to be outdone by Scaurus, C. Curio celebrated the funeral games of his father by erecting two semicircular theaters in timber. Or rather, he *suspended* them. Each theater, claims Pliny, was hung from a large hook, so that "they might bee turned about as a man would have them, approch neare one to the other, or be remooved farther asunder as one would desire." On the morning of the funeral games, Curio had the two theaters hung back to back so that two plays could be put on simultaneously; in the afternoon, he had the two semicircles turned around to face each other, forming one large amphitheater for shows of fencing and swordplay—and all this without the audience having to get up out of their seats.[7] Taking their cue from Cassiodorus, Renaissance poets and

6. Pliny, 36.114–15, trans. Philemon Holland as *The Historie of the World* (London, 1601), pp. 583–84.
7. Pliny, 36.116–18, trans. Holland, p. 583.

painters found in the ruined theaters of antiquity ripe oppor-
tunities for evoking and lamenting just such instances of
departed grandeur as Pliny describes. In "The Ruines of
Time" Spenser, for example, has Verlame (London) count
"goodly theatres" among the "high towers," "faire temples,"
"princelie pallaces," and "sacred sepulchers" that once
adorned her.[8]

Among the ancient theaters to be seen in person and not just
in poems, the best known in the sixteenth century was the
Theater of Marcellus in Rome. The standard Renaissance
guidebooks all describe its exterior (its interior had been con-
verted into a noble house) and offer the same potted lesson in
architecture, noting the difference between a *theatrum* (semi-
circular) and an *amphitheatrum* (circular or oval).[9] Vignola
includes a short section of the theater's façade in his *Regola
delle cinque ordini dell'architectura* (1562) to illustrate the Doric
order.[10] Views of the entire theater figure in both sets of the
sixteenth-century engravings that first made Roman statues
and Roman buildings part of the cultural heritage of all edu-
cated Europeans: Giovanni Battista de'Cavalieri's series *Anti-
quarum statuarum urbis Romae*, begun in the early 1560s and col-
lected in book form in 1585 and 1594, offers a view of the
Theater of Marcellus in its actual delapidated condition; an
attempted full-scale reconstruction by Pyrrhio Ligorio is
included in Antoine Lafréry's series *Speculum Romanae magnifi-
centiae*, begun in the 1540s and finished in the 1580s.[11] (See
Figures 4 and 5.)

8. Spenser, "The Ruines of Time," 1192–98, ed. Charles G. Osgood and
Henry G. Lotspeich in *Works*, Vol. 2 (Baltimore, 1947): 39.

9. Lucio Mauro, *Le antichità della città di Roma* (Venice, 1558), pp. 40–41;
Lucio Fauno, . . . *Delle antichità della città di Roma* (Venice, 1548), pp. 139–40,
provides a similar account.

10. *Vignola: Or the compleat Architect*, trans. Joseph Moxon (London, 1655),
pp. 34–35.

11. Francis Haskell and Nicholas Penny, *Taste and the Antique: The Lure of
Classical Sculpture 1500–1900* (New Haven, 1981), pp. 18–21, discuss the
prints published by Lafréry and Cavalieri and the influence those images
exerted all over Europe in the sixteenth and seventeenth centuries.

II

For technical advice in turning the Theater of Marcellus's crumbling stone walls back into a practicable playing place Ligorio, like all Renaissance humanists, looked to one source above all: Vitruvius's *De architectura*. For clarification of details they could consult two old medieval standbys: Book XVIII of Isidore of Seville's encyclopedia (early seventh century) and, rather more reliably, the treatise *De comoedia* by Donatus. After 1541 there was also Rudolph Walter's Latin translation of Pollux's *Onomasticon*. Only Vitruvius, however, considered the whole matter systematically. Set down in the late first century B.C., during the time of Julius Caesar, the account of theater buildings in Vitruvius's Book V postdates Plautus's scripts by two centuries, Terence's by one, and Cicero's theatrical anecdotes by a generation; but its influence, theoretical if not always practical, was enormous from the very start of the Renaissance.

The first critical edition of *De architectura*, edited by Giovanni Giocondo (Venice, 1511), was followed in short order by Cesare's Cesariano's translation into Italian (Como, 1521). Further Latin editions, not to mention later Italian translations by Giovanni Caporali (Perugia, 1536 et seq.), Daniele Barbaro (Venice, 1556, 1567, 1584, 1629, 1641), and Giovanni Rusconi (Venice, 1590), added thicker and thicker frames of commentary to clarify every detail. Jean Martin's sumptuously printed translation *Architecture, ou art de bien bastin* (Paris, 1547) appeared just at the climax of François Ier's campaign to acclimatize Italian Renaissance art to France. Walter Hermann Ryff's edition of the Latin text (Strasburg, 1543) was followed five years later by his *Vitruvius Teutsch* (Nürnberg, 1548). In Spanish, Miguel de Urrea published a version in 1582.[12]

To this vast European readership, Vitruvius in Book V offered a tantalizingly brief and cryptic account of ancient theater buildings. Practical architect that he is, Vitruvius

---

12. Herbert Koch, *Vom Nachleben des Vitruv* (Baden-Baden, 1951) provides a general survey of Vitruvius's Renaissance reputation and influence.

Pars Theatri Marcelli inter Capitolium, et Tiberim, ubi nunc aedes Sabellorum, hoc ab Augusto Marcelli nomine extructum capiebat hominum octoginta millia.

FIGURE 4. Theater of Marcellus, Rome, from Giovanni Battista de'Cavalieri, *Antiquarum Staturam Urbis Romae* (1585).

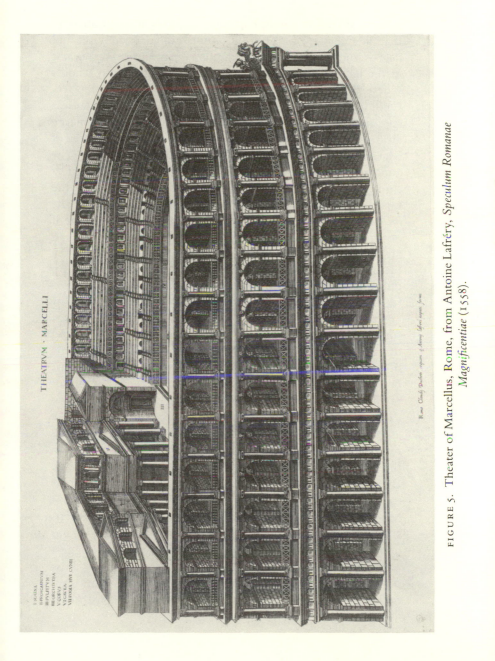

FIGURE 5. Theater of Marcellus, Rome, from Antoine Lafréry, *Speculum Romanae Magnificentiae* (1558).

mainly discusses how to engineer acoustics and sightlines so that an audience of tens of thousands can adequately see and hear—crucial concerns in the theaters of ancient Rome but not in the halls of Renaissance palaces, universities, and schools where most modern productions of classical plays took place. On important matters like the design of the stage he is far less specific. The main features that Vitruvius mentions emerge clearly enough in Ligorio's reconstruction of the Theater of Marcellus published in Lafréry's *Speculum*. (See Figure 5.) The audience, seated in the semicircular cavea (VI; mislabeled IV through reversal of the design on the plate) confronts the raised *pulpitum*, or stage (III), across the open space of the *orchestra* (IIII). In Greek theaters of Sophocles' time, some if not all of the action had taken place in the orchestra—an arrangement not unlike medieval European acting in "the place"—but by Vitruvius's time, the action had moved up onto the pulpitum. Behind this raised stage stands the *scaena* (I). In the earliest Greek theaters the *skēnē* (literally, "hut" or "tent") had been a makeshift structure which the actors used for costuming themselves and for making their entrances and exits—again, an arrangement not unlike the booth at one side of "the place" in medieval practice—but by Vitruvius's time it had evolved into the focal point of the entire theater, a monumental construction with an elaborate façade (the *proscaenium*, II).

Superficially classical and correct as it may appear, Ligorio's reconstruction misconstrues Vitruvius in two telling ways: in the shape of the whole structure and in the design of the stage. By making the cavea half an oval, not half a circle, Ligorio fails to catch the geometrical unity of Vitruvius's design. His freest handling of the verbal evidence, however, occurs in his reconstructed proscaenium: its projecting bays, its deep recesses under the colonnade, and its second-story windows suggest nothing so much as a contemporary Renaissance palace. Possibly Isidore is responsible here, since he argues from etymology (correctly, for once) that the scaena was "constructed in the manner of a house."[13] The two side bays stick out so far onto the stage that Ligorio's façade in fact suggests *three* houses, not one. If so, his design was perfectly compatible with the medieval staging convention of a separate "mansion" for each main character.

About doorways Vitruvius is sketchy enough to have made such compatibility seem possible. When Vitruvius specifies that the middle door is adorned like a royal palace (*mediae valvae ornatus habeant aulae regiae*) and the two doors on either side like lodgings for strangers (*hospitalia*), he might to a Renaissance reader seem to be making distinctions on the basis of character, not place. Only when he describes the two outermost doors as "approaches" (*aditus*) leading in one direction to the forum and in the other direction to foreign parts (*a peregre*) does Vitruvius endow the stage with the kind of fixed locality that Plautus's and Terence's scripts assume.[14] While agreeing with Vitruvius about the directional associations of the two outermost doors, Pollux is even looser in the identities he assigns to the three central doors. He positively invites the assumption that the playing-place is no one place in particular: "Of the three scene doors . . . the middle opened either into a palace, grotto, hall, or whatever was of first distinction in the play; the right-hand door was a retreat for the next in rank; and the left, which had a very miserable aspect, led to some desolate temple, or had no house. In tragedy, strangers entered at the right-hand door; and the left was a prison. In comedy, next to the house there was a "tent" [*tentorium*], represented in draperies, and it was a stable for beasts."[15] Partic-

---

13. *Etymologiarum*, 18.43, in Migne, *Patrologiae Latinae*, 82 (Paris, 1850), col. 658.

14. Vitruvius, *De architectura*, 5.6.8, ed. Frank Granger, Loeb Library (London and New York, 1931), 1: 288, my translation. Future references are cited in the text.

15. Julius Pollux, *Onomasticon*, 4.19, trans. (into Latin) Rudolph Walter (Basel, 1541), fol. BB4, my translation into English. The only readily available English translation of Pollux's chapters on the theater, first published as an appendix to a late-eighteenth-century edition of the *Poetics* and reprinted in

ularly intriguing is Pollux's insistence on the literally "sin-
ister" aspect of the left-hand door.

Add to this confusion Vitruvius's famous description of the
three kinds of scenes, and the stage is set for two hundred
years of improvisation. Comic, tragic, or satiric, the *ornatus*
has arranged for it on the proscaenium a special place between
the doors for strangers and the approaches at either end of the
stage. Three-sided revolving machines called *periacti* (Greek:
periaktoi) display the ornatus, turning according to changes in
the stories (*fabularum mutationes*) or the appearance of gods
"with sudden thunderings" (*seu deorum adventus, cum tonitribus
repentinis*). Concerning these scenic devices Pollux is only
slightly more specific: "At each of the two doors which were
in the middle of the scaena there were likewise two others, one
on each side, to which were joined turning machines [*versatiles
machinae*], the right one showing things outside the city, the
left one a prospect of the city itself [literally, *ea quae ex urbe
ducit*, 'things which extend out of the city'].''[16] By revolving,
these two machines could change the place (*locus*) of the
action. Not mentioned at all by Vitruvius but prominent in
Pollux's account is an astonishing array of machines for spe-
cial effects: a watchtower, a wall, a turret, a lightning tower, a
thunder machine, the throne of the gods, a hanging crane,
Charon's steps, trapdoors. Taken altogether, Pliny, Cassio-
dorus, Vitruvius, Pollux, Donatus, and Isidore of Seville pro-
duced a far from coherent view of the ancient stage. Out of
the confusion emerged two centuries of ingenious compro-
mises between ancient and modern ideas.

III

The earliest producers of classical playscripts seem not to have
seen any need for compromise at all. Without our own histor-
ical hindsight to confuse them, Renaissance enthusiasts like
Pomponius Laetus must have found classical playscripts

A. M. Nagler, *Sources of Theatrical History* (New York, 1952), pp. 7–15, is not
trustworthy in details and omits whole sentences without comment.

16. 4.19, trans. Walter (Latin), my translation.

readily performable in medieval terms: multiperson choruses
in Greek tragedies may not have had any medieval counter-
part, but otherwise the characters in classical comedy and
tragedy talk as freely and directly to the audience as medieval
dramatic characters are wont to do; the machines required for
descending gods in Euripides, in Seneca, in Plautus's *Amphi-
truo* were already stock in trade for producers of the great Bib-
lical cycles; and the palaces and temples of tragedy, as well as
the houses and brothels of Roman comedy, could just as easily
be realized as medieval stage-mansions grouped around an
open "place" as they could as doors in a single façade. In the
medieval view, the fact that the space in front of the tragic
hero's palace or the spaces between the houses belonging to
comic protagonists could be regarded as fixed locations, as a
public square or as a city street, would seem merely inci-
dental—a matter of no particular dramatic advantage.

Indeed, the evidence we have for several productions of
classical scripts in England suggests just this transfer of the
play from Roman street or Greek forum to the undefined
"place" of medieval drama. Among the expenses itemized in
the Revels accounts for court festivities during Christmas
1567–1568, for example, is money for the construction of
"Orestioes howse." Likely acted by boys from Westminster
School, who were under royal orders to prepare one Latin
play each Christmas, the script for which this "howse" was
prepared was almost certainly a Latin version of Euripides'
Orestes.[17] Euripides' play requires that first Orestes and later
Apollo appear on the roof. The precise terms used in the
Revels entry imply a practicable structure: the structure is a
"howse," the technical name for stage-mansions, not a
"palace," as it is called in the text of the play; it is, further-

17. Albert Feuillerat, ed., *Documents Relating to the Office of the Revels in the
Time of Queen Elizabeth* (1908; repr. Vaduz, 1963), p. 119. Entries from the
Revels accounts for each play Elizabeth is known to have seen, together with
eyewitness descriptions and other relevant documents, are usefully assembled
in Carter Anderson Daniel, "Patterns and Traditions of the Elizabethan Court
Play to 1590" (Ph.D. diss., University of Virginia, 1965). *Orestes* is discussed
on pp. 133–36.

more, not the palace of Argos, or Agamemnon's palace, as the
dramatic fiction would have it, but "*Orestioes* howse," identi-
fying it with that specific character, as stage-mansions are
identified by medieval convention. Whatever its identity, the
structure had to be strong enough to support first Orestes and
later Apollo on the roof. Interpreting the "howse" this way
fits with the essentially medieval staging arrangements that
obtained when other plays were put on before the queen.[18]
Financial records of Cambridge colleges are likewise filled
with disbursements for constructing stage "houses," not only
for performances of Plautus and Terence but for productions
of the modern scripts that the ancients inspired. A payment
for "*orname[n]ta [a]edium*" for a Plautus play at Queens' Col-
lege in 1522–1523 is the first in a series of regular payments
that continue as late as 1612–1613 at Trinity College—long
after perspective scenery had transformed the staging of plays
in Italy and France.[19]

When Renaissance producers did take into account the
peculiarities of the ancient theater, the most obvious and usual
strategy was simply to preserve medieval staging arrange-
ments and give them a cosmetic "classicizing." In doing so,
producers were doing on the stage what the scholars were
doing to Vitruvius on the printed page.[20] Giovanni Giocon-
do's *editio criticus* of 1511 copies uncritically the sketch illustra-
tions that appear in late antique manuscripts of Vitruvius's
text.[21] Ignoring Vitruvius's elaborate geometrical scheme that
relates cavea to pulpitum through a series of equilateral trian-
gles inscribed within a circle, Giocondo's illustrator is still
thinking of the theater in organic medieval terms, if not

18. Bereblock's account is reprinted and analyzed in Wickham, *Early Eng-
lish Stages* (New York, 1959), 1: 355–59. See also Daniel, "Patterns and Tra-
ditions," pp. 78–79.

19. Alan H. Nelson provides a judicious summary of the financial records
in "Conditions of College Drama" in *Records of Early English Drama: Cam-
bridge* (Toronto, 1988).

20. Cf. Molinari, *Teatro*, pp. 110–40.

21. Heinrich Rottinger, *Die Holzschnitte zur Architektur und zum Vitruvius
Teutsch des Walter Rivius* (Strasburg, 1914), pp. 13–23, disentagles the snarled
pattern of which Renaissance editions of Vitruvius copied which.

actually imagining the theater set up temporarily in a rectangular space like a great hall, when he encloses the ground plan in a rectangle. As Vitruvius requires, five entranceways onto the stage are provided, but their relationship to the "backstage" area of the scaena is curious: each door opens out from a separate chamber, labeled "*scena*" in the case of the central door and "scenae membra" in the case of the two outer doors on each side. The two outermost entrances appear not at the oblique or right angle that Vitruvius implies but in the same plane as the other doors in the proscaenium façade. And they, too, communicate with separate little rooms. Looking at the scaena as a series of separate little chambers, each with its own entrance onto the stage, we cannot avoid the impression that these are simply medieval stage-mansions that have been pushed together into a tidy classical row. That expedient is hardly enough to turn the undefined space of medieval staging into the structured space that Vitruvius specifies. Misconceived as they are, Giocondo's illustrations were nonetheless widely copied in other editions of Vitruvius throughout the sixteenth century: Latin editions published by Giunta at Florence (1513 and 1522), Italian translations by Durantino (Venice, 1524) and Francesco Lucio (Venice, 1535), Jean Martin's French version (Paris, 1547), and Miguel de Urrea's Spanish translation (1582) all reproduce Giocondo's ground plan without questioning how it misrepresents details—not to mention how it omits Vitruvius's rational geometry altogether.

The other set of widely reproduced illustrations, first published with Cesare Cesariano's Italian translation (Como, 1521), shows a similar misunderstanding of doorways as stage-mansions. To his credit, Cesariano's illustrator grasps Vitruvius's geometrical scheme and inscribes the ground plan within a circle. But his views of the exterior and interior of the theater, despite their correctly ordered columns and round-headed arches, belong to the same realm of Gothic fantasy as the more famous illustrations of Roman theaters in the Terence editions of Trechsel (Lyon, 1493) and Grüninger (Strasburg, 1496), which probably inspired them. Like Giocondo's, the illustrations in Cesariano's edition were uncritically copied elsewhere: immediately in Giovanni Carporali's Italian translation (Perugia, 1536) and farther afield in Walter Hermann Ryff's edition of the Latin text (Strasburg, 1543), as well as in his German translation (Nürnberg, 1548).

For ideas about what Plautus's and Terence's Roman citizens looked like, illustrators of the plays as they were printed by Trechsel and Grüninger turned to illuminations in manuscripts like "Le Térence des Ducs" (MS Bibliothèque de l'Arsenal 664), where houses conventionally have the outsized doors of medieval stage-mansions but where no firm distinction is made between scenes drawn in performance and scenes drawn as narrative events. Once in print, of course, the illustrations in editions of Plautus and Terence, like those in Vitruvius, tended to inspire copies and adaptations rather than a fresh look at the evidence of any actual performances.[22] Like Ligorio in his reconstruction of the Theater of Marcellus, like the illustrators of Vitruvius, the illustrator of Trechsel's Terence has cleverly reconciled fluid medieval staging conventions with Vitruvius's requirement for a solid proscenium wall simply by pushing several medieval stage-mansions together in a row. The result is prominently labeled "Proscenium" in the frontispiece. What might appear to be a unified composition of arched and curtained openings is in fact a row of separate little houses, each identified with an individual character by a placard over the door. Just how these houses figure in the action can be seen in the illustrator's handling of the opening of *Phormio*. (See Figure 1.) Terence's play requires three houses, for Chremes, Demipho, and Dorio; these the illustrator has supplied and labeled. Pride of place is given to the house of Chremes, whose recognition of Phanium as his daughter makes the happy ending possible. But first of all, the

22. T. E. Lawrenson and Helen Purkis, "Les Éditions Illustrées de Terence dans l'Histoire du Théâtre: Spectacles dans un Fauteuil?" in Jean Jacquot, ed., *Le Lieu théâtral à la Renaissance* (Paris, 1964), pp. 1–23, demonstrate how fifteenth- and sixteenth-century illustrations to Terence have as much to do with earlier illustrations as they do with actual stage practices. See also Gascoigne, *World Theatre*, pp. 96–114; Molinari, *Teatro*, pp. 110–40.

slave Davos appears and fills the audience in on the plot afoot: "Geta my greatest friend and countriman too, came to me yesterday, for there was a little peece of money left long since of a certaine reckoning betwixt us, that I might gather it up, and I have done so, and now doe bring it him. For I heard that his masters sonne shall marrie, and I beleeve this money is scraped togither for his use. . . . But doe not I see [G]eta!"[23] Since Davos is supposed to be coming from town, he is shown entering, not out of one of the three houses, but, as Vitruvius and Pollux require, from the right. Interrupting him, Geta comes rushing out of Demipho's house while still talking to someone inside: "If any redde head shall seeke me [. . .]." Davos catches his attention:

GETA: Ho, I laboured Davus to meete thee.
DAVUS: Lo, hold you: its currant, there wants not a penie of that I ought you.
GETA: I beare you good will, for that you have not neglected my busines I give you heartie thanks.
DAVUS: Especially in this corrupt age, for the world is come to this passe, that a man must give him thankes, that paieth him his owne. But why are you sadde?

For whatever reason, the illustrator has made Geta come out of Chremes' house rather than that of his master Demipho, but he has demonstrated how the curtained arch functions as a house, and by making Geta glance away furtively, he has indicated how the area in front could be imagined as a street— or as the unlocalized "place" of medieval drama.

Even so thorough a scholar and so influential an authority as Alberti shows the same capacity of taking classical details and giving them an essentially medieval interpretation. Alberti's treatise *De re aedificatoria*, first printed at Florence in 1485 and reprinted in widely read editions at Paris in 1512 and Strasburg in 1541, takes Vitruvius as the ultimate authority in the design of theaters as of other structures. But in buildng up the scaena from Vitruvius's ground plan, Alberti has his

23. Terence, *Phormio*, 1.35–40, 50, trans. Richard Bernard in *Terence in English* (Cambridge, 1607), fol. CC2.

eye on the mansions of the medieval stage. In both Greek and
Latin theaters, Alberti notes, "the Stage was adorned with
Rows of Colonnades one over another, in Imitation of
Houses, with their proper Doors and Windows, and in Front
was one principal Door with all the Dress of the Door of a
Temple, to represent a Royal Palace, with other Doors on
each Side for the Actors to make their Entrances and Exits
according to the Nature of the Drama."[24] Windows? Vitruvius
mentions them only in relation to the ornatus for comedy, not
in relation to the design of the permanent proscaenium itself.
Writing several years before anyone had attempted to revive
an ancient play in production, Alberti interprets Vitruvius,
naturally enough, in light of the dramatic conventions he
already knew firsthand. The result is a curious compromise:
"houses" with workable windows and doors, despite Vitru-
vius's mentioning them among the ornatus for comedy, are
medieval staging devices; "Colonnades one over another" rep-
resent a classicizing attempt to impose on those devices a uni-
fied architectural order. Johannes DeWitt's famous sketch of
the Swan Theater (1596)—with its grand Vitruvian labels of
"orchestra," "proscaenium," and "mimorum aedes" applied
most incongruously to the Swan's homely English realities—
is altogether typical of how Renaissance viewers could mis-
apply classical names to medieval things.

The staging arrangements in Trechsel's Terence were
turned to practical advantage when producers of classical
scripts had to transform a great hall or college chapel into a
temporary theater. For Plautus's *Aulularia*, one of four plays
planned for Queen Elizabeth's reception at Cambridge on her
summer progress of 1564, a stage five feet high was erected
across the full width of King's College Chapel. The *scaenae
frons* became arches in the nave's north side; the queen as chief
spectator sat on the opposite side of the stage where she could
both see and be seen.[25] Framed by pillars, the two arches in

24. Leon Battista Alberti, *De re aedificatoria*, 8.7, trans. James Leoni (1726),
ed. Joseph Rkywert (London, 1955), p. 177.

25. An eyewitness account by Matthew Stokys, registrar of the university,

front of the side chapels served as stage-mansions for the two houses required in Plautus's play, one for the heroine's father Euclio and one for Megadorus, the lusty old bachelor who seeks her hand in marriage. If the two arches were hung with curtains—as most likely they were—the effect would have been exactly that in Trechsel's illustrations.

In the great halls of most schools, colleges, and palaces such logistical ingenuity as shown at Cambridge would not be required, because in most cases there was a wooden screen running the width of the hall. Arched openings—usually two or three—in the hall-screen offered a ready substitute for individually constructed stage-mansions—and, ironically enough, a medieval equivalent of Vitruvius's scaenae frons. That handy coincidence was probably not lost on Trechsel's illustrator or on the schoolmasters and university dons all over Europe who had to put on classical plays with far less money to spend for scenic devices than princes or dukes. Payments in the Revels accounts for "paper[,] inke and colores for the wryting of greate letters" in connection with Plautus's *Miles Gloriosus*, performed at court by boys from Westminster School at Christmas 1565, perhaps were for the placards inscribed with characters' names that could instantly turn an archway in the hall-screen arch into a stage-mansion.[26]

Whether the acting space in front of the screen was "the place" or *a* place seems to have been an accident of the particular play being produced rather than a settled convention. For example, Euripides' *Phoenecian Women*—or rather George Gascoigne and Francis Kinwelmershe's version of Ludovico Dolce's version of Euripides' *Phoenecian Women*, acted at Gray's Inn during the Christmas revels of 1566–1567—calls for three entrance ways. Whether they were three arched openings in the hall-screen or three individual mansions is not altogether clear. The description printed with the text narrates what happened on the night of performance: "JOCASTA the

---

is analyzed in Glynne Wickham, *Early English Stages*, Vol. 1 (New York, 1959): 355–59.

26. Daniel, "Patterns and Traditions," pp. 90–93.

Queene issued out of hir house, beginning the first Acte, as followeth. JOCASTA the Queene issueth out of her Pallace, before hir twelve Gentlemen, following after hir eight Gentlewomen, whereof foure be the *Chorus* that remayne on the Stage after hir departure."[27] Most entrance and exit directions thereafter specify one of two city gates. "Note (Reader)," the collaborators point out at the end of the text, "that there were in *Thebes* fowre principall gates, wherof the chief and most commonly used were the gates called *Electrae* and the gates *Homoloydes.*"

Kinwelmershe's curious way of narrating the opening action twice—Jocasta is said to enter first "out of hir house" and in the next sentence "out of her Pallace"—probably reflects two different ways of looking at that action, first in theatrical terms and then in fictional terms. "House" is the technical name for a stage-mansion; "palace" is how the house figures in the story, just as the twenty actors are, in fictional terms, "gentlemen" and "gentlewomen," four of whom become, in theatrical terms, the Chorus. The diction suggests, then, that there may have been three painted stage-mansions grouped behind an open playing space in the manner of medieval morality plays and Tudor interludes. Gascoigne and Kinwelmershe do tend to associate each of the characters with only one of the three openings. Thus Eteocles is always instructed to enter and exit via the gates of Electrae, Polyneices and Creon by the gates of Homoloydes, and, with the exception in 4.1 of their exit out the gates of Homoloydes to persuade the brothers not to fight, Jocasta and Antigone by the palace. All these arrangements suggest, of course, a sense of the acting area as the medieval "place." But Gascoigne and Kinwelmershe also observe Vitruvius's distinction between the directions of stage right and stage left: Eteocles always enters and exits via the gates of Electrae, presumably stage left, because that is where the seat of government is (surely in Euripides' play the royal palace and the seat of government are

---

27. George Gascoigne and Francis Kinwelmershe, *Jocasta*, repr. in John W. Cunliffe, *Early English Classical Tragedies* (Oxford, 1912), p. 69.

one and the same place); Polyneices always enters and exits via the gates of Homoloydes, presumably stage right, because that is where the besiegers' camp is, outside the city. Was the playing area, then, not "the place" of medieval convention but a specific fictional locale, the square in front of the royal palace of Thebes? Probably it was both, just as it must have seemed to be in Vitruvius.

The same genial confusion marked a famous production in the same room nearly thirty years later. For the performance of "a Comedy of Errors (like to *Plautus* his *Menechmus*)" at Christmas 1594, a platform stage was erected. As with Gascoigne and Kinwelmershe's *Jocasta*, the stage directions in Shakespeare's play require three "houses": the Priory, the brothel, and the house of Antipholus. Whether realized as separate stage-mansions or as the three openings in the hall-screen, these three houses bordered a playing space just as ambiguous as that in *Jocasta*: references to the "mart" (1.2.74, etc.) and the "street" (3.1.36, etc.), as well as the classical stage direction "Enter Dromio Sira. *from the Bay*," suggest the fixed locale of Roman comedy, yet Act Three, Scene One, has Adriana entertaining the wrong Antipholus inside the house while the real Antipholus cries for entry outside—a shift of scene from outside to inside that is easy enough in medieval terms but hard to imagine if the stage represents a fixed location.[28]

If such an ambiguity would seem intolerable to late-seventeenth-century critics who had studied Aristotle and knew all about the unities, it was hardly remarkable to sixteenth-century Englishmen gathered around a platform stage, for reasons we have seen already: Elizabethan audiences thought about the play, not as an object that needed to be placed in perspective, but as a rhetorical event, an act of direct verbal communication between actor and audience. Where does the dramatic event take place? Elizabethan audiences, tutored by Cicero and Horace, would have answered that question

28. R. A. Foakes notes these classical features in his introduction to the New Arden Edition (London, 1962), pp. xxxiv–xxxix.

simply enough: "Right here in front of us." Later audiences, corrected by Aristotle, would have answered differently: "On a public square in Thebes, on a street in Rome." These two different philosophical contexts for looking at the play have their counterparts in the two different conceptions of theatrical space that we have been observing: on the one hand, an organic, intuitive sense of space that places player and spectator in direct contact and, on the other, a constructed, rational sense of space that separates them as viewer and object. Clearly, actors and audiences in these mid-sixteenth-century productions of Greek and Roman scripts thought of the play in that first sense, as a rhetorical event, and positioned themselves in that first sense of space, as speaker and listener in immediate contact with one another. They may have taken over some of the trappings of classical staging, but they carried the whole thing off in an essentially medieval spirit.

Certain architects and theatrical designers, especially later in the sixteenth century, went beyond cosmetic classicizing to work out genuine compromises between medieval and classical ideas about theatrical space. Serlio's famous illustrations of Vitruvius's three kinds of scenes (tragic, comic, and satiric) occur in his neo-Vitruvian *Architettura*, Books One and Two of which were published in Paris in 1545 while Serlio was serving in the army of Italian artists that François Ier had assembled at Fontainebleau. The specific concern of Book Two is the rational science of perspective: it is in that special context that Serlio considers theater design. His purpose at the end of Book Two is not to reconstruct the theaters of antiquity with archaeological exactitude but to advise on staging arrangements in princely great halls, using the information in Vitruvius: "for that a man can hardly finde any Halls how great soever, wherein he can place a Theater without imperfection and impediment; therefore to follow Antiquities, according to my power and abilitie, I have made all such parts of these Theaters, as may stand in a Hall."[29] If the illusion of

29. Sebastiano Serlio, *The Book of Architecture*, 2.3, trans. Robert Peake

perspective depth is to work, Serlio must perforce rationalize
the space of the hall in which the theater is set up. But in doing
so, he neatly rearranges devices that were already familiar in
medieval staging. Vitruvius, for example, seems to think of
ornatus primarily as atmospheric; Serlio thinks of such things
in terms of actual houses. Concerning comedy, Serlio follows
Vitruvius's description of "private houses" and "city walls"
quite literally; concerning tragedy, however, Serlio turns
Vitruvius's vague "columns and pediments and old statues
and regal things" into well-defined buildings and connects
them specifically with characters in the play: "Houses for
Tragedies, must bee made for great personages, for that
actions of love, strange adventures, and cruell murthers, (as
you reade in ancient and moderne Tragedies) happen always
in the houses of great Lords, Dukes, Princes, and Kings.
Wherefore in such cases you must make none but stately
houses . . ." (fol. 25ᵛ). The very idea of matching particular
characters with particular "houses" is, of course, one of the
most prominent features of medieval staging. Even though
the flats that make up Serlio's illusionistic space recede with
the slope of the raked stage, the "houses" closest to the front
may have been practicable for making entrances and exits.
Serlio's original illustrations carefully distinguish between
blackened windows and doors and those filled in with glass or
closed doors. Copies after these 1545 illustrations do not
always preserve this distinction. The blackened spaces, the
woodcuts imply, are to be left open, perhaps to accommodate
from behind the elaborate colored lights that Serlio goes on to
describe, but perhaps to provide entrances for the characters
appropriate to each house. These openings serve to remind us
that the ultimate models for Serlio's houses are the mansions
of medieval staging. The illustrators of Giocondo's and Ce-
sariano's editions of Vitruvius and of Trechsel's Terence take
these structures out of the medieval round and arrange them

(London, 1611; repr. New York, 1970), fol. 24. Future quotations are taken
from this translation and are cited in the text.

in a plane parallel to the viewer; Serlio goes one step further by organizing the houses in perspective space.

Like most revolutions in European history, Serlio's had only a delayed and moderate effect in England. As late as 1611, long after illusionistic scenery had triumphed on continental stages, Serlio's first English translator Robert Peake interprets details of Serlio's text in light of medieval staging conventions. He seems to miss, for instance, Serlio's implication that a curtain is raised or that a pair of flats pulled aside "to discover the decoration of a scene" ("il discoprirsi lo apparato di una Scena"):

Among all the things that may bee made by mens hands, thereby to yield admiration, pleasure to sight, and to content the fantasies of men; I thinke it is placing of a Scene, as it is shewed to your sight, where a man in a small place may see built by Carpenters or Masons, skillful in Perspective worke, great Palaces, large Temples, and divers Houses, both neere and farre off; broad places filled with Houses, long streets crost with other wayes: tryumphant Arches, high Pillars or Columnes, Piramides, Obeliscens, and a thousand fayre things and buildings, adorned with innumerable lights, great, middle sort, and small.   (fol. 24)

The Dutch translation attributed to Peter Coeke van Aelst (Antwerp, 1553; Amsterdam, 1606), which Peake acknowledges as his source, cannot altogether be blamed for this lapse.[30] Neither does Coeke's Dutch translation quite explain why Peake imagines Serlio's houses as individual structures, each with its own roof. Describing the private houses appropriate to comedy, Serlio observes that the scenery (*apparati delle Scene*) is usually set up at the end of a hall where there is

30. Coeke's Dutch is closer to Serlio's Italian: "Fra l'altre cose fatte per-mano degli huomini che si possono riguardare con gran contentezza d'occhio, & sattisfattione d'animo, e (al parer mio) il discoprirsi le apparato di una Scena . . ." (*Tutte l'Opere d'Architettura* [Venice, 1619; repr. Ridgewood, N.J., 1964], fol. 44) becomes "Onder alle ander dingen die van menschen handen gemaecht mogen worden / om met verwonderinge t'aenschouwen en der oogen ende den geeste te contenterene / dat is na mijn duncken dre toerustinghe van eender Scenen als mense gaet ont decken . . ." (*Architettura*, trans. Peter Coeke van Aelst [Amsterdam, 1606], fol. 25).

a room behind for the actors to use. Taking literally Serlio's idiom for "is set up" (*si fanno al coverto*, "they make sheltered"), Coeke has it in Dutch that the houses themselves (*huysingen*)—not Serlio's illusionistic *apparati*—are "made under the roof in a hall" (*ond dac maect in enige sale*). Compounding Coeke's misconstruing of Italian idiom, Peake's English goes yet one step further from Renaissance Italy and gives each of these houses its own roof: "I will first entreat of the Comicall, whereof the Houses must be made as if they were for common or ordinarie people, which for the most part must be made under roofes in a Hall, which at the end thereof hath a chamber for the pleasure or ease of the personages . . ."[31] (fol. 24). Though Inigo Jones and Ben Jonson had introduced perspective scenery to the Jacobean court in *The Masque of Blackness* six years earlier, Robert Peake's theatrical imagination was still comfortably lodged in 1611 on the organic open space of the Elizabethan stage.

While English audiences were watching classical drama in essentially medieval circumstances, Andrea Palladio was busy measuring ruins, studying Vitruvius precisely, and collaborating with the scholar Daniele Barbaro to produce an edition of Vitruvius in Italian that would change the course of European theatrical history. Surely, few changes of such importance have turned on a small grammatical point. "Secundum autem spatia ad ornatus comparata"—the first word in Vitruvius's phrase is apparently used adverbially to mean "then." By the syntactically dubious device of taking "secundum" as a preposition, the word just could in this context mean "behind": in the middle are the doors decorated like a royal palace, left and right the *hospitalia*, "behind the spaces pro-

31. Compare Serlio's Italian ("io trattero al presente della Comica, i casamenti a laquale volton essere di personaggi privati, liquali apparati per la maggior parte si fanno al coperto in qualche stata, che nel capo di essa vi sia camere perla commodita de i dicitori . . ." [fol. 44]) and Coeke's Dutch ("so sal ic nu tracteren vande comica / vande welcke dat de huysingen naden gemenen man moeten gemaect worden / welke dingen dat men meestendeel ond dac maect / in enige sale die t'eynden een camer heeft tot gerief vanden personagien . . ." [fol. 25]).

vided for ornatus." That is exactly the reading that Palladio and Barbaro argue in *Di Marco Vitruvio Poilione i dieci libri dell'architettura commentati da Mons. Barbaro* (Venice, 1556), and in their ground plan the three-sided periaktoi appear *within* the three middle doors.[32] Presumably the actors must make their entrances and exits through the *versurae* to the extreme left and right. Palladio and Barbaro's solution may seem merely clever on the ground plan, but when we look at their projection of the scaenae frons, we see with a shock just how revolutionary their proposal was. (See Figure 6.) In their central doorway is the beginning of the proscenium arch of the eighteenth- and nineteenth-century stage; behind it is the illusionistic world that became so fascinating that actors eventually decamped from the forestage altogether, entered the illusion beyond the central arch, and left behind them the immediacy, the easy give-and-take of medieval theater-in-the-round. Less than twenty years after their Vitruvius first appeared (it was reprinted in 1567, 1584, and 1629), Palladio and Barbaro's compromise was turned into bricks, mortar, and plaster when Palladio designed the Teatro Olimpico for the antiquarian Academia Olimpica at Vicenza. Rather than as painted panels, the perspective illusion beyond the arches was realized as city streets built up in radically foreshortened relief by Palladio's pupil Scamozzi. The practical influence of the Teatro Olimpico (it stood unused for thirty-three years after the inaugural production of Sophocles' *Oedipus Rex* in Italian translation in 1585) was small beside Palladio and Barbaro's inspired misreading of Vitruvius. Placement of the periaktoi behind the doors soon became dogma and remained so throughout the seventeenth century. The reason is fairly obvious: Barbaro and Palladio managed to honor scholarly scruples at the same time that they satisfied the modern passion for illusionistic scenery.

In his theatrical designs, as in the name he adopted after he

32. In *Andrea Palladio's Teatro Olimpico* (Ann Arbor, 1981), pp. 1–26, J. Thomas Oosting demonstrates how Palladio adapted Vitruvius's prescription to Renaissance stage practice, particularly by enlarging the central door to accommodate illusionistic scenery.

returned from Italy, Inigo Jones managed to reconcile new ideas from Italy with traditionally English ways of doing things. The theater projects that John Orrell has brilliantly reconstructed from Jones's drawings show us the same spirit of compromise we find in Palladio and Barbaro.[33] For the plays that greeted King James at Oxford in 1605, Jones improvised a theater in the great hall of Christ Church that included, for certain, the first raked stage in English theatrical history and, probably, a system of periaktoi that dispensed with archways altogether and placed the painted panels next to one another to produce a box set. In arranging where the spectators sat, as where the actors acted, Jones attempted to take the rectangular organic space of the hall and turn it into something like the circular geometric space of neoclassical theaters in Italy. English tradition thwarted him. When certain courtiers complained that Jones's trapezoidal arrangement of the seats to the left and the right of the throne would keep them from seeing the king, Jones was forced to compromise. All seats but the throne were pushed back against the side walls, just as they always had been when the Tudor monarchs watched plays. Most spectators sat at a right angle to the stage—but straight on to the king, whose chair displaced the stage as the focal point of the whole scheme.

For the old Cockpit in Drury Lane, reconstructed and fitted out as a commerical theater in 1616, Jones devised a more workable compromise between classical and medieval ideas. He retained the thrust stage of Elizabethan and Jacobean playhouses, but he also made provision for a temporary proscenium arch and for painted scenery, should any ever be required. On most occasions they were not. Even when Thomas Heywood, ever on the lookout for new material, took two of Plautus's Latin comedies out of the hands of schoolmasters and university dons and put them on the stage of the Cockpit, he taught Plautus's Romans to conform to Jacobean staging conventions. In *The Captives* (1624), which

33. John Orrell, *The Theatres of Inigo Jones and John Webb* (Cambridge, 1985), pp. 24–77, 90–112.

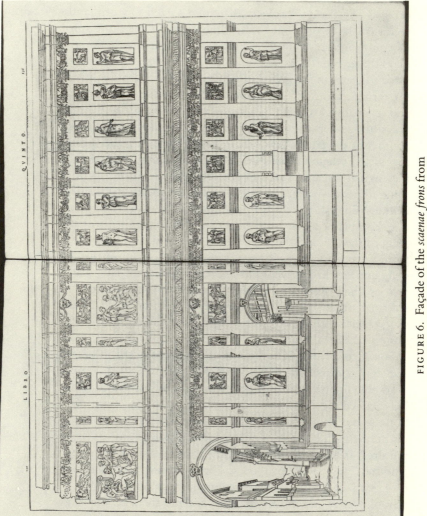

FIGURE 6. Façade of the *scaenae frons* from
Vitruvius, *I dieci libri dell'architettura*, ed. Daniele Barbaro
(Venice: F. Marcolini, 1556).

incorporates the plot and some of the speeches of Plautus's *Rudens*, Heywood's Anglicized Romans have given up both the three localized doors of Vitruvius's scaenae frons and the stage-mansions of Elizabethan great halls and make do instead with the Cockpit's two stage doors, which can serve as any two different places that may be required. Thus in Act Three, Scene Two, one door, in true Roman fashion, serves for the procurer Mildewe's brothel; the other, in true English fashion, for peasants who crash onstage to raid the house: "*A tumult within and suddein noyse. Enter att one doore* GODFREY, *with coontry fellowes for there reskewe, at the other* MILDEWE, SARLA BOYS [his friend], PLESTRA, SCRIBONIA [two of his courtesans]." Elsewhere in the play the same two doors serve for two entirely different locations in the play's subplot, drawn from an Italian novella.[34] *The English Traveler* (1627), Heywood's adaptation of Plautus's *Mostellaria* crossed with another Italian novella, likewise uses the familiar features of the Elizabethan and Jacobean public stage: two doors, an arras to hide behind, props like a table and stools, directed to be "set out" with "lights" to simulate a banquet. The implication of Heywood's stage directions is clear enough: just as classical playscripts in the sixteenth century were adapted to the staging conventions that usually obtained in the great halls of English palaces, colleges, and schools, so in the early seventeenth century those scripts were adapted to the customary playing arrangements on the English public stage. Johannes DeWitt with his Latin labels notwithstanding, the sense of space in the public theaters of Renaissance England was more organic than rational. The fact that *The Captives* and *The English Traveler* were, in part at least, classical comedies, seems not to have demanded any special considerations at all—hardly surprising, when we consider the marginal place such classical adaptations occupied in the repertories of Jacobean and Caroline professional companies.

The compromise worked out by Palladio and Barbaro in

34. John Heywood, *The Captives; or, The Lost Recovered*, 3.2.S.D., ed. Alexander C. Judson (New Haven, 1921), p. 85.

their edition of Vitruvius is precisely the one adopted by Inigo
Jones in his design for the remodeled Cockpit-in-Court
(1630): within the innovative curve of his scaenae frons, Jones
incorporated Vitruvius's five doorways, but with a glance
perhaps to Palladio and Barbaro's Vitruvius, perhaps to actual
theaters he had seen firsthand in Italy, perhaps even to the
space "within" in Jacobean public playhouses, Jones consid-
erably enlarged Vitruvius's central door, probably with an eye
to using that space for illusionistic scenery.[35] What we have in
Jones's designs are three English variations on an Italian
theme, three ingenious attempts to reconcile English staging
traditions with classical ideas imported from Italy.

    Even when neoclassical taste triumphed at the Restoration,
neoclassical architectural ideas still had to be accommodated
to English idiosyncracies. Dryden and Lee's *Oedipus* (1678),
John Crowne's *Thyestes* (1680), Sir Charles Sedley's *Bellarmira*
(an adaptation of Terence's *Eunuchus*, 1687), Dryden's *Amphi-
tryon* (1690)—all of these ancient plays with modern improve-
ments were acted on stages that were modeled ultimately on
Vitruvius but more immediately on the compromise arrange-
ments of Palladio/Barbaro and Inigo Jones. If the design for a
playhouse among Sir Christopher Wren's drawings is indeed
that of the new Drury Lane Theater, opened in 1674, we can
observe the very structure in which all these adaptations, with
the exception of *Oedipus*, were mounted.[36] (See Figure 3.)

    One Vitruvian detail is especially remarkable: Wren's cross
section shows not one but two doors opening onto the stage
on the far side, at a right angle, perhaps even an oblique angle,

35. In addition to Orrell, *Theatres*, pp. 90–112, see D. F. Rowan, "The
Cockpit-in-Court," in *The Elizabethan Theatre*, ed. David Galloway
(Toronto, 1968), pp. 89–102, and "The English Play-house: 1595–1630," in
Renaissance Drama, ed. S. Schoenbaum, N.S. 4 (Evanston, Ill., 1971): 37–51.

36. The physical properties of Restoration theaters and conventions of
staging are discussed in Allardyce Nicoll, *A History of English Drama 1660–
1900*, Vol. 1 (Cambridge, 1952): 25–63, 78–83; Richard Southern, *Changeable
Scenery* (London, 1952); Sybil Rosenfeld, *A Short History of Scene Design in
Great Britain* (Oxford, 1973), pp. 39–59; and Richard Southern, "Theatres and
Scenery," in *The* Revels *History of Drama in English*, ed. John Loftis et al., Vol.
5 (London, 1976): 83–118.

to the audience—just in the position of the versurae Vitruvius describes. Paired with the two unseen doors on the opposite side, these two entrances bring the total number of openings onto the stage to the requisite Vitruvian five, if we count the proscenium arch itself as a development of Barbaro and Palladio's central door. In Wren's design this central door has further expanded to the entire width of the stage. Behind this proscenium arch, Wren indicates seven ranks of flats that slide in parallel grooves. By pulling aside the flats in succession, Restoration producers achieved two different effects: they could reveal successive changes of scene or, as the diminishing heights of the flats suggest, they could offer an illusion of perspective depth.

At the very center of Wren's design, however, is a survival of the medieval, organic sense of theatrical space: in front of the proscenium arch Wren shows a forestage projecting a full twenty feet into the auditorium. This feature was peculiarly English. Not only Wren's drawing but the evidence of Restoration scripts demonstrates that much of the action on Restoration stages took place in front of the proscenium arch, not behind it. Restoration actors thus kept something of the close physical communication with audiences that players and spectators were accustomed to in English public playhouses before the Civil War. Entrances and exits were made customarily through the pairs of side doors, only on exceptional occasions through the scene behind the arch. Thus the script's statement of a scene's location usually indicates not a wing set within which the actors speak their lines, but a single pair of painted flats pushed together somewhere in the dimly lit space behind them. Act One of Dryden's *Amphitryon*, for example, takes place in front of a pair of closed flats on which is painted "Amphitryon's Pallace"; Act Two, in front of a "*Night-Scene of a Pallace*"; Act Three, in front of the same "Scene, before Amphitryon's Pallace" that presumably also served in Act One.[37] With spectacular effect, such pairs of flats could be

37. John Dryden, *Amphitryon; or, The Two Sosias* (1690), in *Works*, ed. Earl

drawn aside to reveal another scene behind. So in Act Two of Dryden and Lee's *Oedipus* when Haemon, Alcander, and Pyracmon are cataloging the cosmic disturbances that attend Thebes' sufferings, they no sooner mention heavenly apparitions of "The perfect Figures of a man and Woman: / A Scepter bright with Gems in each right hand, / Their flowing Robes of dazling Purple made," than "*The Scene draws and discovers the Prodigies*" looming just as Haemon has described them.[38]

Studying the often elaborate stage directions that were designed to make Restoration playscripts salable and readable as well as actable, we get the impression that scenic revelations like this one in *Oedipus interrupt* the forestage action rather than *contain* it. Thus in Act Four of Crowne's *Thyestes*, acted at Wren's Drury Lane Theater in 1680, the dialogue comes to a complete halt while Antigone marries Philisthenes in a dumb-show that seems almost Elizabethan: "*The Scene a Temple. Priests at the Altar. Enter* Atreus, Aerope, Thyestes, Philisthenes, Antigone, Peneus, *Attendants. The Nuptial Ceremony perform'd; they come out of the Temple. The Scene continues.*"[39] And so the dialogue recommences. Apparently it does so only when the actors have come from behind the proscenium arch ("*they come out of the Temple*"), back onto the forestage where most of the play's action transpires. Other Restoration adaptations of Greek and Roman scripts communicate the same impression that these spectacular scenes are set pieces during which the "real" action of the play is suspended. Restoration theaters thus had not one but two focal points, one on the forestage and one behind the proscenium arch, and in the course of a play the focus of the audience's attention could shift from one to the other. Those two focal

---

Miner, Vol. 15 (Berkeley, 1976): 239, 246, 264. Future references are cited in the text.

38. John Dryden and Nathaniel Lee, *Oedipus: A Tragedy,* in *The Dramatic Works,* ed. Montague Summers, Vol. 4 (1932; repr. New York, 1968): 371–72. Future references are cited in the text.

39. John Crowne, *Thyestes: A Tragedy* (London, 1681), Act Four, p. 41. Future references are cited in the text.

points imply two different senses of theatrical space. As a survival from the Elizabethan and Jacobean public playhouses, the forestage is the focal point for the same intuitive, organic sense of space we have encountered in the great halls of palaces, colleges, and schools; as the product of Renaissance study of the ancient theater, the space behind the proscenium arch figures as the focal point for the rational, constructed sense of space we have followed from Vitruvius through Barbaro, Palladio, Serlio, and Jones to Wren. Into these two different senses of theatrical space were fitted two different ideas of drama: Cicero's sense of the play as a rhetorical exchange between speaker and listener, who share the same undifferentiated space, and Aristotle's sense of the play as an object, viewed by an observer who stands, or sits, apart from the play. On the English Restoration stage we discover, then, not a total triumph of classical principles but yet another compromise between ancient and medieval ideas of the theater, physical ideas as well as philosophical.

Unlike the narrative and allegorical dumb-shows of Elizabethan drama, which they superficially resemble, the scenes of spectacle in Restoration drama have less to do with the philosophical program of the play than with its emotional effect. In tragedy such scenes often coincide with the catastrophes of the plot. Thus in Crowne's *Thyestes* the hero's gruesome meal provides an occasion for brilliant spectacle effects: "Thyestes *drinks; a clap of Thunder, the Table oversets, and falls in pieces; all the lights go out.*" The death of the hero in the amorous subplot of the play comes in a moment of literal revelation. "Open the Temple Gates," commands Atreus, likely giving the cue for a pair of flats to be pulled aside. "*The Temple is open,*" say the stage directions that follow, "Philisthenes *lyes bloudy.*" Similarly in Dryden and Lee's *Oedipus*, "*Scene draws, and discovers Jocasta held by her Women, and stabb'd in many places of her bosom, her hair dishevel'd, her Children slain upon the Bed.*" In moments of such intense emotional appeal we have visual evidence of how neoclassical tragedy aspires to epic.

Such moments were not, however, limited to tragedy. A dazzling convocation of gods begins Dryden's *Amphitryon* like the bravura overture to an opera. "Know you the Reason of this present Summons?" asks Phoebus of Mercury as the two "*descend in several Machines*." " 'Tis neither Council-day, nor is this Heav'n; / What Business has our *Jupiter* on Earth?" In a moment Jupiter himself "*descends*" and sets in motion the plot's complications. As the confusions have begun with grand spectacle in Act One, so they end in Act Five: "*It Thunders; and the Company within doors*, Amphitryon, Alcmena, Polydas, *and* Tranio, *all come running out, and joyn with the rest, who were on the Theatre* [i.e., on the forestage platform] *before*." After "*A second Peal of Thunder*," Jupiter himself "*appears in a Machine*" and stage-manages the happy ending. Far from functioning as the choruslike interlude that the dumb-shows in *Jocasta* do, the sensational spectacles in these Restoration productions are designed as moments of climax within the play itself, moments when the audience's attention is focused most sharply. It is in just these crucial moments that Restoration actors, spiritually if not physically, leave the medieval forestage behind and carry the play into the Renaissance world of illusion beyond the proscenium arch. In such emotionally and intellectually charged moments the audience must give up the closeness, the wholistic immediacy with which they have taken in the action on the forestage. With the shift of the play into perspective illusion, all the rational geometry of Wren's design goes to work, shifting the audience, physically and psychologically, into the position of aesthetic observers, just when the emotional effect threatens to take them in. The result is dramatic irony of a peculiarly neoclassical sort: one sees the epic vision beyond the arch, but at the same time one measures the aesthetic distance that separates that vision from reality.

To appreciate just how different this sense of the play is from the medieval sense, we can return to Pacuvius's lost *Orestes* and imagine how it would have been done on the Restoration stage. Instead of following Tiptoft's King Thoas as he searches "the place" over and closes in finally on Pylades and Orestes, we should probably find ourselves sitting back in surprise and delight at the spectacular moment when a pair of flats is pulled back to discover "*The Palace of* Thoas, *King of Taurica Chersonesus*," displayed in sinister splendor and full perspective depth. Pylades' gallant attempt to pose as Orestes and so draw the penalty of death away from his friend and onto himself is the kind of grand gesture that Restoration audiences would have applauded as loudly as Cicero's Romans or Tiptoft's fifteenth-century Englishmen; we would see that action, however, not as a matter-of-fact happening right in front of us but as an heroic performance belonging to the splendid, larger-than-life world beyond the proscenium arch. Quite literally, we would have put the event "into perspective." Our view of the play before us would have shifted from rhetorical event to aesthetic object, our sense of the space around us from organic to geometric, our psychological stance from involvement to detachment.

These two different kinds of space enclose not only different physical and philosophical realities but different social realities, as well. In the sixteenth century, great halls still kept something of their original importance as the place where an entire medieval household lived, ate, and slept. At Hampton Court in 1526, it was the "household" of Henry's court who gathered to watch Plautus's *Menaechmi*. Henry's courtiers may no longer have lived and slept in that one room, as their medieval predecessors had done, but they assembled there to eat, drink, watch plays, dance, and in the process affirm their identity as a social group. The geometric design of the Drury Lane Theater, with its separate spaces of pit, gallery, boxes, middle gallery, and upper gallery, was designed not so much to bring people together as to set them apart, aesthetically from the play and socially from each other. The philosophical and physical contexts of drama in the sixteenth and seventeenth centuries contain a third context, even more decisive in how it structures plays in performance: the social context of the people who watch, listen, and respond.

III · Social Contexts

C. Attilius Serranus, and *L. Scribonius Libo*, Aediles of the chaire, were the first that exhibited the Stage-plaies called Megalesia. And the Romane plaies or games represented and set out by these Aediles, the Senate now first & never before beheld apart from the rest of the people. And this (as all novelties and new fashions) ministred much talke: whiles some gave their opinion and said, That now at length that was given to this most noble and honorable State, which long agoe was due; others againe construed thus, and gave out, That whatsoever was added to the majestie of the Senators and nobles, was derogatorie from the dignitie of the people: and that all such kind of distinctions, whereby estates and degrees are severed one from another, are prejudiciall as well to common peace as publicke libertie. For these five hundred and eightie yeeres say they, these plaies and games have been beheld and looked upon pell mell, without any such precise difference. What new accident is suddainely befallen, why the Nobles should not be willing to let the Commons be intermingled with them in the Theatre? and why a rich man should disdaine his poore neighbour to sit by him? This is a new appetite and straunge longing of theirs indeed, full of pride and arrogancie, a thing never desired nor taken up and practised by the Senate of any nation whatsoever.

IN THE END, Livy reports, Scipio Africanus repented that he had allowed "this new fashion" to come about during his consulship. For half a millenium, Roman drama had been a *civic* event, in every sense of the word. As a way of marking festival occasions, competitions and plays brought together in one place all strata of Roman society. To try and change that, to give the senators their own plays apart from the commonality, was to challenge the whole society's self-definition. "So hard a matter it is," Livy concludes, "to alter an old custome, and make a new order to be well liked of."[1]

Although different in other respects, drama in Athens and

---

1. Livy, 34.44, trans. Philemon Holland as *The Romane Historie Written by T. Livius of Padua* (London, 1600), p. 878.

in Rome was the same in two important ways: it was occa-
sional, and it was communal. It was this public character of
ancient drama that Pomponius Laetus and his collaborators
wanted to reinstate in modern times. When they reintroduced
tragedy to Rome for the first time in more than a thousand
years, they made a special point of staging the first perform-
ance of Seneca's *Hippolytus* in a public square before they
moved play, players, and props to the Castel Sant'Angelo for
a second performance before the Pope and then on to Cardinal
Riario's palace for a third performance before an assembly of
cardinals and nobles. Despite Pomponius's symbolic gesture,
public performances of ancient drama turned out to be all but
nonexistent. More typical of how Greek and Latin playscripts
were revived in the sixteenth and seventeenth centuries are the
second and third performances of *Hippolytus* before the Pope
and before Cardinal Riario's friends. Restored to the stage,
comedy and tragedy may have kept the occasional character
they had in ancient times—in Renaissance Europe, as in fifth-
century Athens and republican Rome, the productions were
customarily a way of celebrating a coronation, a marriage, a
military victory, or a season of the year—but they addressed a
vastly smaller, infinitely more selective audience. All over
Renaissance Europe, productions of classical plays were
almost always private affairs, for two very good reasons: they
called for erudition, and they called for money. Academicians
and their students provided the former; princes provided the
latter.

From the very first performance of a classical script in
modern times, we are faced, then, with a polarity between
public audience and private audience, between the social inclu-
siveness of comedy and tragedy in ancient times and the social
exclusiveness of their revival in modern times. This polarity
poses some large and difficult questions. First there is a theo-
retical issue. If, as Cicero and Horace imply, drama is a rhe-
torical event, an exchange between speakers and listeners,
who constitutes the audience? If comedy and tragedy repre-
sent certain ways of structuring experience, just *whose* experi-
ence is being structured? Trained to think about plays as rhe-

torical events, Renaissance and neoclassical producers possessed an awareness of audience that was as critically central to their understanding of drama as an awareness of readers is to a contemporary deconstructionist's understanding of printed texts. Just who *is* that audience? All of mankind? Learned men only? Good men only? Whoever turns up to watch the play? Cicero, Horace, and Aristotle gave conflicting testimony, leaving theorists to reconcile the contradictions and producers to cope as they could. This abstract question about audience shades off into some solid practical questions about staging. What happened to ancient scripts when they were translated from the pluralistic "open" context of ancient public theaters into the homogeneous "closed" contexts of Renaissance schools, colleges, and noble households? What reflections of their own identity did these social in-groups find in the plays they paid for, watched, and often themselves acted? What happened to the still-emerging patterns of comedy and tragedy when Pomponius's ambitions were finally realized, not in Rome but in Shoreditch and Southwark, and spectators ranging from vagrants to lords thronged to the first permanent public theaters anywhere in Europe since Roman times? How, finally, were these tensions between private and public, between in-group and society at large, resolved in the pages of neoclassical critics and in the pit, boxes, and galleries of Restoration theaters?

I

About ancient audiences the Renaissance inherited two contradictory views. The political anecdotes recounted in Cicero's letters and speeches made the theater of his day sound almost like a courtroom that could accommodate all the city. Actors would use emphasis in delivering their lines, special gestures, even interpolated speeches to draw parallels between the mythic heroes they were impersonating and real political personages who played out their power struggles in the senators' portico next door; audiences would hoot, clap, and yell their verdicts. Before this theatrical tribunal, Pompey, Clodius, Brutus, even Cicero himself passed in turn. The social diversity of Roman audiences was suggested not only in Livy's account of the Megalesian games but in a story Plutarch tells of how the common people rebelled when Marcus Otho decreed that knights should henceforth sit, not among the common people as before, but with the senators in a special section all to themselves. Otho's new law, says Plutarch, "the people . . . took grievously, as a thing done to discountenance them: insomuch that Otho coming afterwards into the theatre, all the common people fell a whistling at him, to shame him withal. The knights also in contrariwise made him room amongst them, with great clapping of hands, in token of honour. Therewith the people fell a whistling louder than before, and the knights in like manner to clapping of their hands, and so grew to words one with another: that all the theatre was straight in uproar with it."[2] Within the theater's walls, Plutarch indicated, there was assembled a microcosm of the whole of Roman society, and the stratified order of the seating reflected the stratified order of society outside the walls. It was just such indications of ancient drama's public vigor that prompted Pomponius to stage the premiere of *Hippolytus* in a city square.

Horace gave a different impression:

> If now the phrase of him that speakes, shall flow
> In sound, quite from his fortune; both the rout
> And Roman Gentrie, jearing, will laugh out.[3]

Horace may mention "the rout," but the arbiters of what will go and not go in a play are clearly the "Roman Gentrie," cultivated gentlemen like Horace himself. The *real* audience for classical drama, Horace implies, was a small, select group of cognoscenti. Quintilian furthers that impression. When Quintilian refers to actors at all, they are the Roscius and Aesopus of Cicero's day, not the mimes, jugglers, and

2. Plutarch, Life of Cicero, trans. Thomas North in *The Lives of the Noble Grecians and Romans* (1579), ed. Paul Turner (Carbondale, Ill., 1963), 2: 77–78.

3. Horace, *Ars poetica*, 112–13, trans. Ben Jonson, ed. William B. Hunter in *Complete Poetry* (New York, 1963), p. 285.

variety-show *artistes* who had displaced legitimate actors in
Quintilian's own time. Where Cicero is enthusiastic about the
public character of the theater, Quintilian is openly contemp-
tuous of its vulgarity.[4] In large part Quintilian's attitude
reflects differences in the Roman theater in imperial times and
in republican times, but read by scholars fifteen hundred years
later, his discriminations must have seemed not so much his-
torical as social: serious drama, he implies, is not compatible
with public performance. As false to historical fact as it was,
this view of classical drama proved amazingly tenacious in the
Renaissance.

The *social* distinction set in place by Horace and Quintilian
became with most Renaissance critics a *moral* distinction.
Robortello, for one, attributes Horace's intellectual snobbery
to Aristotle. What does Aristotle mean by describing tragic
heroes as men "like ourselves" (53.a.5), Robortello asks.

> Fear is aroused, indeed, when we behold someone like ourselves who
> has fallen into misery. Aristotle means like the auditors themselves,
> almost all of whom are judged to be good [*boni*]; or else he speaks
> only of the good ones. For it is out of their souls that the rule for
> writing tragedy is derived, nor must any poet ever be mindful of the
> wicked, but he must adapt everything he writes to the nature of good
> men. Good men, then, when they see evil things happen to some
> good man, fear—since they understand that he is like themselves and
> that they are like him—lest the same thing at some time befall them,
> as they live in the same circumstances.[5]

In imagining the audience of ancient drama, Renaissance
critics were more likely to pay attention to Horace and Quin-

4. Quintilian, *Institutio oratoria*, 11.3.111–16, trans. H. E. Butler, Loeb
Library (London, 1921), p. 4. The debased state of the theater during the
Empire is discussed by William Beare, *The Roman Stage*, 2d ed. (London,
1955), pp. 223–30.

5. Francesco Robortello, *In librum Aristotelis de Arte Poetica explicationes*
(1548), facsimile reprint. (Munich, 1968), p. 128, my translation. Horace is
clearly the inspiration for this advice. Compare *Ars poetica*, 193–96, trans.
Jonson, p. 293: "An Actors parts, and Office too, the Quire / Must maintaine
manly; not be heard to sing / Betweene the Acts, a quite cleane other thing /
Then to the purpose leades, and fitly 'grees. / It still must favour good men,
and to these / Be wonne a friend. . . ."

tilian than to Cicero for the simple reason that Horace and Quintilian more closely described the social circumstances in which Greek and Latin plays were acted in the sixteenth century. It was not in the *orchestrai* of ancient theaters but in the refectories of schools and colleges and in the great halls of princes' palaces that the heroes of Greek and Roman drama spoke again after a millenium of silence.

The social exclusiveness of Horace and Quintilian and the moral uprightness of Renaissance critics like Robortello explain why classical drama found a place in the curriculum of Renaissance schools.[6] Like so much else in Renaissance education, justification for acting plays in school came ultimately from Cicero. In *De officiis*, probably the most widely read of Cicero's philosophical writings during the Middle Ages and the Renaissance, Cicero discusses pleasures and pastimes, plays included, in the context of reason controlling appetite. *Homo sapiens* should stay firmly in control of *homo ludens*. "For lyke as we gyve not to chyldren all wanton lycence to play / but suche play as is not exorbytant fro[m] the exercyse of honesty / so that in this selfe jestyng some lyght of laudable disposycion may apere." Cicero goes on to distinguish two different kinds of "jestyng." Comedies like Plautus's belong to the "higher" sort:

There is utterly but two maner of jestynges / that one carterly / scoldyng / vycious / and abhomynable. The other clenly / manerly / wysely / and with mery borde. In the whiche maner not onely Plautus our countreyman and the olde comedy of Athenes / but also the bokes of philosophers that folowed Socrates be replenyshed. And many wordes of dyvers manerly spoken / as those whiche were gathered of Cato in his olde age / whiche he called i[n] greke Apothegmata. Therefore it is an easy distinctyon of a gentyll bourde & of a carterly jestyng. The one if it be done in tyme and with a mery stomake / becometh a gentyll man. The other unfyttyng for a gentyll

6. On the place of drama in Elizabethan grammar schools, see T.H.V. Motter, *The School Drama in England* (London, 1929), pp. 85–104; M. L. Clarke, *Classical Education in Britain 1500–1900* (Cambridge, 1959), pp. 9ff.; and Lawrence Tanner, *Westminster School: A History* (London, 1934), pp. 55–59.

man / if so be that vyle termes be joyned to the leude ded of the thynges.[7]

"Gentyll bourde" and "carterly jestyng": the two terms Cicero actually uses are *ingenuus*, "native, free born, worthy of a free man," and *illiberalis*, "mean, unworthy of a free man." Robert Whittinton's English translation of 1534 catches the nice balance between style and social status in this distinction. For gentlemen there are "bourdes" with an elegant French vowel; for riffraff there are "jests" with two hard consonants. Ingenuus, in the sense of "native," did not enjoy the same cachet in sixteenth-century England as it did in republican Rome. Translating *De officiis* a quarter century later, Nicholas Grimalde imposes a typically Renaissance reading on this same passage when he sees Cicero's distinction not as social or stylistic but as moral: "To be short, after twoo sortes is the maner of jesting: the one, unhonest, rayling, hurtful, bawdie: the other, fine, civil, wittie, pleasaunt. . . . Easie therfore is the difference bitwene honest, and unhonest jesting. The one is meete for an honest man, if it be done in season, and with a light hert: the other, meete for no man, if the unclenlinesse of the mater be encreased with filthinesse of wordes."[8] The point for educators was clear: playacting was a pastime that conduced to style, social breeding—and morality.

Quintilian had even more specific things to say about the place of playacting in education. For Cicero, as we have seen, acting and oratory were allied arts. As a student learning to gesture and declaim, Cicero is supposed to have studied the techniques of Roscius the comedian and Aesopus the tragedian. Quintilian thus feels no hesitation in recommending that would-be orators follow the great master onto the stage. With his goal of making the orator a vir bonus, Quintilian gives Cicero's ideas an additional twist by insisting that acting out

7. Cicero, *De officiis*, 1.29.103–104, trans. Robert Whittinton as *The thre bookes of Tullyes offyces* (1534), fols. F7–F7ᵛ.

8. *De officiis*, 1.29.103–104, trans. Nicholas Grimalde as *Marcus Tullius Ciceroes thre bokes of duties*, 2d ed. (1556), fols. E8ᵛ–FI. Grimalde was the author of two school plays, *Christus Redivivus* (Cologne, 1543) and *Archi-propheta* (Cologne, 1548).

plays is morally good for the actors themselves as well as for the audience:

Some time is also to be devoted to the actor, but only so far as the future orator requires the art of delivery; for I do not wish the boy, whom I educate for this pursuit, either to be broken to the shrillness of a woman's voice or to repeat the tremulous tones of an old man's. Neither let him imitate the vices of the drunkard, nor adapt himself to the baseness of the slave; nor let him learn to display the feelings of love, or avarice, or fear; acquirements which are not at all necessary to the orator, and which corrupt the mind, especially when it is yet tender and uninformed in early youth; for frequent imitation settles into habit. It is not even every gesture or motion that is to be adopted from the actor.

Quintilian goes on to give Renaissance educators five practical tips on how to coach their charges in eloquent declamation.[9] However high-spirited the comic complications, however deep the tragic passion, one never loses sight of the fact that plays are a way to argue a moral point—and that the lesson will not be lost on the actors themselves.

There were practical reasons, of course, for Renaissance students to learn to speak Latin—as the language of statesmanship, commerce, and learning, it enjoyed the same international currency as English, French, and German do today— but there were compelling theoretical reasons, too. To the Renaissance view, the orator seemed uniquely able to join together man's wit to know the truth and his will to make it a social reality. The playscripts of Greek and Roman antiquity spoke to both of man's capacities. Attended to for their moral lessons, the plays instructed the philosopher's wit to know; declaimed on the stage, they exercised the orator's will to act. For schoolboys, Plautus and Terence in particular were a natural: the dramatic heroes themselves were youths, and, at least as Erasmus, Melanchthon, and other humanist educators saw them, they offered their impersonators lessons in good breeding and good deeds as well as in good speaking.

The same sense of putting on classical plays as a Ciceronian

9. Quintilian, *Institutio oratoria*, 1.11.1–3, trans. Butler, 1: 184–87.

exercise in jesting "clenly / manerly / wysely and with mery borde" obtained in the colleges of Oxford and Cambridge. When William Gager, don at Christ Church, Oxford, and writer of neo-Latin plays himself, attempted to defend college plays from Puritan attack late in the sixteenth century, he turned to Cicero's observation that the orator has much to learn from the actor and Quintilian's insistence that a player has much to learn from plays. Ancient professional entertainers, Gager will concede,

came upon the stage . . . of a lewd, vast, dissolute, wicked, impudent, prodigall, monstrous humor, wherof no dowte ensued greate corruption of manners in them selves, to say nothinge heere of the behowlders. We contrarywise doe it to recreate owre selves, owre House, and the better parte of the *Universitye*, with some learned *Poeme* or other; to practyse owre owne style eyther in prose or verse; to be well acquantyed with *Seneca* or *Plautus*; honestly to embolden owre pathe; to trye their voyces and confirme their memoryes; to frame their speeche; to conforme them to convenient action; to trye what mettell is in evrye one, and of what disposition thay are of; wherby never any one amongst us, that I knowe was made the worse, many have byn muche the better; as I dare reporte me to all the *Universitye*.[10]

Implicit in Gager's remarks about trying his students' mettle is a sense of the larger political context in which classical plays were acted in Renaissance schools and colleges. The occasions may have been fun; they also taught future statesmen about the structure of Elizabethan society. We can see this political dimension of drama in the statutes with which Tudor monarchs reformed educational institutions and founded them anew after Henry VIII's break with Rome had transferred control of education from church to state. Henry VIII's statutes for St. John's College, Cambridge (1545), for example, call for "*dialogos aut festiva aut litteraria spectacula*" as part of the college's Christmas celebrations.[11] When she

10. Quoted in Frederick S. Boas, *University Drama in the Tudor Age* (Oxford, 1914), pp. 235–36.
11. Ibid., p. 8.

refounded Westminster School in 1560, Queen Elizabeth commanded that every year two plays be put on at Christmas, one in Latin and one in English. Most seasons during the 1560s and 1570s she came to see one of the plays—or, more usually, had one of the plays brought to her. Thus, in January 1565 the Westminster School boys took their production of *Miles Gloriosus* to Whitehall; the next year Elizabeth came to the school, accompanied by Princess Cecilia of Sweden, to hear an "original" Latin play on a Biblical theme, *Sapientia Solomonis*; and during Christmas 1567–1568 the Westminster scholars came again to Whitehall to mount Euripides' *Orestes*. The merging of "households," the queen's and the school's, on these festive occasions shows how each was structured in imitation of the other.

The Christmas king or Lord of Misrule who presided over the seasonal revels in Renaissance schools and colleges ruled over no lawless utopia but a copy, in miniature, of the kingdom at large. Like the ruler of the realm, the Christmas king was provided with counselors and officers; like the queen at Whitehall, he commanded the Christmas play as part of his royal entertainment. At Westminster School the Christmas king was called Paedonomus. Payments to a tailor in 1571 and 1573 for "the showe at Padonomy, the Childrens Lorde, his creation" show us how lavishly this court microcosm was staged to resemble the court of the realm. Paedonomus was dressed in black silk with gold lace and silver buttons and flourished a cloak of "ritch taffata of Carnation in graine." Guards armed with halberts surrounded him as he presided over the revels. To take the Westminster Christmas play to Whitehall was only to exchange one court context for another—and not altogether the facetious for the factual.[12]

The court of Padonomy may have been a parody of the court of the realm, but it was a *serious* parody. The rigor of the usual Renaissance school regime positively demanded an

12. On the tradition of boy bishops, see Motter, *School Drama*, pp. 85–104. The court of Padonomy in particular is discussed by Tanner, *Westminster School*, pp. 9–10.

escape valve, an institutionalized way of letting off steam. Yet paradoxically, the jubilant release during the Christmas revels did not undermine the power structure that obtained the rest of the year: it confirmed it. In a survey of a variety of cultures and a variety of historical periods, Victor Turner has demonstrated how common such occasions of temporary role reversal are in highly structured societies. The result, always, is a return to normal society with a renewed sense of commitment. Kings humbling themselves in a plain smock before the coronation, the fasting and all-night vigil of knights before their dubbing, the shared hardships and glories of pilgrims regardless of their social rank, the seasonal sway of boy bishops and Christmas lords—in all these ways medieval and Renaissance society compensated for its hierarchy and rigid structure and fostered social health that seems conspicuously absent from our own less structured but also less self-assured society.[13] Far from challenging the rigid social structure of Westminster school and Elizabethan society, the court of Padonomy consolidated it. And it provided a social context for classical drama that was as parochial as a school refectory and yet as broad as Elizabethan society itself. Acting out classical plays in such a context, Renaissance schoolboys could never forget that they were acting out in fiction what they would act out in fact when as young men they ventured outside the walls of the school into the world beyond. When the queen herself came to see the play, metaphors came very much to look like realities. The little household of the school reflected as in a convex mirror all the values, rules, and mores of Renaissance society at large.

As in Renaissance schools, at Oxford and Cambridge the comedians of Aristophanes, Plautus, and Terence and the tragic heroes of Sophocles, Eurpides, and Seneca appeared onstage at the command of a Christmas prince who reigned over a topsy-turvy court that parodied the court of the realm. Anthony a' Wood offers an account of how the prince was

13. Victor Turner, *Dramas, Fields, and Metaphors: Symbolic Action in Human Society* (Ithaca, 1974), pp. 166–271.

elected at Merton College, Oxford. On November 19, the vigil of St. Edmund, the bachelor fellows would choose one of their number to be Rex Fabarum. "The King of the Beans" alludes to the Twelfth Night custom, widely observed in England, of baking a single bean in a large cake and letting whoever chanced to get it in a slice be king for the nonce.[14] The Rex Fabarum carried out his duties in pompous state: "He had always a chair provided for him, and would sit in great state when any speeches were spoken, or justice to be executed, and so his authority would continue till Candlemas, or much about the time that the Ignis Regentium was celebrated in that college."[15] In most Oxford colleges the Christmas prince was enjoined by the college statutes to get up the Christmas plays himself; at Cambridge the persons responsible were more often fellows of the college, but the fiction was still the same: the plays were put on for the pleasure of the Christmas king and his court.

As riotous as the students could sometimes be—the expense accounts are filled with disbursements for smashed windows—the court of the Christmas king in Oxford and Cambridge colleges, no less than in Elizabethan schools, served to confirm the social hierarchy of Renaissance English society and to set in place the conservative program of values according to which audiences laughed at Roman citizens, passed judgment on tragic malefactors, and took pity on suffering kings. This telescoping of microcosm and macrocosm was made graphically clear when queen and court came to Oxford and Cambridge during her summer progresses over the realm. When Elizabeth visited Cambridge in August 1564, for example, the comedies and tragedies mounted for Her Majesty's pleasure included Plautus's *Aulularia*. Even the seating arrangements in King's College Chapel kept always before the audience's eye the hierarchical social structure

14. John Brand, *Observations on the Popular Antiquities of Great Britain* (London, 1849), 1: 22–28.

15. Quoted in Boas, *University Drama*, pp. 4–5. Wood himself was at Merton in the 1640s, but his account undoubtedly refers to practices traditional in the sixteenth century.

against which, quite literally, they were to view Plautus's play.
Eyewitnesses make it clear that the queen sat enthroned on the
stage itself, facing the side chapels that served as a backdrop
and tiring houses.[16] To her right on the stage sat the noblemen
of her court; to her left, on the floor of the nave of the chapel,
stood the students. Thus no one but the queen enjoyed a
front-on view of the play. Everyone else, however, enjoyed a
simultaneous view of the play *and* of the queen who presided
over it. As we shall see when we reconstruct the performance
in detail, the queen's presence on this occasion likely trans-
formed Plautus's lustiest comedy into a celebration of chas-
tity. So powerfully could social context transform dramatic
text. It was just such considerations of social hierarchy that
wrecked Inigo Jones's scheme to turn Christ Church hall,
Oxford, into a Vitruvian theater when James I came to see the
students put on plays in 1605.[17]

If the court of Padonomy at Westminster School strikes us
as schoolboy whimsy and the courts of the lords of misrule at
Oxford and Cambridge as an undergraduate rag, the courts of
the Christmas princes at the inns of court must appear consid-
erably closer to the real thing. The description of the Inner
Temple revels of 1561–1562 in Sir William Dugdale's *Origines
juridiciales* (1666) shows us how precisely these little courts
were set up in imitation of the court of the realm. Beneath
Robert Dudley, who took for the occasion the cognomen Pal-
laphilos, "Lover of Wisdom," there were a Lord Chancellor, a
Lord Treasurer, a Lord Privy Seal, two Chief Justices, a Chief
Baron of the Exchequer, and twelve household officers
(including Christopher Hatton as Master of the Game),
besides eighty of the Guard and, Dugdale notes, "divers
others not here named." In one respect at least Pallaphilos's
court was even more extravagant than the court of young
Queen Elizabeth: there were not one but four Masters of the

16. See Glynne Wickham, *Early English Stages*, Vol. 1 (New York, 1959):
355–59.

17. John Orrell, *The Theatres of Inigo Jones and John Webb* (Cambridge,
1985), pp. 24–38.

Revels.[18] With up-and-coming men like Robert Dudley (later
Earl of Leicester) and Christopher Hatton (later Lord Chan-
cellor) playing the roles, "parody" does not seem quite the
word to describe the relationship between the court of the
Christmas prince and the court of the realm.

Like schools and colleges, the inns of court enacted plays as
a ritual for affirming the conservative moral and political
values that undergirded society at large. The account of the
Gray's Inn revels of 1526–1527 in Edward Hall's chronicles
(1542), for example, shows us that the barristers had their eyes
fixed beyond the confines of Clerkenwell:

This christmas was a good disguisyng plaied at Greis inne, whiche
was compiled for the moste part, by master Jjon Roo seriant at the
law .xx. yere past, and long before the Cardinall had any aucthoritie,
the effecte of the plaie was, that lord governance was ruled by dissi-
pacion and negligence: which caused Rumor Populi, Inward grudge
and disdain of wanton sovereignetie, to rise with a greate multitude,
to expell negligence and dissipacion, and to restore Publik welth
again to her estate, which was so done. This plaie was so set furth
with riche and costly apparel, with straunge devises of Maskes &
Morrishes that it was highly praised of all menne, savyng of the Car-
dinall, which imagined that the plaie had been divised of hym.[19]

Wolsey was never one to underrate his own importance, but
Hall leaves no doubt about the political lesson in the Gray's
Inn revels, ad hominem or not.

Made up largely of sons of gentlemen, the households of
the inns of court could "keep Christmas" some years in a style
rivaling the royal court. Desmond Bland has dicovered in the
accounts of Furnivall's Inn, the oldest house records to sur-
vive, payments from 1412 onward for dramatic performances
by hired professionals.[20] Once humanists had established the

18. William Dugdale, *Origines juridiciales* (1666), excerpted in John
Nichols, *The Progresses and Public Processions of Queen Elizabeth*, 2d ed.
(London, 1823), 1: 131–41.

19. Edward Hall, *The Union of the Two Noble Families of Lancaster and York*
(1550; repr. Menston, England, 1970), fol. c–54ᵛ.

20. Desmond S. Bland, "Interludes in Fifteenth-century Revels at Furni-

value of acting for developing a student's memory, elocution, and deportment, the gentlemen themselves might act plays. It was as part of the Inner Temple's Christmas revels of 1560–1561, just a year before Robert Dudley presided as king of arms, that Thomas Sackville and Thomas Norton's *Gorboduc*, the first neoclassical tragedy in English, was mounted before Queen Elizabeth. This landmark production was followed in later years at the inns of court by at least two other neoclassical tragedies (*Gismond of Salerne in Love*, Inner Temple, 1566, and Thomas Hughes's *The Misfortunes of Arthur*, Gray's Inn, 1588) and by at least one classical tragedy in English translation (George Gascoigne and Francis Kinwelmershe's version of Euripides' *Phoenician Women*, Gray's Inn, 1566). The fact that *Gorboduc*, *Gismond*, and *Arthur* were all acted in the presence of Queen Elizabeth shows us again how closely connected were the court of the Christmas prince and the court of the realm. As the vital place where the world of the academy and the world of state affairs touched orbits, the inns of court provided a particularly important context for performances of classical tragedy. The progression from school to university to an inn of court to the court of the realm marked out the ideal career for a Renaissance statesman. In that progression he moved through a series of successively larger but tightly interlocked social structures that shared three characteristics: their exclusiveness, their hierarchy, and their commitment to conservative moral and political values. These closed social contexts left their decisive marks on the reemerging forms of comedy and tragedy.

An astonishing feature of the *real Politik* that governs these social contexts is how beguilingly disguised it is. Schools, colleges, the inns of court, or the court of the realm itself: all of these Renaissance households liked to think of themselves in images taken from medieval romance. The Inner Temple revels of 1561–1562 offer a particularly striking instance. Henry Machyn was a rapt witness when Robert Dudley and

---

vall's Inn," *RES*, N.S. 3 (1952): 263–68. A. Wigfall Green offers a general account in *The Inns of Court and Early English Drama* (New Haven, 1931).

the other barristers and benchers rode in procession through the streets of London as if they were royalty indeed: "The xxvii day of Desember cam ryding thrugh London a lord of mysrull, in clene complett harnes, gylt, with a hondred grett horse and gentyll-men rydyng gorgyously with chenes of gold, and there horses godly trapytt, unto the Tempull, for ther was grett cher all Cryustynmas. . . ."[21]

Another eyewitness was attracted by the cannon shots that greeted this mock-royal procession. In his treatise on heraldry, *The Accedens of Armory* (1562), Gerard Legh concludes his disquisition on Pegasus as an heraldic emblem by describing the 1561–1562 Temple revels in some detail. His account shows us how the benchers' mock-court shared with the court of the realm not only its hierarchical structure and conservative political values but its devotion to the neomedieval myth that gave those values imaginative life. The treatise as a whole is cast as a dialogue between Gerard "the Herehaught" and Legh "the Caligat Knight," and the account of the Inner Temple revels is worked in as a tale of Gerard's search "throughe the Est parts of th[']unknowen world, to understa[n]d of deades of Armes."[22] Especially before his naive pupil Legh, Gerard figures as a kind of academic knight errant. The sound of cannon leads the terrified Gerard to a passing citizen of London and to the news that a great prince is going in procession.

Enthralled, Gerard makes his way to the Temple, where one Pallaphilos takes him on tour. On the way to "the Pallace of his Prince," Pallaphilos tells Gerard a story that in effect provides the background plot to the spectacle the visitor is to see that evening. The *Romance of the Rose* is as vital in Pallaphilos's tale as it was three hundred years before. From Eulos, "the breath of fame," a gentlemen named Desire first learns about Dame Beauty's gifts. Eager to possess these gifts but unsure how to go about it, he is comforted and tutored by

21. Henry Machyn, *Diary*, ed. J. G. Nichols (London, 1848), pp. 273–74.
22. Gerard Legh, *The Accedens of Armory* (London, 1562), fol. 204^r. Future references will be cited in the text.

Governance and Grace, who escort him to the Tower of Doctrine, where Comely Countenance lets him in and Dame Congruity receives him. There Desire chances to see Dame Beauty passing to and fro in the Tower of Solace, but her door is guarded by Danger. Desire makes suit to Counsel, who advises him that the best way to foil Danger and Fortune is through wisdom. So Desire proceeds to "the howse of Chivalrye"—an obvious alias for the Inner Temple. There he is let in by the porter Strength and embraced by Youth and Pleasure. The presence chamber in this "hall of auncient foundacion" shows us what place the subjects of classical tragedy occupy in such a world. Pallaphilos's description of the Inner Temple hall reflects the fantasy in which the benchers liked to project themselves: "Richelye arrayed and tappesed withe Arras curiouselye wrought, conteynynge the siege of Thebes, where sate knightes, passing the tyme at chesse. There were Philosophers and Astronomers whoe drove the daye a waye with theyr Studiouse games, And in the middes under a ryche clothe of auncient and sumptuouse woorke, satte Chayerd, Honour. To whome the Gentilmanne humblye hym enclyned, shewing hys long desyer to see hys majestye, who welcomed him" (fols. 209^v–10^r). This is the Thebes, not of Sophocles, but of Statius, Chaucer's "Stace."

At Honor's command, Due Desert dubs Desire a "knight of the fielde." Audacity bears his helm, Courage his breastplate, Speed his spurs; Truth gives him a charge. Accompanied by Courtesy and Nurture, he passes to the Palace of Comfort, where he meets Fellowship and Knighthood and Perseverance. Armed by Hardiness, he goes forth to vanquish a serpent with nine heads "wheron weare carrected these ix. severall names. Dissimulacion, Deley, Shame, Misreporte, Discomfort, Variance, Envye, Detraction, and doublenes, enemyes to knighthod." At long last he receives as his due reward the hand of Lady Beauty. As Pallaphilos concludes his tale, Desire is installed, after years of glorious action, among the virtuous in Heaven.

What Gerard saw that evening in the Inner Temple hall was an enactment on a grander scale of Desire's investiture. Mar-

shaled by Pallaphilos, twenty-four young men were invested
as Knights of Pallas, complete with pompous processions and
allegorical disquisitions on each piece of their regalia, just as
in Pallaphilos's tale. Tilting, masking, and dancing concluded
the evening's pleasures:

Al which observances finished, Palaphilos biddeth them go offer to
Pallas, the first fruites of their gotten vertues, geving thankes to the
goddes with sacrifice. And so they departed towardes the Temple, in
suche order as they came, saving accompanied with two noble men,
to every of them. And before them wer all sowndes of Marce his
musike & officers of armes in their order, their sacrifice done, they
returned in like sort to Palaphilos hall, where they prepared prices of
honour, for Tylt, Turney, and such knightley pastimes. And after for
theyr solace, they masked with Bewties dames, with such heavenly
armony, as Appollo and Orpheus had shewed their cunnyng.

(fols. 224^v–25^r)

Pallas, we begin to suspect, may not have been only a goddess
in the fiction but the young sovereign to whom these
"knights" owed their allegiance in fact. For all its misty
romanticism, Desire's investiture reflects solid political reali-
ties: it marks the last stage in a career that leads from school
to college to inns of court to the court of the realm. It is a
lesson in statesmanship.

The Gray's Inn revels of 1594–1595—grandly set forth in
print with the mock-heroic neomedieval title *Gesta Gray-
orum*—enact the same romantic myth. Francis Davison's
"Masque of Proteus" may look forward to the self-deceptive
dreams of the Stuart court, but the overall program looks
backward over a century or more of revelry in the service of
political reality. The "High and mighty PRINCE, HENRY, Prince
of Purpoole, Arch-Duke of Stapulia and Bernardia, Duke of
High and Nether Holborn, Marquis of St. Giles and Tot-
tenham, Count Palatine of Bloomsbury and Clerkenwell,
Great Lord of the Cantons of Islington, Kentish-Town, Pad-
dington and Knights-bridge, Knight of the most Heroical
Order of the Helmet, and Sovereign of the Same" is only a
prince for the nonce, his supposed journey to Russia between

New Year's and Candlemas and his triumphant procession through the streets of London are both great fun, but the speeches Francis Bacon provided for the prince's six debating counselors are as full of sharp observations and usable advice as any of Bacon's essays. The seriousness of Bacon's speeches, not to mention the extravagant lengths to which he and his cohorts carried the fiction that the Prince of Purpool was a prince in fact, serve to remind us that it was more than geographical proximity that allied the inns of court with the court of the realm. It was in this romantic but politically charged context that the Lord Chamberlain's Men put on *The Comedy of Errors*.

   To follow the future statesman as he proceeds from school to college to one of the inns of court to the court of the realm is to pass through a series of ever grander rooms in which the decor remains constant. It was to King Arthur's court, not to Caesar Augustus's Rome, that Henry VII, Henry VIII, and Elizabeth looked for an *inhabitable* fiction. The entertainments that attended Henry VII's knighting of London's Lord Mayor at Twelfth Night 1494 establish not only the chivalric myth in which the Tudors liked to cast themselves but the range of diverse delights that constituted an evening's pastime. After the king and his party entered the hall at about an hour before midnight, there was first of all "a goodly Interlude" put on by "the kyngys players." Before the players had quite finished their play, however, "Cam in Ridyng oon of the kyngys Chapell namyd Cornysh apparaylid afftyr the Fygure of Seynt George, and aftir Folowid a Fayer vyrgyn attyrid lyke unto a kyngys dowgthyr, and ledyng by a sylkyn lace a Terryble & huge Rede dragun, the which In Sundry placys of the halle as he passyd spytt Fyre at hys mowth. . . ." When he had ridden before the king, Cornish declaimed "a certayn speche made in balad Royall." Then "wyth lusty Corage" he and some of his fellows of the Chapel Royal, who had assembled near by, sang an antiphon addressed to St. George. After this spectacular emblem underscored with political sentiment, Cornish and his dragon disappeared, the rescued virgin was led to the queen's box, and from the end of the hall came suddenly the music of "a small Tabert & subtyle Fedyll." In came twenty-four "Costiously & goodly dysguysid" ladies and gentlemen who danced an artfully choreographed ballet to conclude the evening's sport.[23]

It was into this milieu of dragons, rescued virgins, speeches in ballad royal, and dancing in masquerade that Cardinal Wolsey attempted to introduce classical drama at the court of Henry VIII. With all his ecclesiastical, political, and cultural ties with Italy, Cardinal Wolsey figures as the closest thing in sixteenth-century England to a Renaissance Italian prince—and a particularly Machievellian one, at that. Wolsey was likely responsible for the "goodly commedy of Plautus" that entertained Henry and his court on March 7, 1520—the earliest recorded performance of a classical play at the English court. Eyewitnesses credit him specifically with sponsoring performances of the *Menaechmi* by "the Cardinal's gentlemen" at Hampton Court in January 1527 and of *Phormio* by St. Paul's boys a year later.[24] In the courts of Italy such early productions of Greek and Latin plays inspired a flourishing vernacular tradition of *commedie erudite*; in the court of England, mythic kings and Roman citizens never quite won out against St. George and the dragon. Throughout Elizabeth's reign, belated morality plays instructed her; when her host had academic pretensions, imitations after classical tragedy admonished her; but another dramatic kind entertained her. Though the plays themselves are almost all lost, most titles mentioned in the Revels Office accounts during the 1570s and early 1580s point to a rich and well-worked mine of romance narrative.[25]

23. *The Great Chronicle of London*, ed. A. H. Thomas and I. D. Thornley (London, 1938), pp. 251–52. The occasion is analyzed by Sydney Anglo, "William Cornish in a Play, Prison, and Politics," *RES*, N.S. 10 (1959): 347–60, as the first that sets up the paradigm of play-pageant-dance that became customary at the court of Henry VIII.

24. The political program behind the productions that Wolsey sponsored is studied by Sydney Anglo, "The Evolution of the Early Tudor Disguising, Pageant, and Mask," *RenD*, N.S. 1 (1968): 3–44.

25. Information on all the plays Elizabeth is known to have seen is assembled in Carter Anderson Daniel, "Patterns and Traditions of the Elizabethan Court Play to 1590" (Ph.D. diss., University of Virginia, 1965). C. R. Bas-

Sir Clyomon and Sir Clamydes, perhaps revived near the end of the century and then put into print, is virtually the only survivor of a genre that enjoyed royal favor for at least fifteen years, long after Wolsey and his academic successors had led Phormio, the Menaechmus twins, Orestes, and Ajax out of the Mediterranean sunshine and into northern candlelight.

The dramatic fictions that engrossed Elizabeth and her court in the middle and late years of her reign are part of the neomedievalism that Roy Strong, Frances Yates, Mark Girouard, and others have discerned as a general characteristic of Elizabethan art. English painting in the sixteenth century, Roy Strong has shown, moves in a decidedly un-Renaissance direction: painters during Elizabeth's long reign discarded the psychological verisimilitude of Hans Holbein's portraits of Henry VIII's courtiers in favor of the iconographical remoteness of Nicholas Hilliard's jewellike miniatures and Elizabeth's official portraits. Mark Girouard has described a similar pattern in sixteenth-century English building. Incipient classicism in such buildings as Longleat House (begun 1559) gives way to romantic fantasy in Elizabethan dream castles like Wollaton Hall (begun 1580). The grand displays of chivalry on Queen Elizabeth's Accession Day every year proceeded from the same impulse to deck the political expediencies of the present in the myth of an heroic past.[26] Behind these romantic fantasies were solid political realities: the Arthurian myth celebrated strong monarchy, it focused religious devotion on the Virgin Queen, it transported courtiers into a wish-fulfilling realm where dreams, political as well as amorous, could always be realized.

---

kervill, "Some Evidence for Early Romantic Plays in England," *MP* 14 (1916–1917): 229–51, 467–521, is still the best discussion of the vogue for romantic plays in the sixteenth century and the probable continuity of conventions and audience taste from the fifteenth century. See also L. M. Ellison, *The Early Romantic Drama at the English Court* (Chicago, 1917).

26. Roy Strong, *The English Icon* (London, 1969), pp. 5–21, and *Portraits of Queen Elizabeth I* (Oxford, 1963), pp. 33–41; Mark Girouard, *Robert Smythson and the Architecture of the Elizabethan Era* (London, 1966); Frances Yates, "Elizabethan Chivalry: The Romance of the Accession Day Tilts," *JWCI* 10 (1957): 4–25.

Not only physically, but socially and philosophically, the great halls of Westminster School, of Oxford and Cambridge colleges, of the Inner Temple, of Whitehall Palace were more constricted places than Pompey's theater and the Theater of Dionysius. The households who included classical plays in their celebrations of Christmas and Shrovetide were small, closed societies whose hierarchical structure and conservative political and moral values replicated and reinforced each other. Morally instructive, politically didactic, the newly revived comedies and tragedies of Greece and Rome were played before audiences who liked to disport themselves amid trappings of medieval romance. The plays of Sophocles, Euripides, Plautus, Terence, Seneca, and their English imitators had to fit in with a program of education in moral wisdom and virtuous action. Particularly in the inns of court, the lively point of contact between humanist ideals and political realities, the tragedies of Greece and Rome were expected to yield the kind of political dogma an audience could carry away from Skelton's *Magnificence* or from the debate of Bacon's six counselors in the *Gesta Grayorum*. By Cicero's own testimony, classical drama was calculated to provide just that.

As a strategy for satisfying such demands, one can see how *Gorboduc*, with its music, its emblematic dumb-shows, and its homilies on political prudence, would score a triumph. Read on the page, Sackville and Norton's neoclassical tragedy seems tedious; seen in its social context, it is charged with imaginative power. The court of King Gorboduc is a court within a court within a court: surrounding the court depicted in the play is the court of the Christmas prince, and surrounding the court of the Christmas prince is the court of the realm. All three of these courts coincided when *Gorboduc* was acted a second time before Queen Elizabeth at Whitehall on January 18, 1562. On such an occasion the correspondences among the three courts must have been visually as well as philosophically clear. The tale Pallaphilos tells Gerard and the titles of court plays listed in the Revels accounts during Elizabeth's reign remind us that surrounding the three courts of play, the Christmas prince, and the monarch of Britain there is still a fourth court which, though never present physically, nonetheless structures the Christmas revels as powerfully as the other three. That fourth court is the inspiration for the Inner Temple's self-image as "the howse of Chivalrye," the inspiration for the annual tilts on Elizabeth's Accession Day, the inspiration for the Earl of Leicester's neomedieval Kenilworth Castle and *The Princely Pleasures* provided there for the queen in 1575, the inspiration for Spenser's *The Faerie Queene*, perhaps even the inspiration for legendary British history as the subject of Sackville and Norton's tragedy. The outermost frame around play, academic household, and royal court is the court of King Arthur. It was in the cultural half-light of this romance world that English audiences first encountered Phormio, Pamphilus and Charinus, Oedipus, Hippolytus, and Orestes.

II

The Theater: as the first purpose-built permanent playing place anywhere in Europe since ancient times, the structure that James Burbage erected in Shoreditch in 1577 had a claim to the definite article. Physically, The Theater and its successors in Southwark stood outside the city of London; socially, they stood outside the structure of Elizabethan society. In the perfectly articulated hierarchy of schools, colleges, the inns of court, and the court of the realm, public playhouses had no fixed place. The audiences who assembled in the great halls of Westminster School, Christ Church, Oxford, the Inner Temple, and Whitehall Palace were closed societies, households of individuals who knew each other and were confident of the values they shared; to join the crowd at the Globe only one thing was required: an ability to pay. Where the spectators sat in great halls was dictated by the hierarchy of Elizabethan society. For the performance of *Aulularia* at Christ Church, Oxford, in 1564, we have seen, there were three distinct places for the three distinct ranks of viewers who were present: Queen Elizabeth as chief spectator sat enthroned on one side of the stage where she could both see and be seen; courtiers and university dignitaries sat to her right; the students stood to her left. The traditional hierarchy of society was an observable physical fact. There was a hierarchy of viewing places in public playhouses, as well, but it was pence, not social position, that determined who went where. This open seating arrangement was one of the things that the Swiss traveler Thomas Platter singles out for special mention when he describes a visit to one of the suburban theaters in autumn 1599: "The playhouses are so constructed that they play on a raised platform, so that everyone has a good view. There are different galleries and places, however, where the seating is better and more comfortable and therefore more expensive. For whoever cares to stand below only pays one English penny, but if he wishes to sit he enters by another door, and pays another penny, while if he desires to sit in the most comfortable seats which are cushioned, where he not only sees everything well, but can also be seen, then he pays yet another English penny at another door."

In such an arrangement, as M. C. Bradbrook has observed, *everyone* becomes chief spectator. [27] By dressing up and paying the required sum, imposters from the lower orders could, and did, pass as gentlemen and sit on the stage. Ann Jennalie Cook has called into question Alfred Harbage's too neat distinction between the aristocrats who patronized indoor theaters and the commonality who thronged outdoor playhouses, but the "privileged" playgoers who made up the regular audience at both kinds of theaters were, by Cook's own account, "tremendously varied, reaching from bright but impoverished students, younger sons of gentry families set to a trade, and minor retainers in noble households all the way up to lords, ambassadors, merchant princes, and royalty itself." [28] Most

27. *Thomas Platter's Travels in England 1599*, trans. Clare Williams (London, 1937), p. 167; M. C. Bradbrook, *The Rise of the Common Player* (Cambridge, Mass., 1962), p. 100. In addition to Bradbrook's account of "The Creation of the Common Audience," pp. 96–118, see E. K. Chambers, *The Elizabethan Stage* (Oxford, 1923), 2: 518–57; Alfred Harbage, *Shakespeare and the Rival Traditions* (New York, 1952); and Ann Jennalie Cook, *The Privileged Playgoers of Shakespeare's London, 1576–1642* (Princeton, 1981).

28. Cook, *Privileged Playgoers*, p. 272. When the Privy Council ordered a

of this regular audience may have been thoroughly familiar with plays and playacting from schools, colleges, and the inns of court, but in suburban playhouses like the Globe, they encountered drama in a totally new social context. Here, for the first time since antiquity, was public theater as Livy describes it: in Shoreditch and in Southwark plays were "beheld and looked upon pell mell, without any such precise difference."

Idolatry, godlessness, crime, disease, rebellion—the charges brought against playacting were many, but at bottom the thing that made public theaters so suspect to the conservative authorities was their separateness from the traditional hierarchy of Elizabethan and Jacobean society. The diverse audience had no fixed place in the traditional social order, nor did playacting every day in the week fit in with the traditional order of communal holidays. The authorities' fears were not altogether groundless. There was the famous occasion when the Earl of Essex's supporters hired the Lord Chamberlain's Men to perform the overthrow of Richard II as a dress rhearsal of their attempted overthrow of Queen Elizabeth. Less spectacular but more typical are the numerous occasions when scuffling broke out in the playhouse. Blamed in almost every recorded case is the traditional rivalry between apprentices and serving-men, individuals who were next to each other in the hierarchies of household and kingdom.[29] Bound to take orders from their masters during their indenture, apprentices must have resented their social proximity to serving-men; serving-men, for their part, must have resented the prentensions and upward mobility of apprentices. Standing or seated side by side in public playhouses, without the usual social restraints to

sweep of the public playhouses in 1602, the haul included "Gentlemen and servingmen, lawyers, clerks, countrymen with law causes, ay the Queen's men, knights, and as it was credibly reported, one Earl" (quoted in Bradbrook, *Common Player*, p. 116).

29. Bradbrook, *Common Player*, pp. 103–16. On the social mobility of apprentices vis-à-vis servingmen, see Cook, *Privileged Playgoers*, pp. 45–49, 218–22, and Keith Wrightson, *English Society 1580–1680* (New Brunswick, N.J., 1982), pp. 40–44.

keep them apart, apprentices and serving-men gave free reign to their mutual resentment.

There were, to be sure, social tensions within academic and noble households, but there were also legitimate, carefully controlled ways of easing those tensions. In a symmetrical inversion of the usual social order, Christmas princes and their courtiers could give symbolic play to the frustrations they naturally felt as bottom men in the social hierarchy and yet pose no real threat to the idea of hierarchy itself. No such control, no traditional means for resolving social tensions, governed the diverse audiences who came together in public playhouses. The result, just as the authorities feared, was often violence. In Scipio's Rome it was an insistence on the "distinctions, whereby estates and degrees are severed one from another" that threatened "common peace"; in Shakespeare's London, it was just the opposite—or so conservatives thought. In both places Livy's conclusion rings true: "So hard a matter it is to alter an old custome, and make a new order to be well liked of."

Socially the public theater freed audiences to sit where they liked; philosophically it liberated their imaginations—and the imaginations of the playwrights who wrote for them—to explore more widely than was possible in the constricted spaces of great halls. In schools, colleges, the inns of court, and the court of the realm, plays were expected to reinforce the household's self-identity by affirming the moral and political values its members held in common. As there was no such group identity in the public theater, so was there no such program of values. When called to the bar by civic dignitaries and Puritan divines, the common players of Elizabethan and Jacobean England could muster only the conventional defenses of drama that everyone already knew from Cicero: plays, they protested, teach moral and political truth, as Thomas Heywood claims in his *An Apology for Actors* (1612). Whatever defenders of plays may say in print, whatever authors or publishers may say in prefaces, most scripts for the Elizabethan and Jacobean public stage do not set out primarily to argue a moral position or to support a political program. Therein lies their suspiciousness for sixteenth- and seventeenth-century authorities—and their fascination for us. The public stage freed playwrights, actors, and audiences to see that love-struck youths might engage sympathy, not censure, and that kings who make wrong choices might still deserve pity. To us in our own time, distressed that the humanist values of the past four centuries are embattled, alarmed at the values, or lack of values, that seem to be replacing them, the proposition that literature in general and stage plays in particular might actually subvert the dominant ideology of a society is inter-esting, even heartening. Professors of "the new historicism" are divided, however, about just how real the possibilities were for subversion in the culture of sixteenth- and seven-teenth-century England. Adopting the terms of Victor Tur-ner's anthropology, Louis A. Montrose sees plays for the public stage as "anti-structures," time out from the rules of everyday existence, a liminal space in which traditional roles and traditional values could be challenged and, on occasion, changed. Looking at the same plays with Michel Foucault's structuralist theories and Jacques Lacan's sense of how lan-guage and discourse limit the possibilities for self-definition, Stephen Greenblatt proposes that Renaissance literature, and stage plays in particular, create subversion in order to contain it. Elizabethan society, in Greenblatt's view, was a quietly effi-cient system for co-opting rebellion.[30]

Given the diversity of Shakespeare's audience, the choice between these alternatives could never be verified, even if more than one eyewitness of the original productions could be called for testimony. Simon Forman—the sole surviving

30. Louis A. Montrose, "The Purpose of Playing: Reflections on a Shake-spearean Anthropology," *Helios*, N.S. 7 (1979–1980): 51–74; Stephen Green-blatt, "Invisible Bullets: Renaissance Authority and its Subversion," *Glyph* 8 (1981): 40–61, rev. and repr. in *Political Shakespeare*, ed. Jonathan Dollimore and Alan Sinfield (Manchester, 1985), pp. 18–47; and Peter Erickson and Coppélia Kahn, eds., *Shakespeare's "Rough Magic"* (Newark, Del., 1985), pp. 276–302. Jean Howard puts Montrose and Greenblatt into a larger historical context, notes their sources, and draws out the contrast between them in "The New Historicism in Renaissance Studies," *ELR* 16 (1986): 13–43.

witness, in writing, among the many thousands who must have seen Shakespeare's plays at the Globe—shows an amazing blindness to the complexities that engage us as watchers and readers of Shakespeare's plays today. However painstaking Forman may have been about details of his dreams and his sex life, his diary entries about *Macbeth*, *Cymbeline*, *Richard II*, and *The Winter's Tale* as performed at the Globe in 1611 are mainly concerned with remembering the story. About *The Winter's Tale*, for example, Forman writes out an incomplete plot summary (how could he forget Hermione's statue coming to life?) and concludes with this memorandum about Autolycus: "Beware of trusting feigned beggars or fawning fellows."[31] Nothing here about Bohemia as a version of pastoral or Autolycus as an archetypal trickster.

Whatever the possibilities for subversion, Shakespeare seems to have thrived on the diversity of his public audience. His prologues and epilogues, on the rare occasions when he felt the need to address the audience directly, speak with assurance and an easy familiarity. Ben Jonson's quandary about his audience stands in the sharpest possible contrast. It was not just the public audience's lust for rant and special effects that Jonson feared, but the threat that such a diverse audience posed to communal, conservative values. Like all Renaissance playwrights, Jonson was caught between two theoretical views of the audience and two practical traditions of theater. On the one hand, Jonson must have known from Cicero about the vast public audiences that found political allegory in the deeds of stage-kings and cried out their approval or displeasure. On the other hand, Horace gave Jonson a comfortable, reassuring sense that the real audience for good writers was a small group of learned men who shared the playwright's erudition and ethical values. As a graduate of Westminster School, Jonson would have known firsthand about in-house audiences who watched their colleagues act out Latin plays and in the process reaffirm the household's common values.

31. Forman's four diary entries are reprinted in A. L. Rowse, *Simon Forman: Sex and Society in Shakespeare's Age* (London, 1974), pp. 303–307.

As a man who made his living with his pen, however, Jonson had to face the teeming, multifarious audiences at the Globe. His prefaces and his persistence in writing plays let us know that he never really resolved these tensions in defining his audience. Like Robortello, Jonson thought of his ideal audience not just in terms of learning and taste but in terms of morality. In its disastrous performance at the Globe, *Sejanus* "suffered no less violence from our people here than the subject of it did from the rage of the people of Rome," says Jonson in his dedicatory epistle to the printed version of the play, "but with a different fate, as (I hope) merit. For this hath outlived their malice, and begot itself a greater favor than he lost, the love of *good* men."[32] The hostility of the Globe audience, he implies, was not just a want of taste but an error in moral judgment. Not once do we hear such a lecture from Shakespeare. It is hard to avoid the conclusion that Shakespeare thought of his audience in Aristotle's terms, as all of mankind, while Jonson thought of his audience in Horace's terms, as good and learned men only. That difference in perspective has tremendous consequences, as we shall see when we compare the different ways in which Shakespeare in *Titus Andronicus* and Jonson in *Sejanus* acclimatized classical tragedy to the public stage.

III

The more that sixteenth- and seventeenth-century critics learned about the differences between Horace and Aristotle, between drama conceived as a rhetorical event and drama conceived as an aesthetic object, the more crucial became the question of who constituted the audience. Aristotle himself does not supply much help. Clearly enough, he cannot be thinking only of the fifth-century Athenian citizens who assembled in the Theater of Dionysius, since, as he observes so casually, tragedy can work its emotional effects just as aptly when read as when performed. Who, then, *is* the audience?

---

32. Jonson, *Sejanus*, ed. Jonas Barish (New Haven, 1965), p. 25, emphasis added.

Looking at the question with the moral bias of the Roman rhetoricians, Robortello decides that Aristotle must mean *good* men, since only they can sympathize with the plight of a virtuous man who suffers undeservedly. Looking at the question with the scholarly detachment of a philologist, Daniel Heinsius decides, more probably, that Aristotle means the generality of mankind. People may like to think the best of themselves, Heinsius says, and they may expect virtue to be rewarded, but "there is no doubt that the greater part of mankind are good in the middling way."[33] The definition of the audience that Heinsius articulates in *De tragoediae constitutione* (1611) became dogma for seventeenth-century neoclassical critics like Thomas Rymer. Against the universal applicability of Aristotle's precepts, "objectors urge . . . that *Athens* and *London* have not the same *Meridian*." Not so, says Rymer in *Tragedies of the Last Age* (1677): "Certain it is, that *Nature* is the same, and *Man* is the same, he *loves, grieves, hates, envies,* has the same *affections* and *passions* in both places, and the same *springs* that give them *motion*. What mov'd *pity* there, will *here* also produce the same effect."[34] With that universal yardstick, Rymer proceeds to measure the shortcomings he finds in the tragedies of Shakespeare and of Beaumont and Fletcher. These English playwrights fail, claims Rymer, because they fail to produce the universal effects of pity and fear in approved universal ways. They succeed, counters Dryden, because they produce these universal effects in ways peculiar to the audiences for whom they wrote:

Shakespeare and Fletcher have written to the genius of the age and nation in which they lived; for tho' nature, as he objects, is the same in all places, and reason too the same, yet the climate, the age, the dispositions of the people to whom a poet writes, may be so different that what pleased the Greeks would not satisfy an English audience.

33. Daniel Heinsius, *De tragoediae constitutione*, 2d ed. (1643), trans. Paul R. Sellin and John J. McManmon as *On Plot in Tragedy* (Northridge, Calif., 1971), pp. 49–50.

34. Thomas Rymer, *The Tragedies of the Last Age Consider'd and Examin'd by the Practice of the Ancients, and by the Common Sense of All Ages* (1678), ed. Curt A. Zimansky (New Haven, 1956), p. 19.

And if they proceeded upon a foundation of truer reason to please the Athenians than Shakespeare and Fletcher to please the English, it only shows that the Athenians were a more judicious people; but the poet's business is certainly to please the audience.[35]

That precisely was what Dryden set out to do. In his prologues as in his critical essays Dryden shows himself as self-assured about his audience at Drury Lane and the Dorset Garden as Jonson was dubious about audiences at the Globe.

Dryden could be so assured when Jonson could not partly because the public-theater audience after the Restoration was so much smaller and better defined than the public-theater audience before 1642. The young king and his young courtiers, home from political exile and polite education in France, may not have been old enough or serious enough to form the "Roman Gentrie" that Horace had in mind, but they constituted a coterie who controlled the theater legally through the patent monopoly system, financially through their frequent attendance, aesthetically through the blend of refinement and raffishness they expected to hear in comic dialogue, philosophically through the strong monarchs they expected to see in tragedy, and socially through the promotions that they offered to the actresses and orange-molls who became their mistresses and to the military, professional, and business men who aspired to courtier style by going to the theater.

Just how many of these military, professional, and business men in fact cast off their Puritan drab and dressed themselves up for Drury Lane and the Dorset Garden is a matter of debate among theater historians.[36] As in public theaters before 1642,

35. John Dryden, "Heads of an Answer to Rymer" (1677), in *Of Dramatic Poesy and Other Critical Essays*, ed. George Watson (London, 1962), 1: 214.

36. On the social composition and performance manners of the Restoration audience, see Allardyce Nicoll, *A History of English Drama 1660–1900* (Cambridge, 1952), 1: 5–25; Montague Summers, *The Restoration Theatre* (London, 1934), pp. 54–93; John Wilson, *A Preface to Restoration Drama* (Cambridge, Mass., 1965), pp. 31–42; John Loftis, "The Social and Literary Context," in *The Revels History of Drama in English*, ed. John Loftis et al., Vol. 5 (London, 1976): 1–40; and Harry William Pedicord, "The Changing Audience," in *The London Theatre World, 1660–1800*, ed. Robert D. Hume (Carbondale, Ill., 1980), pp. 236–52. Against Nicoll's view of the audience as

it was price that determined who sat where, but each of the four price ranges apparently attracted its own distinctive audience. The distinctions were partly a matter of sex, partly a matter of refinement, but mostly a matter of social status: fops pranced and preened themselves in the pit; royalty and ladies and gentlemen of quality reposed in the boxes; middle-class spectators settled in the middle gallery to observe the *two* spectacles that separated them from the stage; footmen huddled in the upper gallery. A lingering sense of Horace's snobbery survives in Dryden's critical essays—in the preface to *All for Love* he distinguishes "the crowd" and "every one who believes himself a wit, that is, every man" from the true judges of tragedy, "poets"—but on the whole Dryden aims his comedies and tragedies at the box tier, particularly at the center box from which the king and queen commanded stage and auditorium alike.[37]

As a military and professional man who found his way first into the upper gallery and later into the middle gallery and pit, Pepys is the perfect witness to the social context into which Dryden introduced Sophocles' *Oedipus*. On December 21, 1668, Pepys first went to Holborn to see a Danish hermaphrodite.

Thence to the Duke's playhouse and saw *Mackbeth* [likely Davenant's adaptation]; the King and Court there, and we sat just under them and my Lady Castlemayne, and close to the woman that comes into the pit, a kind of loose gossip, that pretends to be like her, and is so something. And my wife, by my troth, appeared I think as pretty as any of them, I never thought so much before; and so did Talbot and W. Hewer, as they said, I heard, to one another. The King and Duke of York minded me, and smiled upon me at the handsome woman near me: but it vexed me to see Mall Davis, in the box over his and my Lady Castlemaynes head, look down upon the King and he up to

entirely aristocratic, more recent commentators have stressed an increasing number of middle-class attenders, especially after the Popish Plot in 1678. Steele's soft sentimentality certainly suggests a reaction of middle-class taste against brittle Restoration wit.

37. Dryden, Preface to *All for Love*, ed. Watson, 1: 225–26.

her; and so did my Lady Castlemayne once, to see who it was; but when she saw her, she blushed like fire; which troubled me.[38]

Clearly, the spectacle of royalty was far more important to Pepys than the play was. Not only that: *he* was noticed, and by the king, no less. What bothers Pepys about the king's flirtation with Moll Davis? Outrage that a former actress should now be the king's mistress? Envy? Embarrassment at the couple's public flirtation in front of Lady Castlemayne? Pepys may admire courtly fashions, but in such moments the durable middle-class cloth shows up under the embroidered frock coat. Describing another theater visit about a year earlier, Pepys leaves behind an even sharper image of himself as a middle-class social climber. At a performance of Dryden's *Sir Martin Mar-all* at the Duke's Theater on January 1, 1668, Pepys balks at "a mighty company of citizens, prentices, and others; and it makes me observe that when I begin first to be able to bestow a play on myself, I do not remember that I saw so many by half of the ordinary prentices and mean people in the pit, at 2*s*–6*d* apiece, as now; I going for several years no higher then the 12*d*, and then the 18*d* places, and though I strained hard to go in then when I did—so much the vanity and prodigality of the age is to be observed in this perticular" (9: 2). Pepys leaves no doubt about the social cachet of going to the theater: a play is a luxury to be "bestowed." The brash new arrivals discountenance the self-bred *arriviste*; the carefully calculated treat in Pepys's own case becomes "vanity and prodigality" in the fellow travelers who clamber in after him. However many military, professional, and business men may have gone to the playhouses, however much their numbers may have increased toward the end of the century, they, like Pepys, came to the theater because they shared the aspirations of the theater's noble patrons. Only a merchant who fancied himself a man of taste would have laughed at the "cits" ridiculed so contemptuously in Restoration comedy; only a mili-

---

38. *The Diary of Samuel Pepys*, ed. Robert Latham and William Matthews, Vol. 9 (Berkeley, 1976): 398. Future quotations are taken from this edition and are cited in the text.

tary man who supported the monarchy would have marveled at the emperors glorified so flawlessly in Restoration tragedy.

Footmen may have paid their shilling to enter the upper gallery, middle-class observers their shilling and six pence for the middle gallery, and fops their half crown for the pit, but it was the four-shilling patrons in the boxes who dominated the public theaters that opened after the Interregnum. Restoration drama was coterie drama as absolutely as academic and court drama had been in the sixteenth century. Even the violence was intramural. In place of the *class* rivalry that led serving-men and apprentices to bait each other, Restoration audiences witnessed *personal* rivalries between courtiers. The fight at the Duke's Theater between the Duke of Buckingham and Henry Killigrew that Pepys describes on July 22, 1667, is only one of many times that denizens of the pit took their private quarrels onto the public stage (8: 348).

In their own way, then, the public audiences at Drury Lane and the Dorset Garden were as homogenous as the private audiences who gathered in sixteenth-century great halls. In place of the conservative moral and political program that unified academic and court audiences in the sixteenth century, the Restoration stage presented two distinct but complementary versions of the new courtier ideal: in comedy, the fantasy of free movement in a demimonde of witty repartee and sexual license; in tragedy, a celebration of the grand passions and monumental individuality of epic heroes. The neomedieval romance world in which sixteenth-century productions had set both comedy and tragedy became, in like manner, two distinct but complementary places: in comedy, an immediate contemporary world crowded with familiar place names; in tragedy, a distant timeless world of vast, uncharted possibilities. Tutored by Sedley, Terence's Romans learned to speak like seventeenth-century courtiers; transported by Dryden and Lee, Sophocles' Oedipus played out his suffering in a vision of Thebes that shares the exotic grandeur of India, Mexico, and Persia. Neither of these ideals, neither of these imagined places, is without its political implications. John

Loftis reads revenge in the way Restoration comedies attack middle-class proprieties: the "cits" who made their fortunes out of the confiscated estates of royalists are laughed at for their cautionary minds and manners, the Puritans who executed Charles I are mocked for their sexual scruples.[39] The epic heroes of Restoration tragedy, paragons of principle and passion, testify to the strength of monarchy.

As decisively as for sixteenth-century academic drama, the restricted social context for Restoration drama marked out a restricted field within which dramatists and audiences could exercise their imaginations. There is a certain paradox here. In settings, characters, and situations, Restoration drama would seem to expand, not contract, the boundaries of earlier seventeenth-century drama: comedy moves farther downstage to include more immediate, more sharply observed mores, tragedy moves upstage, beyond the proscenium arch, to include places and personages physically distant in the New World and the Orient and chronologically distant in ancient history. But in the range of attitudes to those settings, characters, and situations, Restoration drama represents a retrenchment. Restoration audiences may have traveled farther, but they saw less when they got there. As a closed society with a sharp sense of its own identity, the audiences at Drury Lane and the Dorset Garden had very definite ways of judging the characters and situations represented onstage—ways of judging that may have been different from those of private audiences in the sixteenth century but were finally just as delimiting. The result was the same kind of one-dimensional view of comic plotters and tragic sufferers in which sixteenth-century viewers took refuge. Restoration drama may have been public drama in no longer being tied to specific occasions, but it returned to the communal closeness of academic drama in the sixteenth century.

By choosing a public square for the first modern perform-

39. Loftis, "The Social and Literary Context," pp. 33–40, and "Social and Political Thought in the Drama," in *The London Theatre World*, ed. Hume, pp. 253–63.

ance of an ancient play, Pomponius Laetus and his collabora-
tors were being true to the very nature of drama. Of all exer-
cises of human imagination that involve writing, drama is the
most public, the most social. Since the rise of middle-class lit-
eracy in the eighteenth century, the two dominant literary
forms have been kinds that an individual can read by himself:
lyric poetry and the novel depend for their effect upon inti-
macy between reader and text. Drama, however, demands
people: actors to perform and an audience to watch and listen.
Philosophically minded critics may try to pin such things
down, but comedy and tragedy have no abstract existence:
they present two distinctive ways of impersonating characters
and acting out events that answer the imaginative needs of the
people who act them and the people who watch and listen. In
sixteenth- and seventeenth-century England those needs were
vastly different from what they had been in fifth-century
Athens and second- and first-century Rome. To be rehabili-
tated as ways of structuring experience, ancient tragedy and
ancient comedy had to answer modern needs. The sixteenth-
and seventeenth-century social contexts of plays in perform-
ance fit within two larger contexts, critical and spatial, that
also determined the direction taken by tragedy and comedy as
rediscovered paths of the imagination. Between 1500 and
1700, none of these three contexts was fixed: each involved a
dynamic between polarities, each was constantly changing.
The play-as-rhetorical-event competed with the play-as-aes-
thetic-object. Organic ways of organizing theatrical space
competed with geometric ways. The social and ethical closed-
ness of private households competed with the social and eth-
ical openness of public theaters. In the dynamic of all three
contexts we can witness on a small scale that larger competi-
tion between medieval and classical models that vitalized Ren-
aissance civilization in general. Interplay between polarities
was the very condition that brought comedy and tragedy back
to imaginative life in the theater. Adapted to address the con-
trarieties in modern experience, comedy and tragedy have sur-
vived to our own day.

IV · *Comedy*

CARDINAL WOLSEY'S banquet was just beginning when into the great hall at Hampton Court burst some uninvited guests—a company of shepherds. No wayfarers from the muddy January fields outside, these merrymakers; they claimed to speak no English and asked for a French interpreter. "Havyng understandyng of thys yoᴿ tryhumphant bankett," their translator explained to Wolsey, "where was assembled such a nomber of excellent fayer dames [they] cowld do no lesse under the supportacion of yoᴿ grace but to repayer hether to vewe as well ther incomperable beawtie as for to accompany them at Mume chaunce And than After daunce wᵗ them And so to have of them acquayntaunce. . . ."[1] At the end of their game of mumchance, Wolsey had to confess to the French interpreter his suspicion that "there shold be among theme some noble man whome I suppose to be myche more worthy of honor to sitt and occupie this rome & place than I to whome I wold most gladly (yf I knewe hyme) surrender my place accordyng to my dewtie. . . ." There was indeed such a man, the shepherds reported through their interpreter, but Wolsey would have to pick him out. The cardinal chose wrong. Delighted, King Henry VIII jerked off his visor "& dasht owt wᵗ suche a pleasaunt Countenaunce & cheare that all noble estates there assembled seying the kyng to be there amoong them rejoysed very myche. . . ." After this grand chivalric gesture, the "shepherd"—such an admirer

---

1. George Cavendish, *The Life and Death of Cardinal Wolsey*, ed. R. S. Sylvester (London, 1959), pp. 25–28. In this and other quotations in old spelling I have made the consonants *v* and *j* accord with modern orthography. Cavendish does not date the incident he recounts here, but King Henry's flamboyantly dramatic entry in disguise is a prominent event in the Venetian secretary's account of Wolsey's banquet and entertainment at Hampton Court on January 3, 1526–1527. With a few changes, Shakespeare incorporates this famous incident into *Henry VIII* (1.4).

of noble ladies—doffed his disguise, changed to royal attire, and stayed on for the evening's entertainment.

The royal sports Henry enjoyed that January night in 1526–1527 began with a performance, in Latin, of Plautus's *Menaechmi* by some of the gentlemen of the cardinal's household. The whole affair was impressive enough for the Venetian ambassador's secretary, Gasparo Spinelli, to write home about it the next day. It was not the play but what came afterward that impressed Spinelli the most. The end of the play was immediately set off with speeches: one by one the actors bowed before the king and declaimed Latin verses in his praise. Then, after a pause for refreshments, the audience was treated to an amorous mythological afterpiece. Elegant oratory, brilliant trumpet music, beautiful dancing, and a chariot entry reminiscent of Petrarch's *Triumph of Love* were combined in a dramatic event that was essentially a debate. Spinelli was charmed:

a stage [*uno solaro*] was displayed, on which sat Venus, at whose feet were six damsels, forming so graceful a group for her footstool, that it looked as if she and they had really come down from heaven. And whilst everybody was intently gazing on so agreeable a sight, the trumpets flourished and a car appeared, drawn by three boys stark naked, on which was Cupid, dragging after him, bound by a silver rope, six old men, clad in the pastoral fashion, but the material was cloth of silver and white satin. Cupid presented them to his mother, delivering a most elegant Latin oration in their praise, saying they had been cruelly wounded; whereupon Venus compassionately replied in equally choice language, and caused the six nymphs, the sweethearts of the six old men, to descend, commanding them to afford their lovers all solace, and requite them for past pangs. Each of the nymphs was then taken in hand by her lover, and to the sound of trumpets they performed a very beautiful dance.[2]

2. Spinelli's letter is calendared and translated in *Calendar of State Papers Venetian*, 4: 2–3, from which I take my subsequent quotations. I have checked this translation against the Italian original, reprinted in *I Diarii di Marino Sanuto*, ed. F. Stefani, Vol. 43 (Venice, 1890): cols. 703–704, from which I have occasionally inserted the Italian in parentheses. Productions of Plautus and Terence at Henry VIII's court receive only passing mention in F. P. Wilson, *The English Drama, 1485–1585* (Oxford, 1969), pp. 102–103. In *Spec-*

Afterwards the king and his favorites joined in, and the dancing became general. Never a passive viewer but always an eager participant in court revels, Henry had favored such grand conclusions to an evening's pastime since the precedent-setting occasion in 1512 when, "after the manner of Italy," the audience and maskers danced together at the end of the pageantry.[3]

Wolsey's production of the *Menaechmi* was thus framed by two masking devices: a *pastourelle* at the beginning, and a Petrarchan "Triumph of Love" at the end. At first glance the "classical" trappings of these two shows might suggest a complement to the "classical" atmosphere of Plautus's comedy; a second look, however, tells us that we are in "The House of Chivalry," the courtly romance world we have just explored. Henry and his fellow shepherds have wandered into the great hall at Hampton Court not from a Virgilian eclogue but from one of John Lydgate's mumming devices; the Venus who presides over the invitation to the dance is not the Venus of Quattrocento painting but the Venus of Chaucer's *Knight's Tale*. If there is a common theme in the varied disports of the evening, it is disguise. Mistaken identities furnish the fun in Plautus's comedy, just as dressing up—or, rather, dressing down—as shepherds gave Henry and his courtiers such evident delight.

Disguise may be a key element in both play and pageants, but there is an important distinction between the two in the ends toward which disguise is used. If delight in disguise is the motive behind the "Triumph of Love," the whole thrust of Plautus's play is toward the casting off of disguise, toward the unveiling of true identities. The *Menaechmi*, like other Roman comedies, delights us with the ironic disparities between character and situation: typically realistic characters, speaking typically realistic language, moving around in typically realistic settings, run into extraordinarily unrealistic confusions and

---

tacle, *Pageantry, and Early Tudor Policy* (Oxford, 1969), Sydney Anglo studies these productions as political propaganda.

3. On the controversy surrounding "after the manner of Italy," see Sydney Anglo, "The Evolution of the Early Tudor Disguising, Pageant, and Mask," *RenD*, N.S. 1 (1968): 4–8.

coincidences. The two conventional boundaries of geograph-
ical place on the Roman stage describe also the two imagina-
tive boundaries of Roman comedy: to the right lies the harbor,
the connection with the unknown, the landing place of long-
lost brothers, the source of all the fantastic unexpected things
that define Roman comedy's romantic side. To the left lies the
country, the *comae* or villages where comedy was first devel-
oped out of joking attacks on abuses and foibles, the here-and-
now realities that define Roman comedy's satiric side. The
world of Roman comedy revolves on the axis of these two
imaginative poles.

The *Menaechmi*, like other Roman comedies, ends by
affirming these here-and-now realities at the expense of illu-
sion. In Wolsey's frame devices, on the other hand, it is not
reality that is affirmed but illusion. The pastourelle and
"Triumph of Venus" define a chivalric dream world to which
Henry and his courtiers aspired to belong. Instead of ending
as Plautus's play does with the dispelling of illusion and a
return to everyday reality, the "Triumph of Venus" ends with
the spectators getting up from their seats and joining the
maskers in a vision of heart's desire where Venus's votaries
are always victorious and fair ladies always show favor.
Despite their superficial "classicism," the world of Plautus's
play and the world of the masques that frame it represent two
different versions of experience from two different historical
eras. One is a world of satirically observed realities; the other,
a world of romantically imagined ideals. One has its origins
on the Roman stage; the other, in the court revels of medieval
Europe. As they define two different orders of experience, so
each of these two worlds engages our imagination in two dif-
ferent ways: the detached ridicule with which we laugh away
illusion in satiric comedy contrasts with the sympathetic
delight we take in the romantic ideals of masking devices. In
the optimistic views they offer of human experience, both of
these dramatic patterns are versions of comedy. The interplay
between them in the sixteenth century shaped the reemer-
gence of comedy as a way of structuring dramatic events and
of structuring audience responses. We can observe that inter-

play in all three social contexts in which classical comedies were staged between 1500 and 1700: in schools, colleges, the inns of court, and the court of the realm; in Elizabethan and Jacobean public theaters; and in the playhouses of Restoration London.

I

Although the *Menaechmi* that Wolsey sponsored in 1526 is the first English production of a classical script, tragedy or comedy, that we know by name, Hall's chronicle describes one earlier occasion when "a goodly commedy of Plautus" was performed at court. At Oxford and Cambridge, records of productions of Terence go back at least fifteen years. Beginning with expenses recorded *"pro comedia Terentii in Ludo"* at King's Hall, Cambridge, in 1510–1511, the financial accounts of Cambridge colleges, discontinuous and incomplete as they are, testify to dozens of productions of Greek and Latin comedies in the sixteenth and seventeenth centuries.[4] About most of them we know nothing besides how much they cost. It was not just the best known plays that engaged students' acting skills. Along with such obvious choices as Terence's *Adelphi* (Queens', 1547–1548; Trinity, 1562–1563; Jesus, 1562–1563), *Phormio* (Trinity, 1562–1563), and *Eunuchus* (Queens', 1547–1548, 1554–1555; Jesus, 1563–1564), and Plautus's *Miles Gloriosus* (Trinity Hall, 1522–1523; Queens', 1542–1543), *Amphitruo* (Trinity, 1560–1561), and *Menaechmi* (Trinity, 1551–1552 and 1565–1566), the college accounts mention productions of such relatively obscure plays as Plautus's *Penulus* (Queens', 1548–1549), *Rudens* (Trinity, 1556–1557), *Asinaria* (Trinity, 1565–1566), *Stichus* (Queens', 1553–1554; Trinity, 1564–1565), *Mostellaria* (Trinity, 1559–1560), *Curculio* (Jesus, 1562–1563), *Pseudolus* (Trinity, 1562–1563), *Trinummus* (Trinity, 1563–1564), *Bachides* (Trinity, 1563–1564; Jesus, 1579–1580), and *Persa* (St. John's, 1582–1583). Nor were the productions

---

4. They are cataloged in the Chronological Table that accompanies G. C. Moore Smith's *College Plays Performed in the University of Cambridge* (Cambridge, 1923), pp. 50–72.

limited to Latin comedy. From references independent of college financial records we know that Aristophanes' *Plutus* was acted, in Greek, at St. John's in 1536. John Dee refers to another Aristophanes comedy, *Pax*, as having been acted at Trinity College, probably in 1547–1548. Perhaps it is more than the chance survival of good records that marks off the 1550s and 1560s as a particularly strong period for classical comedy at Cambridge. Most of these college productions, alas, are no more to us than names, dates, and shillings disbursed. Concerning sixteen other academic productions we have firmer information. To follow these sixteen productions chronologically would tell us less about the emergence of modern comedy than to consider, first separately and then together, the two different dramatic traditions, the two different kinds of comedy, that Cardinal Wolsey brought together in the great hall of Hampton Court in 1526. We shall first survey, then, how Plautus's and Terence's scripts were brought to dramatic life in the moralistic context of sixteenth-century schools and colleges before we explore the marvelous sea change these plays suffered when they were transported into the romantic context of court performance.

The prologues and epilogues that humanist scholars wrote for particular performances in schools and colleges show us how decisively events onstage were shaped by the printed format in which Renaissance scholars usually encountered the scripts. Schoolmasters found subtle and not so subtle ways of turning learned commentary into people, speeches, and blocking—all without altering a word of Latin. For example, in the earliest known English translation of a classical script, a version of Terence's *Andria* printed about 1520 with the grandiloquent title of *Terens in englysh*, the anonymous translators are scrupulously faithful to Terence's Latin but take the liberty of sending out before and after the play a figure of their own invention: "The Poet." In a critically self-conscious prologue the Poet calls attention to the medium (the translation is an attempt to enrich the still uncultivated English language) before going on to lay out the matter. In the epilogue the Poet turns to the play's moral *sentence*:

Syth we have playd now this lytill comedy
Before your wisdoms as we pretendyd[,]
To tak it in gre we besech you humbly
And to forgyne us where we hane offendid[.]
The translatours know well it may be Amendyd
By theym that be wyse & wold take the payne
It [to] forrede & to corect agayn[.]

Wherfore the translatours now Req[ui]re you this
yf ought be amys ye wold consyder
The englysh almost as short as the latten is
And still to kepe ryme a dyffycult matter
To make the sentence opynly to appere
Which if it had a long expocyson
Then were it a comment & no translation[.][5]

Though they sound as if they have not quite freed the play from the page when they direct critics to "forrede" the text and correct any errors, the translators of *Terens in englysh* are concerned about how to transpose into dramatic form all the marginal commentary that made Renaissance readers see moral applications in Terence's speeches. They do that by providing their own commentator in The Poet.

At first glance, the devisers of this English *Andria* seem to be doing no more than following Terence's own precedent: Terence is famous for his vituperative prologues. There is one crucial difference, however. Terence's prologues may indeed defend the playwright from his detractors, but the speeches are always spoken by one of the actors. The playwright himself is nowhere to be seen. For the translators of *Terens in englysh*, by contrast, The Poet is the presiding genius of the whole proceeding, a stand-in for the author. By standing, figuratively as well as physically, as a medium between the audience and the fiction, The Poet gives the audience, figuratively as well as physically, their point of view. The play is not allowed to stand on its own. Early sixteenth-century audiences would have expected nothing else. In an age of few printed books, when most literature was still meant to be

5. *Terens in englysh* (London, n.d.), p. 137.

heard in a group, not read in solitude, poets continued to entertain audiences as raconteurs of their own works, just as they had done in the Middle Ages.[6] Not only that; ancient drama itself had been performed in pantomime while the dramatist read the speeches from a pulpit—or so said authorities like Isidore of Seville.[7] Ancient playwrights presided over their plays just as medieval poets presided over the romances they recited for assembled listeners. Long after fifteenth-century humanists like Pomponius Laetus had exploded the encyclopedists' misconception, the frontispieces to Renaissance printings of Terence were perpetuating the iconography of the manuscripts. The Poet is given a literally super-visory position vis-à-vis the players. That is just where we find him in *Terens in englysh*. And that is just where he must have stood, also, in productions of Roman comedy at the universities. An inventory of costumes in the possession of Queens' College, Cambridge, in 1554–1555 includes "the prologes goune" and "the poet[es] gowne" as items in continuous use.[8]

In the prologues that Alexander Nowell drafted for performances of Terence's *Adelphi* and *Eunuchus* at Westminster School about 1545 the presiding genius is not The Poet but The Pedagogue. Terence himself encouraged Nowell to be argumentative. Terence's original prologue to *Eunuchus* answers Luscius Lanuvinus's charge that the playwright has done nothing but plunder Menander for characters and plot devices. In writing a new prologue for the same play, Nowell simply takes up a modern critical controversy and substitutes

---

6. John Stevens, *Music and Poetry in the Early Tudor Court* (London, 1961), pp. 154–202.

7. Cf. Isidore of Seville, *Etymologiarum Liber XVIII*, ch. 44: "*Orchestra autem pulpitum erat scenae, ubi saltator agere posset, aut duo inter se disputare. Ibi enim poetae comoedi et tragoedi ad certamen consceudebant, iisque canentibus, alii gestus edebant*" (*Patrologiae Latinae*, ed. J. P. Migne, Vol. 82 [Paris, 1850]: col. 658). Wilhelm Creiznach, *Geschichte des neueren Dramas* (Halle, 1901) suggests that Isidore got this idea by misreading passages in Livy (7.2) and Valerius Maximus (2.4). On the poet as performer, cf. Ruth Crosby, "Oral Delivery in the Middle Ages," *Speculum* 11 (1936): 88–110.

8. Alan H. Nelson, ed., *Records of Early English Drama: Cambridge* (Toronto, 1988), s.v. 1544–1555.

it for the ancient one—but at a length and with a fervor that outdoes Terence by an English mile. Pagan plays set bad examples for student actors, claim critics. To answer that charge, Nowell's prologue first compliments the academic audience on its *humanitas*, then goes on to make a defense of classical plays that is morally just as rigid as the arguments of drama's "uncivilized" detractors:

these people could, by the same reasoning, prohibit us from reading the sacred scriptures and, what is more, the New Testament itself, for recorded there are vile whores, Herod the child-killer, Judas the traitor, Simon the sorcerer, Herodias the harpist, Ananias the perjurer, and countless others of that ilk. Why don't these men fear for the boys' well-being *there*? Ah, but *these* things are put forward to be avoided, not emulated. The poets had a similar intention in mind—which the outcomes of their stories prove. How uprightly they have expressed the comic spectacle of human life! Out of these plays you can choose examples to follow and examples to avoid. Here you can discern headlong furies, passion, ill-advised judgments, and what in fact is bitterness not love [*vere amarores, non amores*]. Here you may get to know harlots' filthiness, gluttony, greed, all without any danger but with great usefulness and as much delight, so that once you have learned it you will always hate it. Here you may make out, as in a mirror, the alluring but deadly ingratiations of flatterers. Thus may you hear, with ridicule, the boasting of Thrasoes and, in general, deliberately avoid all such harmful things.

Add to that Terence's abundance of *sententiae*, scattered here and there through the play like little flowers, not to mention the purity, simplicity, and elegance of his language, and the dramatic occasion at hand becomes formidable indeed.[9]

9. "[V]estra humanitas[,] viri praestantissimi[,] ea nobis gratior, acceptiorque est, quia non desint etiam hodie homines quidam (si tamen homines illi et non pecudes potis dicendi sunt) quibus pestilens esse videtur, quicquid non est barbarum quique contendunt, totam hanc agendi rationem pueris peniciosam esse, et eos a poetarum fabulis omnibus tanquam a Syrenae scopulis, aut sagarum incantanentis procul arcendos. capire enim flexiles illos aminos, et in peius semper sequaces, viciorum illecrebris, potius quam orationis lenociniis: praestareque linguas illorum minus elegantes quam mores magis corruptos esse. atque haec tanta detonant auctoritate, tanta improbitate passim inculcant, praesertim apud imperitos (apud quos mirum quam sunt facundi infantissimi homines) ut nonnullos ad haec studia segniores reddiderint.

"Flatterers" and "Thrasoes" are, of course, allusions to two particular characters in *Eunuchus*, Thraso the *miles gloriosus* of the play and Gnatho the impecunious dandy who survives by hanging around Thraso and telling him what a valiant soldier he is and how witty his bad jokes are. "Even as sects receive their names from Philosophers themselves," Gnatho declares in Richard Bernard's translation of 1598, "so from me in the same manner Parasites might be called Gnathoes."[10] Guided by Nowell's prologue, the audience at Westminster School was supposed to laugh at this duo's droll dialogue but at the same time to note the didactic lesson they offered:

T[HRASO]. I thinke in my heart truely, its a gifte given me, that every thing should be taken in good part which I doe.

---

quibus vestram autoritatem obviam visse super modum guademus. quis enim nescit ea probare vos, quae spectare dignamini possunt certe nobis eadem ratione, sacrarum literarum, atque adeo ipsius novi testamenti lectionem interdicere. nam et illic meretrices malae, herodes infanticida, iudas proditor, Simon magus: herodiades psaltatricula: periurus ananias. et hoc genus alia innumera memorantur. cur non hic pueris metuunt homines saluti? sed ista certum est deterrendi causa proponi; non ad imitationem, neque alia pro-specto poetis mens fuit. quod abunde fabularum exitus declarant. quanto rectius illi, qui comoediam humanae vitae spectaculum dixere. unde tibi exempla quae sectere, quaeque fugias, sumes. hinc, precipites in venum furores, impetus, inconsulta consilia, et vere amarores non amores intelligas. hinc, meretricum sordes, ingluviem rapacitatem nullo periculo, multa cum utilitate tamenque voluptate minori cognoscas, ut ubi noris perpetuo oderis. hinc, pal-ponum blandum, sed pestilentem gratiorissimum, veluti in speculo cernas. sic thrasonum vanas glorias non sine risu audias. omniaque in universum tamquam pestifera diligentur vites." MS Brasenose College 31 (Bodleian Library, Oxford), fols. 29–29ᵛ–30, my translation. All we have are property lists and expense accounts for Westminster School's other productions of Latin comedy in the sixteenth century. In 1564–1565 the boys acted Terence's *Heauton Timorumenos*, as well as Plautus's *Miles Gloriosus* in a production that they took to court. There were productions of *Menaechmi* in 1566, of *Rudens* in 1567, and of *Mostellaria* in 1569. The school treasurer's accounts keep mentioning plays until 1632. After gaps in the late seventeenth and early eighteenth centuries, Latin plays were resumed in the late eighteenth century and continue as an annual event to this day. See Lawrence Tanner, *Westminster School: A History* (London, 1934), pp. 55–59, and T.H.V. Motter, *The School Drama in England* (London, 1929), pp. 273–74.

10. *Terence in English*, trans. Richard Bernard (Cambridge, 1598), p. 127. Future references are cited in the text by page number.

G[NATHO]. In faith I have perceived so much.

T[HRASO]. Yea the grand Captaine gave me alwaies most heartie
   thankes, for any thing I had done for him: but he did not so to
   others.

G[NATHO]. He that hath the wittie conceites you have, often times
   winnes by wordes great commendations and renowme, which
   others have gotten with their great paines and travell.

T[HRASO]. Thou has me right.   (pp. 138–39)

Boast not, flatter not.

   Rather more radical adjustment of perspective is needed to
condemn the "headlong furies, passion, ill-advised judg-
ments, and *vere amarores, non amores*" that in fact make the play
so funny—not to mention the "filthiness" of Thais. Here is
the whore with a heart of gold, in more ways than one: she
may indeed encourage her two rival clients, Phaedria a
wealthy merchant's son and Thraso the braggart, and play
them off against each other for what they can give her, but she
also wants to restore her slave girl Pamphilia to the free-born
status she lost when stolen as a child by pirates. Phaedria's
brother Chaerea chances to see Pamphilia passing on the
street, falls in love with her on the spot, contrives with the
help of the tricky slave Parmeno to get into Thais's house dis-
guised as a eunuch, manages to bed the girl—and thereby
hangs a tale, in more ways than one. Chaerea's boast to his
friend Antipho about how he proved himself on that occasion
something *other* than a eunuch bothered moralistic critics as
far back as St. Augustine.

   While Pamphilia's maids were preparing her bath, Chaerea
waited behind and spied on the object of his desire as she
studied a painting of Jupiter seducing Danae in a shower of
golden coins. A disguising trick just like the one he was per-
petrating himself—and worthy of the same denouement! Chae-
rea got his chance when the maids brought Pamphilia back
from the bath, laid her on the bed, went off to have a wash
themselves—and left safely sexless Chaerea behind to fan
Pamphilia. As soon as his mistress had fallen asleep, Chaerea
tells Antipho,

I looke a squint thus privily with the fanne, and I prie about to see to other things also, whether they were sure or no: I seeing them to be so, I boult the dore.

A[NTIPHO]. What then?
C[HAEREA]. What then[,] foole?
A[NTIPHO]. I confesse my selfe a foole.
C[HAEREA]. Should I let go such opportunitie and occasion offered me, having so short time to doe it in, so greatly desired, so sudden, and nothing looked for? then was I hee indeede, whome I did counterfait. (pp. 151–52)

With good reason was St. Augustine nervous. Nowell's Prologue would have the audience hear all this with disdain, not delight. We have seen already how the commentators could turn Phaedria's opening speech in the play—"What then shall I doe? shall I not goe? what not now when I am so kindly called? or shall I resolve rather with my selfe, not to put up the despitefull abuses of a filthy drabe?"—into an argument, by negative example, against falling in love. Nowell tries the same strategy in putting *Eunuchus* onstage. Momentarily to be sure, Parmeno does seem to side with Nowell and the other moralists. Near the end of the play the clever plotter stands back and notes with satisfaction how well his strategem has worked:

that's the thing, for which I think my selfe worthy to be crowned, that I have devised a way how a young man may know the naturall disposition and manners of queanes: to the intent that after he knoweth them, he may for ever hate them as long as he liveth. Who beeing abroad out of their owne houses, nothing in the worlde seemes to be more cleane than then they be, nor any thing more demure, nor more proper, who, when they suppe with their lover feed very nicely and daintily, and not but of the best: but to see them how uncleanely they be, the ravening and manching, the sluttish-nesse, penury, and what greedie gripes [when] they are all alone at home: how they will slabber and sosse up browne bread in pottage, such as was left the day before, to know these things are a singular profit to young men. (p. 177)

The "sluttishnesse" of harlots: these are the very words Nowell echoes in his prologue. Choric as this soliloquy may sound, in context it is only a setup for Parmeno's own come-uppance moments later when Thais's servant announces that Pamphilia is not a slave girl after all but a free-born citizen, that Chaerea's father has unexpectedly returned from the country and discovered the outrage his son has committed under Parmeno's tutelege, and that punishment awaits within. So much for smug self-congratulation!

If, as Nowell's Prologue implies, we are to judge the characters by their deeds, how are we to justify the happy ending? Everyone gets what he wants: Chaerea gets to marry Pamphilia, the father gratefully takes Thais into his family's protection, Phaedria gets to enjoy Thais's favors all to himself—at least until Gnatho speaks up. Why not admit Thraso as a kind of permament rival, he asks Phaedria. He'll continue to shower Thais with gifts, and since he "lieth routing and snorting all night and all day," he'll never know he's being cuckolded (p. 189). Agreed. In return, impoverished Gnatho gets free run of Thraso's rich house. Where are the "examples to avoid" that Nowell's Prologue promises? Clearly, a great deal depends on one's point of view. In effect, Nowell's Prologue asks the audience to temper their laughter with moral judgment, to stifle their sympathetic delight in the play's happy ending with ridicule of the characters' follies. Terence's fine balance between satire and romance is upset: the realities of stage left overwhelm the fantasies of stage right. In effect, Nowell's Prologue prepares the audience to look at *Eunuchus* as if it were a modern morality play. This insistence on the play's contemporary "realism" was doubtlessly reflected in the costuming. Inventories of players' apparel stored away in the coffers of Cambridge colleges leave no doubt that Plautus's and Terence's Romans were customarily decked out as sixteenth-century Englishmen. In the St. John's inventory of 1562, "Gnatoes clocke" is a garment in "spanishe fassion of read cotto[n] w[i]th iii gardes of [y]ellow cotton"; "a cote for [M]iles" (Thraso in the same play?) is emblazoned, most anachronistically, "w[i]th a longe St. Andrewes crosse before and behinde."[11]

11. *REED: Cambridge*, s.v. 1562–1563.

Nowell's prologue for *Adelphi* sets up the same moral frame for watching the play's titular brothers win their hearts' desires against the objections of their grumbling old father: Ctesipho gets the lute player who has enchanted him, Aeschinus gets the citizen's daughter he has seduced. *Adelphi* would seem, then, to present the same puzzling polarity as *Eunuchus* between moral didacticism and amorous delight. What are we to make of this disparity? *Did* Nowell's audiences sit back in smug detachment as they followed the fortunes of the love-struck pairs of brothers in these two plays? Did they take no delight in youth and passion winning out over age and caution? Did they not wonder how the protagonists could be adulterers and yet in the end get just what they want? Unless we assume a fundamental change in the nature of human nature between the sixteenth century and now, we must conclude that the opposed comic impulses we outlined at the start—satiric detachment and sympathetic delight—stood in unresolved tension. Later academic producers, as we shall see, attempted to resolve that tension by altering Plautus's and Terence's texts to make the amorous mores of the ancients better fit the moral scruples of the moderns.

The split between the comedy of delight and the comedy of ridicule is especially sharp in *A new Enterlued for Chyldren to playe, named Jacke Jugeler, both wytte, and very playsent,* first printed in 1562 but written perhaps eight years earlier. The deviser of *Jack Juggler* has taken the first scene of Plautus's *Amphitruo*, anglicized the characters and dialogue, and turned the scene into a self-contained raucous farce. To settle an old score, Jack Juggler plays Mercury to Jenkin Careaway's Sosia: just as Mercury intimidates the slave Sosia by confronting him in his own guise, so Jack eavesdrops on Jenkin's carousings, steals some of his clothes, stands him off at the door of his own master's house, forces him to admit that he is not himself, and thus sets up the ne'er-do-well servant for beatings from his master and mistress. The anonymous author of *Jack Juggler*—in the prologue he gives himself the medieval title of "maker"—has borrowed not only Plautus's general situation but also his strategy of first giving the trickster the stage to

himself and letting him take the audience into his confidence.
Provided with an unusually large number of asides and direct
speeches to the audience, *Amphitruo* must have struck an inter-
lude-writer as just his métier. When, for example, Mercury
starts pummeling Sosia with his fists, the beleaguered slave
calls out to the people of Thebes for help (l. 376). True to the
medieval sense of playacting as a game, the servant's appeal in
Jack Juggler is addressed, not to other actors, but to the audi-
ence gathered around him: "who is thy maister now?" asks
Jack after using his fists to drive home his point.

> JENKIN. By my trouthe[,] syr[,] who so ever please you[!]
>   I am your owne, for you bete me soo
>   As no man but my mayster sholde doo[.]
> JACK. I woll handle thee better if faut be not in fyst[.]
> JENKIN. Helpe[!] save my life[,] maisters[,] for the passion of
>   christ[!][12]

These "maisters" are not the citizens of Thebes but the spec-
tators gathered informally around the acting place in the
middle of a great hall. Just as he casually transfers the action
of Plautus's play from the rational distance of the Roman stage
to the organic space of medieval playacting, so the "maker" of
Jack Juggler translates Plautus's Latin jokes into racy, idiomatic
English. "Gentleman[,] are you disposed to eate any fist
met[?]" Jack blusters when Jenkin refuses to open the door (l.
392).

What has such high-spirited farce to do with moral *sentence*?
Nothing, the "maker" assures us in the prologue. He dutifully
cites the advice from *De officiis* that earned classical comedies
a place in school curriculums. "Cicero Tullius[,] a man sapient
and wyse," says in the first book of "an honest man[']s office"
that hearing "the old comedie" is good for you. *This* inter-
lude, however, is no such thing:

> . . . I tell you all, before it bee begone[,]
> That no man looke to heare of mattiers substancyall
> Nor mattiers of any gravitee either great or small[,]

---

12. *Jack Juggler*, ed. Eunice Lilian Smart and W. W. Greg (Oxford, 1933),
ll. 500–509. Compare Plautus, ll. 302–25. Further quotations are cited in the
text.

For this maker shewed us that such maner things
Doo never well besime litle boyes handelings[.]   (ll. 47, 73–77)

We are in for a surprise, for after Jenkin has taken his lumps,
out comes an Epilogue who explains that the whole thing has
been an allegory of the world's deceit, of powerful men taking
advantage of weak men, of poor humble folk being forced to
confess, among other Catholic absurdities, that one man can
have two bodies. What are we to make of the prologue's
pointed disclaimer? Either we have here an especially coy
example of *occupatio* (I'm not going to tell you this, but of
course I'm telling it to you by telling you I'm not going to tell
it to you), or else, as David Bevington suggests, the epilogue
was added for the printed edition and was not part of the orig-
inal play. The play was likely written in the mid 1550s, under
Mary's Catholic reign; it was printed four years after Eliza-
beth's accession, when Protestant propaganda was still aimed
at discrediting the old regime.[13] Whichever is the case, the
knockabout farce of Jack and Jenkin seems worlds away from
the sober *sentence* of the epilogue. In *Jack Juggler* the comedy
of delight and the comedy of satiric ridicule appear to work at
cross-purposes.

Lifelike typicality and moral topicality: along with their
exemplary rhetoric, it was these two features that earned
Roman comedy a place in the in-house revels of sixteenth-
century schools and colleges. Taken in hand by a modern Pro-
logue, sometimes by "The Poet" himself, academic audiences
were encouraged to watch Plautus's and Terence's comedies
as if they were morality plays. By saying that he is not doing
it, the Prologue to *Jack Juggler* may actually be doing just that.
To look at Roman comedies as morality plays is to heighten
the plays' realism in two ways. On the one hand, it means
delighting in the characters' lifelike antics. How like a real
lover Phaedria moans and moons! How like a real courtesan
Thais teases her suitors! How like a real servant Parmeno lays
his plots! On the other hand, it means tempering one's delight
with moral scorn. How wrong Phaedria is to squander his

13. David Bevington, *Tudor Drama and Politics* (Cambridge, Mass., 1968),
pp. 124–26.

father's money! What a bad thing to fall in love with low
women! To transport these bright, solid realities into the can-
dlelit romance world of court revelry was to invite a distinc-
tively Renaissance form of culture shock. Yet on numerous
occasions in sixteenth-century England that meeting of two
worlds did occur. In addition to the gentlemen of his house-
hold, Wolsey called on the children of St. Paul's School to put
on a classical comedy at court; the Children of the Chapel
Royal were regular performers before Henry VIII; besides
calling on these two troupes, Elizabeth several times took
advantage of the annual play required in her statutes for West-
minster School and made a command performance part of her
Christmas revels.

The production of *Menaechmi* sponsored by Cardinal
Wolsey in 1526 was not the first time that Plautus's and Ter-
ence's earthy Romans found themselves face to face with the
denizens of dream visions. Hall describes an earlier occasion,
on March 7, 1520, when Henry and his court watched "a
goodly commedy of Plautus."[14] Hall does not bother to say
just which goodly comedy it was or even who acted it, but he
withholds no essential details of the pageantry and dancing
that followed the play. Henry had an audience of noble French
hostages to impress. Even if they did not appreciate such an
up-to-the-minute humanistic gesture as mounting a Plautine
comedy, they must surely have been impressed with the spec-
tacle that ensued: an entry of sixteen ladies and gentlemen
"tired like the Egipicians very richely." What had these refu-
gees from Mandeville's *Travels* to do with Plautus's adoles-
cent lovers and adamant fathers? The question seems not to
have occurred to Hall any more than it did to Henry and his
French hostages.

The *Menaechmi* at Hampton Court came six years later. Its
combination of pastourelle, play, and Petrarchan pageant is
altogether typical of how court entertainment introduced
satiric comedy into an essentially romantic context. On the

14. Edward Hall, *The Union of the Two Noble and Illustre Famelies of Lan-
castre and Yorke*, ed. H. Ellis (London, 1809), p. 597.

third occasion at Henry's court for which we have production details, the surface splendor of the earlier two occasions was complemented with didactic depth. Just a year after *Menaechmi*, Wolsey sponsored a court performance of Terence's *Phormio*. Spinelli, the Venetian ambassador, was again among the guests at festivities that marked a politically important occasion: the Pope's release from captivity by the Holy Roman Emperor Charles V.[15]After dinner the children of St. Paul's School recited Terence's comedy—and with such spirit (*galanteria*) and good acting (*bona attione*) that Spinelli was frankly astounded. Inscriptions at the front of the hall announced the name of the play, "*Terentii Phormio*," and dedicated the performance "*Honori et laudi Pacifici*," with an unsubtle allusion, as Spinelli realized, to Wolsey's title Cardinal Pacificus.

No sooner were true identities revealed, Spinelli reports, no sooner were irate fathers calmed and lovers allowed to marry, than three "richly clad" maidens appeared: Religion, Peace, and Justice."They complained of having been expelled well nigh from all Europe, by heresy, war, and ambition; detailing the iniquities perpetrated by the enemy, saying they had no other refuge than in the most generous Father, whom they besought to assume their protection and defence. . . ." The same little boy who had earlier pronounced the play's prologue then delivered a Latin oration, praising the Pope's escape from the clutches "of the most iniquitous men in the world, worse than the Turks." All the late calamities proceeded from the lust (*libidine*) of a single man who tried passionately (*cupide*) to subject everyone else to himself. The sexual overtones, the comparison of the emperor and his henchmen to Turks, the portrayal of Religion, Justice, and Peace as maidens—all these details make up a romantic scenario out of *Jerusalem Delivered*. As *Menaechmi* was offset by a "Triumph of Venus" in 1526–1527, so this production of

15. Spinelli's letter is translated in *Calendar of State Papers Venetian*, 4: 115–16, from which I take my quotations. The Italian words in parentheses are taken from the original letter, repr. in *Sanuto*, Vol. 46 (1897): col. 595.

Phormio was offset by a romantic "Triumph of Peace," with Cardinal Wolsey himself as the titular figure.

In surrounding the verisimilar panel of satiric comedy with a gilded frame of romance, the productions of Roman comedy at Henry VIII's court were altogether typical of productions elsewhere in Renaissance Europe.[16] At Ferrara, where classical drama found its most enthusiastic patronage in the d'Este princes, the five acts of comic complications were customarily relieved by interludes of music, mythological disguise, and showy philosophizing that the Italians dubbed *intermedi*. Alternating with the confusions that ensue when a god seduces one's wife, the audience watching a production of *Amphitruo* that celebrated Alfonso d'Este's marriage in 1491 saw a choral dance by ivy-clad youths, Apollo singing an ode in praise of the d'Este house, a rustic farce, an entry of Bacchus and Venus, and a pantomime of the judgment of Paris.

The princely taste for such things could lead only to ever more extravagant displays. Somewhat later in the century the celebrated playwright Antonfrancesco Grazzini ("Il Lasca") had had enough. In a satiric madrigal called "The comedy that aches with *intermedi*," he groans in mock horror at the artistic servitude he finds himself in:

> My grief! Those people who waited on me
> And once for adorning me hung about—
> They're wrecking it all, they're wearing me out!
> Little by little this villainous rout
>   Have taken my breath and vigor
>   And now have so much favor
> That all of them abuse me—they mock and flout.
>   And all this troop demand one thing
>   With gaping stare, with hankering:

16. Alessandro d'Ancona, *Origini del teatro Italiano*, 2d ed. rev. (Turin, 1891), 2: 61 ff., and Ireneo Sanesi, *La Commedia*, 2d ed. rev. (Milan, 1944), 1: 199 ff., offer accounts of classical drama on the Italian stage. Briefer English accounts are found in Marvin T. Herrick, *Italian Comedy in the Renaissance* (Urbana, Ill., 1960), pp. 61–65, and Douglas Radcliff-Umstead, *The Birth of Modern Comedy in Resaissance Italy* (Chicago and London, 1969), pp. 59–63.

The wonder—alas—of *intermedi*,
    "And you'd better have one ready . . ."
Or at once of my life they'll bereave me.
Have pity! Ah Phoebus, help me! help me![17]

On occasion, however, Il Lasca himself could satisfy that "hankering"—and with a measure of artistic integrity, too. For the marriage of Francesco de' Medici and Johanna of Austria in 1565, he collaborated with the composers Alessandro Striggio and Francesco Corteccia in devising a series of intermedi on the fable of Cupid and Psyche for a grand production of Francesco d'Ambra's comedy *La Confanaria*. From Apuleius's fable, Il Lasca and his collaborators chose six episodes, not, apparently, because they were important to the narrative (several key events in the story have to be inferred between the six episodes), but because they were visual and musical emblems in a figurative pattern that began with cosmic accord (Venus descending in her chariot accompanied by the Graces, the Hours, and Cupid), fell into discord (Cupid's abandonment of Psyche; a wild *moresca* danced by Discord, Anger, Cruelty, Rapine, Vendetta, the two Anthropophagi, and the Furies; a tearfully sung lament by Psyche descending to the Underworld), and returned to a triumph of union and renewed concord at the end (a celebration on Mount Helicon and a descent of Hymen).[18] Intermedi could, then, serve some

17. "La Comedia che si duol degli intermezzi": "Misera, da costor che gia trovati / fur per servirmi e per mio ornamento / lacerar tutta e consumarmi sento. / Questi empi e scelerati a poco a poco / preso han lena e vigore / e tanto hanno or favore, / ch'ognun di me si prende scherno e giuoco, / e sol dalla brigata / s'aspetta e brama e guata / la meraviglia, ohime! degli intermedi; / e se tu non provvedi, / mi fia tosto da lor tolto la vita; / misericordia! Febo, aita! aita!" (Antonfrancesco Grazzini, *Le Rime Burlesche*, ed. C. Verzone [Florence, 1882], p. 229, my translation). Grazzini was not unknown in England in the sixteenth century: his comedy *La Spiritata* was translated into English anonymously as *The Bugbears* (repr. *Early Plays from the Italian* [Oxford, 1911]).

18. Il Lasca's description, translated by Theodore Baker, is printed by O. G. Sonneck, "A Description of Alessandro Striggio and Francesco Corteccia's Intermedi 'Psyche and Amor,' " in *Miscellaneous Studies in the History*

kind of choric function at the same time that they delighted
courtly taste—a fleshly "hankering" Il Lasca would have it—
for spectacle, music, and dance.

Capable of serving as a thematic chorus, intermedi could
stand as a kind of frame for helping the audience adjust their
perspective. The problem concerned proportion: intermedi
threatened to take over the play itself. In the prologue to *La
Strega*, Il Lasco brings on two characters, Argumento and
Prologo, who lament such times as these, when intermedi are
more important than the plays they adorn:

ARGUMENTO. . . . I say that in these comedies that are hardly any
    good and hardly worth looking at [intermedi] come in just like
    ugly middle-aged women who, the more they try dressing them-
    selves up in silk and gold, with garlands and pearls, the more they
    try ornamenting themselves, making themselves glitter, and pow-
    dering their faces so they'll look pretty and young, the more they
    show they're really old and dried up.
PROLOGO. No doubt that the richness and beauty of the inter-
    medi—which mostly show muses, nymphs, *amori*, gods, heroes,
    and demigods—darken the comedy itself and make it look poor
    and ugly.
ARGUMENTO. And what a thing this comedy is! All of sudden
    onstage there's an old man, a parasite, a servant, a widow, and a
    serving girl—what a group!
PROLOGO. What can you do? That's how the world is nowadays.
    You just have to get used to the customs.
ARGUMENTO. A *custom*, you say! Once they used to put on inter-
    medi to serve the comedies; now they're doing comedies to serve
    the intermedi—What do you say to that?
PROLOGO. I'm with you. But you and I can't change the minds
    people have today.[19]

---

of Music (1921; repr. New York, 1968), pp. 269–86, from which this quotation
is taken. There is a description of the whole affair in Alois M. Nagler, *Theatre
Festivals of the Medici: 1539–1637*, trans. G. Hickenlooper (New Haven, 1964),
pp. 15–21.

    19. "A. . . . anzi dico che alle commedie poco belle e poco buone, inter-
viene come a certe donne attempate e brutte, che quanto più si sforzano, ves-
tendosi di seta e d'oro, e con ghirlande e vezzi di perle, e ornandosi, lisciandosi

It is clear enough where this gaudy "custom" comes from, Argumento volunteers: from pedants. Replete with opportunities for showing off a humanist's recondite learning, the mysteries of pagan mythology could titillate the mind as well as the senses.

Il Lasca's choice of images in this interchange from *La Strega* is telling. Unflatteringly observed flesh contrasts with splendid ornament; the mundane, very unheroic personages of the play ("an old man, a parasite, a servant, a widow, and a serving girl—what a group!") contrast with the sublime, marvelous creatures of the intermedi ("muses, nymphs, *amori*, gods, heroes, and demigods"). The first set of characters are objects of satiric laughter; the second set are objects of what Il Lasca's madrigal calls "wonder" (*meraviglia*). Play and intermedi present an audience with two sharply juxtaposed worlds. It is just this sharp juxtaposition, in fact, that Trissino, that thoroughgoing Aristotelian, found most objectionable about contemporary drama. In division six of the *Poetica* (1563) he chooses to talk about intermedi as a kind of chorus. Instead of the traditional choruses of tragedy, Trissino complains, "in the comedies that are staged today they bring on songs and dances and other things that intermedi call for—things that are very different from the action of the comedy;

---

e stribbiandosi il volto, di parer giovani e belle, tanto più si dimostrano agli occhi dei risguardanti vecchie e sozze.

"P. Non e dubbio che la ricchezza e la bellezza degl'intermedi, i quali rappresentamo per lo pi'agu muse, ninfe, amori, dei, eroi e semidei, offuscano e fanno parer povera e brutta la commedia.

"A. E di che sorte! veggendosi poi comparirvi in scena un vecchio, un parassito, un servidore, una vedova e una fantesca; bella convenevolezza!

"P. Che vuoi tu fare? il mondo va oggidi cosi: bisogna accomodarsi all'usanza.

"A. Un'usanza da dirle voi! Già si solevon fare gl'intermedi che servissero alle commedie, ma ora si fanno le commedie che servono agl'intermedi: che ne di' tu?

"P. Intendola come te in questa parte, ma ne tu ne io semo atti a riformare i cervelli di oggidi" (Antonfrancesco Grazzini, *Teatro*, ed. G. Grazzini [Bari, 1953], pp. 185–86, my translation).

sometimes they introduce a troupe of jesters and jokers who perform another whole comedy (something very out of place) that does not allow us to savor the theme of the comedy itself, the function of which is to move us to laughter not by means of every possible kind of action, but only by those means peculiar to itself [*col suo proprio*]—that is, by biting at ugly, wicked things and reproving and ridiculing them."[20] The persons of comedy, Aristotle had said, were characters who are "worse" than average; the means by which comedy works, like the means by which tragedy works, are emotional. Tragedy arouses pity and fear; comedy arouses ridicule. Comedy's function (and on this point Horace and Cicero were in agreement with Aristotle) is to "laugh folly out of countenance." With their splendid personages who play on the emotion of "wonder," intermedi failed to satisfy both terms in Aristotle's definition of comedy. From Trissino's critical perspective, intermedi distract attention from those objects that *are* appropriate to comedy; quite simply, intermedi confuse the emotional means by which comedy works.

Trissino may have raged; Italian audiences raved. When we look over a century of productions of the comedies of Plautus and Terence and of the commedie erudite they inspired, we can see in Italian courts exactly that "hankering" for dramatic variety that we have found at the court of Henry VIII. By themselves, Plautus and Terence were unable to supply three things that noble audiences, in England as in Italy, had come to expect: spectacle, didactic message, and love interest. Of these three the last is the most crucial. The wide-ranging mythological allusions and the pretentious allegory of some

20. "[M] in vece di questi tali Cori ne le Commedie, che oggidi si rappresentano, vi inducono suoni, e balli, et altre cose, le quali dimandano Intermedi, che sono cose diversissime da la azione de la Commedia, e talora v'inducono tanti buffoni, e giocolari, che fanno un'altra Commedia, cosa inconvenientissima, a che non lascia gustare la dottrina de la commedia, l'officio de la quale non e di muovere riso per ogni modo che si puo, ma solamente col suo proprio, cioè col mordere, e riprendere, e deleggiare le cose brutte, e viziose" (Giangiorgio Trissino, *Poetica*, in *Tutte le Opere* [Verona, 1729], 1: 122, my translation).

of the intermedi may prompt us to applaud their highbrow classicism, until we realize that almost always the allegory points to a statement in the idiom of courtly love. It was an idiom in which Ovid was well versed and versed well—or so it seemed to his medieval and Renaissance admirers. Italian courtiers, no less than Henry's English courtiers, were doing more than watching plays: they were playing an elaborate and very old social game. Jousts and tournaments with all their medieval romantic trappings remained as popular at Italian courts down through the sixteenth century as they did at the court of Queen Elizabeth.[21] With great displays of ingenuity, the devisers of courtly revels in Italy managed to persuade the unlikely characters of Plautus and Terence to conform with the social code of courteous love. Wolsey was attempting the same thing with his "Triumph of Venus" in 1526. The only difference is that Wolsey failed to carry the business off with quite the artistic integrity of his Italian compeers. Il Lasca's intermedi for *La Confanaria* turn play and pageants into a single artistic whole; *Menaechmi* and the "Triumph of Venus" remain separate entities.

Productions of Roman comedy before Queen Elizabeth later in the century show us a merging of these two dramatic worlds of satire and of romance. The two realms of experience that had remained separate in Henry VIII's revels became one in the productions of Plautus and Terence that Elizabeth saw. Combining the dreams of romance with the realities of Roman comedy, these productions restored the balance between satire and fantasy that seems lost in academic productions of Plautus and Terence. The result is comedy rediscovered as a viable genre, comedy as it flourished on the Elizabethan and Jacobean public stage.

The first of these court performances is a production of *Aulularia* planned for Queen Elizabeth's visit to Cambridge on her summer progress of 1564. We have observed already

21. Elena Povoledo, "Le Théâtre de tournoi en Italie pendant la Renaissance," in *Le Lieu théâtral à la Renaissance*, ed. Jean Jacquot (Paris, 1964), pp. 95–104, with illustrations.

how the college dons improvised a theater in Christ Church Chapel by using the building's side chapels as stage-mansions. Two arches between the nave and the aisle handily provided the two houses required in *Aulularia*, one for the miser Euclio and one for his long-suffering neighbor Megadorus. The dons also set the queen's throne down right onstage so that the audience could see both her and the play at the same time. The dons thus had it both ways: they were classically correct, but they also capitalized on the organic togetherness of medieval playing places.

In the cuts and additions they made to Plautus's play, they worked out a similar compromise between ancient and modern. If anyone already knew the play, he might well have been surprised at what he heard. An account of the performance by an eyewitness, Abraham Hartwell, scholar of King's College, differs in one crucial detail from the plot of Plautus's text. Hartwell describes accurately enough how the miser Euclio stashes his ancestral gold in a pot and almost takes leave of life, not to mention his senses, when the servant of his daughter's suitor sees where he hides the treasure and spirits it away: "The stingy Euclio sleeps on the dug-up gold, and greedily hides his wealth as if he did not have it. Alas the money badly entrusted to Silvanus—it has perished, plundered by the hand of a thievish slave! Stupidly he lost his life with the money and insanely determined to approach the sad Stygian lakes." When Hartwell turns to Euclio's daughter and her suitor Lyconides, however, we seem to be in the presence of rather different characters from those in Plautus's play: "The young man restored the coins, to him the daughter is given in marriage, the chaste daughter of an unworthy father."[22] "Chaste"? A big part of the play's fun is the fact that Lyconides has secretly seduced Euclio's daughter. She in fact is heard offstage laboring in birth pains at the very time Euclio is trying to save her dowry money by marrying her off to his

22. Trans. in Carter Anderson Daniel, "Patterns and Traditions of the Elizabethan Court Play to 1590" (Ph.D. diss., University of Virginia, 1965), p. 68.

old neighbor Megadorus. Unless Hartwell was one of the people who enraged another eyewitness by drowsing off during the performance, the producer of the play, Roger Kelke, D.D., seems to have dropped all references to the daughter's pregnancy and to have given the play a much more romantic twist by keeping the young lovers apart until the end. Perhaps that is why another eyewitness, Nicholas Robinson, remarks "how much charm, in truth, was *added* to the wit of Plautus by the industry and efforts of Dr. Kelke."[23]

Kelke's task was made easier by the fact the play's denouement scene is missing, giving a director license to fill out the metrical plot summary as he will. To make the play fit Hartwell's description, only one scene would have had to be changed drastically. That, unfortunately, is some of the funniest business in the whole play, a scene in which Lyconides apologizes to Euclio for "taking what was not mine"—which Euclio construes, of course, as the gold and not the girl. Did Kelke make these changes with his royal audience in mind? Two of the four plays planned for Elizabeth's entertainment on this occasion, John Halliwell's *Dido* and Nicholas Udall's *Ezechias*, might have had special significance for the queen: Dido is a monumental female protagonist whose love for Aeneas is sacrificed to national destiny, and Udall's play, though lost, must have dramatized King Hezekiah's conversion of the Israelites from pagan deities to the worship of Jehovah—a timely parallel to Elizabeth's championing of the protestant cause against the Roman church. The chastity of Euclio's daughter might have been similarly cast as a compliment to the queen. The effect of these changes in character and circumstance would be a heightening of the play's romantic interest and a blunting of its satiric edge.

That, however, was exactly what Elizabeth and her courtiers expected when they watched classical comedies. Of the several plays that Elizabeth had the Westminster boys bring to court, one was Plautus's *Miles Gloriosus*, acted during the

23. Trans. in Mary Susan Steele, *Plays and Masques at Court* (New Haven, 1926), pp. 17–18.

Twelfth Night revels of 1565. Itemized expenses in the school financial records for pins to fasten costumes, for borrowed armor and a drum, for paper and ink for placards above stage-mansions paint a sumptuous picture of what the production looked like—and perhaps even how it sounded and smelled. Twelve pence was paid "for butterd beere for the children being horse"; one penny was spent for frankincense. But they leave us in the dark as to how the royal audience took in this particularly racy play. The ending, at least, fits the peda-gogues' prescriptions: directed by Palaestrio, the narrator/manipulator of the comedy, a prostitute dressed up as a lady, dupes the braggart soldier into giving up his captive concu-bine so that the concubine can marry her young Athenian lover who lives next door. The just deserts of a Thraso! Did, however, Elizabeth and her courtiers watch the play's first half, in which Palaestrio arranges for concubine and lover to tryst by cutting a hole in the common wall between the houses and convincing the servants that the concubine has a twin sister? *Miles Gloriosus* is Plautus's longest play, and it is possible that the Westminster boys acted only the second, less salacious half when they carried the play to court.[24] If so, romance would again have overpowered satire, just as it did in the expurgated production of *Aulularia* at Cambridge.

However funny Palaestrio's plotting may have been, it was not calculated to appeal to the Elizabethan court's love of romantic adventure. To satisfy that "hankering," a new dra-matic kind emerged that incorporated certain features of Roman comedy but subjugated them thoroughly to drama-tized romance. When Elizabeth made her famous visit to Oxford in 1566, three plays were prepared to mark the occa-sion. Wily slaves were summoned out of Plautus and Terence and made to speak Renaissance Latin in an example of com-media erudita specially written for the occasion, *Marcus Ge-minus*, but Elizabeth for some reason failed to be on hand for

24. Cf. Daniel, "Elizabethan Court Play," pp. 90–93. The treasurer's accounts are reprinted in E.J.L. Scott, "The Westminster Play Accounts of 1564 and 1608," *Athenaeum*, No. 3929 (February 14, 1903): 220.

the performance. She did appear several days later, however, to watch Oxford students enact that unrelieved sequence of horrors that make up Ovid's tale of Progne, Philomel, and Tereus, redacted into a sententious neo-Senecan tragedy by Dr. James Calfhill, a prominent Catholic theologian and a canon of Christ Church. The dramatic highlight of Elizabeth's visit, to judge by the number and the detail of surviving accounts, was neither of these academic exercises, however, but a two-part dramatization of a medieval romance. Richard Edwards, master of the Chapel Royal, took the romantic intrigue of Chaucer's *Knight's Tale*, combined it with high jinks of Roman comedy, and struck just the right balance between satire and romance. Under-plot clowning by a knave named Tercatio caused Elizabeth to exclaim, "God's pity, what a knave it is!" Tercatio may well proclaim his ancestry with his Italian name. Certainly the conniving servants who carry on the comic business in Edwards's earlier court play *Damon and Pythias* leave no doubt that they have migrated to England from Plautus's and Terence's Rome. The main focus in Edwards's play, however, was not on the quipping comedian but just where the d'Este court, Gasparo Spinelli, and Edward Hall would lead us to expect it: on the amorous knights and their adventures. Edwards scored a triumph. Though the text itself has been lost, *Palamon and Arcite* was memorable enough for several eyewitnesses to record it in detail and for Anthony à Wood to give the occasion singular attention when he set down Edwards's biography more than a century later. We know more about the performance and audience reaction on this occasion than we do for many court plays that survive intact. Edwards's plan for *Palamon and Arcite* had variety, unity—and imitators. Most titles in the Revels Office accounts during the 1570s and early 1580s point to a well-worked mine of romance narrative. During these years, Italian princes may have been yawning through commedie erudite, but Elizabeth and her knights and ladies were sitting rapt before the adventures of *Herpetulus the Blue Knight and Perobia* and *The Knight of the Burning Rock.*

Romance looms large in what is probably the most famous

example of commedia erudita in English: *The Comedy of
Errors*. Acted as part of the Gray's Inn Christmas revels in
1594, possibly for the first time, Shakespeare's adaptation of
Plautus's *Menaechmi* is fitted out for performance in "The
House of Chivalry" not only in the staging arrangements that
the script implies but in the romantic vision that overwhelms
Plautus's farce of mistaken identities. Perhaps it is only an
accident of the source, but *The Comedy of Errors* is the only
one of Shakespeare's comedies to observe the unities of time
and place. Indeed, the "place" of the play is the conventional
fixed locale of Roman comedy, with the harbor in one direc-
tion and the city in the other. More than one editor has
remarked how the script can be played out in front of three
stage-mansions, or three openings in a hall-screen, one appro-
priate to Antipholus, one to the courtesan, and one to the Pri-
oress.[25] But the script could just as easily be played out on the
bare open space of a public stage, which, very likely, it was
before or after it was part of the *Gesta Grayorum* Christmas
revels.

The chivalric world of these revels, presided over by a mock
"Prince of Purpoole" whose counselors were provided with
speeches by Francis Bacon, is reflected in the way Shakespeare
has heightened the romance elements in Plautus's comedy.
Shakespeare's play is framed at beginning and end by the story
of Egeon and Emilia, a variant on the romantic tale of "Apol-
lonius of Tyre," likely drawn out of Gower's *Confessio amantis*
and reused in *Pericles*. In place of Plautus's typically scheming
courtesan, the principal female role in *The Comedy of Errors* has
become Antipholus's sympathetic wife Adriana. Perhaps the
subtlest of Shakespeare's romantic changes is his reversal of

25. R. A. Foakes provides a thorough account of the Gray's Inn perform-
ance, of likely staging arrangements, and of changes from Plautus in *The
Comedy of Errors*, New Arden Edition (London, 1962), pp. xvi–xxxix, 109–
17. On the play's sources, see also Geoffrey Bullough, *The Narrative and Dra-
matic Sources of Shakespeare*, Vol. 1 (New York, 1957): 3–11, and Kenneth
Muir, *The Sources of Shakespeare's Plays* (New Haven, 1978), pp. 14–17. *Gesta
Grayorum*, the description of the Christmas revels of which *The Comedy of
Errors* was a part, has been edited by Desmond Bland (Liverpool, 1968).

the relative importance of the twins. In Plautus, interest centers on the citizen-brother and all the farcical confusions he faces. He is an essentially satiric figure. In Shakespeare, the bulk of the lines have been shifted to the wanderer-brother. He, too, faces farcical confusions, to be sure, but he also falls in love with Adriana's sister Luciana, woos her with Euphuistic extravagance, and wins her in the end. Quester and lover, he is an essentially romantic figure.

In all these respects *The Comedy of Errors* is a more romantic play than Plautus's *Menaechmi,* but the romance is edged with the same self-reflective irony that distinguishes Shakespeare's other comedies. Like *Love's Labors Lost* with its postponed denouement and its dialogue between Winter and Spring, like *Twelfth Night* with Malvolio's angry exit, like *As You Like It* with Jacques' refusal to dance and Rosalind's throwing off disguise to speak the epilogue, like *All's Well* with its uneasy reconciliation between Helena and Bertram, *The Comedy of Errors* sets romantic fantasy at a certain ironic distance from the audience. The imagery of sorcery, witchcraft, and deception that fills the play is appropriate not only to what people do in Ephesus but to what actors do on the bare boards of a stage. Certainly the gentlemen of Gray's Inn seem to have picked up the hint when they later apologized for the crowd's rambunctiousness on the night of the performance as a matter of "Sorceries and Inchantments; and namely, of a great Witchcraft . . . whereby there were great Disorders and Misdemeanours, by Hurly-burlies, Crowds, Errors, Confusions, vain Representations and Shews, to the utter Discredit of our State and Policy."[26] Because of Shakespeare's play, as well as the crowd's unruliness, the occasion went down in the official account as "The Night of Error." The romance may be enticing, but *The Comedy of Errors* strikes that special balance between romantic longing and satiric detachment that gives classical comedy its timeless hold on human imagination. *The Comedy of Errors* transcends the narrow social circumstances in which it was first performed. In bringing ancient models to bear on

26. Quoted from *Gesta Grayorum* in Foakes, *Comedy,* p. 117.

modern experience, Shakespeare shows us comedy rediscov-
ered as a viable genre. He is able to do so because his perspec-
tive as a playwright for the public stage extends beyond the
narrow concerns of an in-house audience. Even academic pro-
ducers seem to have realized that. When we turn to later aca-
demic productions, we discover that they are all indebted to
the public theater for the compromise they work out between
satire and romance.

The Birth of Hercules, for example, introduces a "Prologus
Laureatus" who is as much at home in Southwark as he is in
the great hall of an academic household. At first hearing, he
sounds predictably pedantic, proudly identifying the play
with Plautus's *Amphitruo* and dutifully lecturing the audience
on genre, style, and theme. First played in Athens, then five
times in Rome, where it was "Clapt by Consulls and
Emperors," this play "is a Commedie, Or tragicke Comedye,
call yt which you will."[27] Plautus's Mercury, speaking at the
beginning of *Amphitruo*, tosses off that generic confusion as a
little joke to startle the audience (after all, eventualities do look
dire until Jupiter steps in as *deus ex machina*); the Prologus Lau-
reatus is pedagogically precise. Despite such obviously aca-
demic preoccupations, however, the Prologus Laureatus of
The Birth of Hercules seems rather more aware of public-theater
conventions than academic prologues usually are. Would an
academic prologue have to apologize to an academic audience
for giving them a prologue? Long ago prologues were "in
use," but now "Th['] epilogue is in fashion; prologues no
more" (l. 5). However rare they may have been in Southwark,
prologues never went out of fashion in Renaissance editions
of Plautus's and Terence's plays. Then, too, would an aca-
demic prologue have to worry whether some of the audience
might not like "these same translated thinges" (l. 34)? What
did they expect? That the play would be done in Latin? Why,
moreover, would Mercury have to conjure the audience to
imagine it night-time (ll. 59–62), when almost every academic

27. *The Birth of Hercules*, ed. R. Warwick Bond and W. W. Greg (Oxford,
1911), Pro. 17–18. Further quotations are cited in the text.

production we know about was in fact acted at night? Why, furthermore, should Mercury go on to assume that an academic audience was not used to seeing impersonations of pagan gods?

> . . . Soe perhapps
> You would take me for a man,
> But you are deceived, for I am a god;
> And that by this good night: yet I doe not wonder
> You should mistake me: For unles yt be
> the maskinge god *Cupid*, you may well
> Have heard of the ould Goddes, but I thinke
> It is a good while since you see any of us.   (ll. 62–69)

Is Mercury being coy? Surely an academic audience would have more than "heard" about "the ould Goddes." The one thing a strictly academic audience might not have seen is "the maskinge god *Cupid*." The implied milieu there is courtly, not academic. Both of the spokesmen who introduce *The Birth of Hercules*, the Prologus Laureatus and Mercury in his opening soliloquy, seem to assume, then, an audience who know as much about conventions in the public theater as they do about academic drama and who know at least something about masques at court, as well. The one audience who embraced all three traditions—academic, courtly, and popular—were the gentlemen of the inns of court. Perhaps like *The Comedy of Errors*, *The Birth of Hercules* was calculated for that special group, assembled in one of their great halls where three dramatic worlds converged. That venue fits, too, the staging arrangements implied by the script—arrangements that include painted heavens and practicable stage-mansions.

Academic traditions may account for the tidy structure of *The Birth of Hercules*, but like *The Comedy of Errors*, it injects into Plautus's Rome the heady rhetoric and hearty passions of romantic love. Just once Plautus has Sosia tell Amphitruo how much he is looking forward to a reunion with his own "lady friend" [*amica mea*] (l. 659). In *The Birth of Hercules* this single mention is expanded into a flirtation that matches Amphitruo's devotion to Alcmena. In Plautus, Sosia's "lady friend"

is never even specified by name: Thessala exists only to fetch
the cup that Jupiter-as-Amphitruo has given to Alcmena. In
The Birth of Hercules, Thessala becomes Alcmena's confidante,
and together the two women lament their loneliness in terms
more appropriate to Chrétien de Troyes than to Plautus. Like
all life's pleasures, how short the pleasure of her reunion with
Amphitruo, Plautus's Alcmena reflects (ll. 632–33). Her Ren-
aissance counterpart casts herself as the lady left to wait in the
castle while her knight goes off to battle. To bear their absence
is a double "crosse": "For were they absent onely in Ambas-
sage: or as traveylers: or as merchantes: yet they might leave
us hart easinge hope at home to accompanie us till their
returne. But beinge absent as souldiers they leave us pale feare:
a passion that we are lesse hable to endure then grief. . . ." The
passion of the mistress is shared by her maidservant. Thessala
may be living in ancient Rome, but she envisions marriage in
the trappings of medieval chivalry:

> O there cannot be such a crosse in the world to a woman, as to parte
> from her husband. Whie Mistress, he is the husband of her bosome:
> when he is gone, alas how can she but be naked. He is her propp and
> upholder: take him awaie, she cannot chuse but fall. Besides, a soul-
> dier is to his wief a sheild and a buckler to, remove him and she will
> lye open straight to all assaultes.
>   A[lcmena]. T'were pitty but thou haddest a husband *Thessala*, thou
> coulest perswade him soe well to staie at home.   (ll. 819–51)

Though Thessala and Sosia never get a scene to them-
selves—in fact, they never exchange any lines at all—they do
at least show their affection in a bit of amorous byplay when
Alcmena orders Thessala to fetch Jupiter's cup. Mooning at
Sosia "through silent signals," according to the stage direc-
tions, Thessala has to be commanded to her task a second time
(ll. 1242–47). In keeping with her image as the virtuous *chate-
laine*, the Renaissance Alcmena takes Amphitruo's accusations
of adultery much more to heart than Plautus's Alcmena does.
"A strange way for my husband to be acting," observes Plau-
tus's heroine. "To get pleasure out of falsely accusing me of
misconduct! Well, whatever it is, I'll find out soon enough

from Cousin Naucrates" (ll. 858–60). And that's that. The Renaissance Alcmena turns this spunky comeback into a passionate set piece that sets her up as a kind of Patient Griselda: "This is strange to me, that have lived thus longe untainted in the opinion of the worlde: now to be challenged by my lord and husband. The godds I trust, that are wytnesses of myne Innocency will deliver me out of this distresse. It cannot be other wise. I knowe my cousin *Naucrates* is honorable, and loves me. He must needes be wytnes of my side." (ll. 1361–68). The play's happy ending becomes, then, not just a happy ending but an allegory of Innocence Vindicated.

It becomes, in fact, rather more than that. The Prologus Laureatus has prepared us from the start to take pleasure in the play "bycause yt patternes out a highe mistery" (l. 55). At the ending that "mistery" bursts upon us, and we come to understand why the play is called *The Birth of Hercules* and not *Amphitruo*. Lacking any explicit stage directions, Plautus's text does not specify just how Jupiter makes his appearance as *deus ex machina* in the play's final scene and reconciles husband and wife by telling them the whole story of his disguise—and by identifying one of the just-born twins as his own son. Was Jupiter let down in a crane? Did he appear on the roof of the house? Was only his voice heard? Plautus's script does not say. In the absence of such details *The Birth of Hercules* manages the whole thing as a grand theophany: thunder crashes, the music of trumpets or other instruments begins to sound out of the painted heavens, and Jupiter's voice booms out, apparently in disembodied majesty. "This voyce is from heaven," Amphitruo cries as he prostrates himself, "I must doe Reverence" (ll. 2507–08). As Jupiter speaks, a choir gives certain of his lines special emphasis by singing them "as if out of the heavens" (s.d. for l. 2513). Even without the prompting of the Prologus Laureatus, there is no mistaking that these lines echo the accounts of Christ's miraculous birth in Matthew and Luke. "Amphitruo, feare not, but take thy wief againe," commands Jupiter, sounding for all the world like Jehovah reassuring Joseph, "The boyes she is delivered of, one of them was begotten by the, the other by me"—and here the script shifts

to a larger type font to indicate the choir's participation—
"WHOM I WYLL HAVE CALLED HERCULES" (ll. 2511–14), Plautus
mentions nothing about the child's name; that detail comes
from Luke:

> Feare not, Marie: for thou hast founde favour with God.
>
> For lo, thou shalt conceive in thy wombe, and beare a sonne, and
> shall call his name JESUS.
>
> He shalbe great, & shalbe called the Sonne of the moste High, and
> the Lord God shal give unto him the throne of his father David.
>
> And he shal reigne over the house of Jacob for ever, & of his king-
> dome shalbe non end.[28]

With license of Plautus's Latin, Hercules too is destined for
immortali gloria (l. 1140): "Amphitruo, the confusion of thy
house was wrought by me, for my owne pleasure. In
Recompence wherof, I have given the—A SONNE THAT SHALL
CROWNE THY MORTALL HEADE WITH IMMORTALYTIE" (ll. 2517–
21). The joyful tidings complete, the unseen music "seems
gradually to reascend" (s.d., ll. 2530–32), leaving Amphitruo
like one of Luke's quaking shepherds to end the play by
affirming simply, "All rulinge Jupiter, yt shalbe as thou
Comaundest" (ll. 2528–29). As old as the medieval mythog-
raphers, the parallel between Christ and Hercules was com-
monplace as late as the eighteenth century, when Bach found
nothing untoward about borrowing themes from his birthday
cantata "Hercules am Scheidewege" (BWV 213) and incorpo-
rating them in his Christmas Oratorio. In the context of *The
Birth of Hercules*, that "highe mistery" strongly suggests that
the play was part of the Christmas revels of an academic
household, most likely one of the inns of court.

Conventions of the public stage also loom large in Thomas
Randolph's adaptation of Aristophanes' *Plutus*, probably acted
at Trinity College, Cambridge, sometime between 1616 and
1628. In the Renaissance conflict between romance and satire,
Aristophanes posed a special problem. On the one hand, he
commanded respect as the father of comedy. On the other

---

28. Luke 1:30–33, in *The Geneva Bible* (1560), ed. Lloyd E. Berry (Mad-
ison, 1969).

hand, he gave the romantic imagination precious little to feed upon. The *editio princeps* of the Greek text appeared from the Aldine Press in 1498, just three years after four of Euripides' tragedies had been published and well ahead of the first printings of Sophocles and Aeschylus. Between 1498 and 1624, presses all over Europe issued no fewer than thirteen separate editions of Aristophanes' comedies, many of them with a Latin trot and a panoply of Latin commentaries printed alongside. Ben Jonson's copy of one of these bilingual texts, edited by Odoardus Bisetus and Aemilius Portus (Geneva, 1607), is now in the Fitzwilliam Museum, Cambridge. Aristophanes' appeal was not limited to scholars, as Jonson's possession of this text and the example of his own plays show.[29] Long before Jonson's time, however, Aristophanes had appeared onstage in England. As early as 1536 the scholarly discussions about "trew Imitation" that Roger Ascham, John Cheke, and their colleagues carried on at St. John's College, Cambridge, bore fruit in a production of *Plutus* that used Cheke's rules for Greek pronunciation. This production is, in fact, among the earliest productions of classical drama of any kind in England: it is preceded only by two unspecified comedies of Terence at King's Hall, Cambridge, in 1510–1511 and 1516–1517 and by an unspecified "*comedia Plauti*" at Queens' College, Cambridge, in 1522–1523. Aristophanes' *Pax* was produced, likewise in Greek, at Trinity College ten years after *Plutus*. According to the producer, John Dee, the production, if not the play itself, was the talk of the university: "I did sett forth (& it was seene of the Univ[er]sity) a Greeke Comedie of Aristophanes, named in Greek Eirene, in Latine Pax. with the p[er]formance of the Scarabeus his flying up to Jupiters Pallace, with a Man & his Basket of victualls on her Back: whereat was great wondering, & many vaine report[es] spread

29. Louis E. Lord, *Aristophanes: His Plays and His Influence* (New York, 1927), pp. 102–15; Coburn Gum, *The Aristophanic Comedies of Ben Jonson* (The Hague, 1969), pp. 9–18; Aliki Lafkidou Dick, *Paedeia Through Laughter* (The Hague, 1974), pp. 1–10; David McPherson, *Ben Jonson's Library and Marginalia; An Annotated Catalogue, SP* 71 (1974): item 8, pp. 25–26. The markings in this copy seem not to be Jonson's.

abroad, of the meanes how that was effected."[30] With *Pax* at
Trinity the record of productions of Aristophanes ends for a
hundred years. These two early stagings are the only ones on
record until Thomas Randolph took *Plutus* in hand in the
1620s. In that gap of a century there were, by contrast, literally
scores of productions of Roman comedy.

The reason that Aristophanes ran Plautus and Terence a dis-
tant third in academic popularity is not hard to seek: he pro-
vided no romantic interest whatsoever. With the shift from
romance to satire that distinguishes Elizabethan sensibility
from Jacobean sensibility, Aristophanes came into his own.
He suited the age of Donne and Jonson perfectly: as a device
for bringing on a succession of fools, Aristophanes' loosely
connected episodes were much more serviceable than Plau-
tus's and Terence's tightly knotted plots. And for an eager sat-
irist what an assortment of eccentric fools Aristophanes pro-
vided! Here was a far richer variety than the stock types—*miles
gloriosus, servus, adolescens*—that crop up again and again in
Plautus and Terence. Unfortunately, Aristophanes also pro-
vided impenetrable allusions and intractable Greek idioms.
The one play that was freest of these drawbacks was *Plutus*.
Just as it was the most frequently copied play in Byzantine and
European manuscripts, so *Plutus* became far and away the
Renaissance favorite among Aristophanes' comedies. Even
before the Aldine edition appeared, Leonardo Bruni had called
for a Latin translation. Franciscus Passius's version appeared
in 1501; by midcentury there were at least ten other versions
in Latin. The Greek text attracted the editing skills of Petrus
Mosellanus, Thierry Martens, and Melanchthon, all of whom
published separate editions in the first decades of the sixteenth
century.

What Renaissance scholars, actors, and audiences liked
about *Plutus* was the very thing that makes it the least admired
of Aristophanes' plays today: its similarity to new comedy.
The play's utterly fantastic plot device, free of any parallels
with actual events, brings to the stage a parade of universally

30. *REED: Cambridge,* s.v. 1546.

recognizable types rather than thinly disguised historical individuals who need footnotes to introduce them. Unhappy in his own financial affairs, the poor but honest Chremylus has asked the Oracle of Apollo whether his son ought to live virtuously like himself or become an opportunistic knave like everyone else. The oracle, cryptic as usual, has advised Chremylus to follow the first man he meets when he leaves the temple—which is just what he is doing when the play opens. The first man he sees is a miserable blind man, who turns out to be none other than the god of wealth. Guided by Chremylus and his friends to Aesculapius' temple, Plutus gets back his sight, sees how he has been rewarding all the wrong people, and rights his mistake by turning paupers into patricians and patricians into paupers. It is these assorted patricians and paupers, all portrayed as new comedy character types, who give the play its satiric verve. Marshaling the motley procession is Chremylus's servant Cario, the prototype for all the wily slaves in Plautus and Terence. Add the play's moral premise to these features already familiar from Roman comedy, and the Renaissance success of *Plutus* was assured.

The author of two original plays for his fellow undergraduates at Trinity College, Cambridge, Thomas Randolph likely devised *Plutophthalmia* for a college production sometime between 1626 and 1628. The text of the play as published nearly a quarter-century later is a palimpset literally, socially, and generically. Though described on the title page as "Translated out of Aristophanes his *Plutus*" and credited to Randolph, *Hey for Honesty, Down with Knavery* (1651) has been "augmented" by a mysterious "F.J.," who provides Royalist jabs at Roundhead absurdities in the form of added speeches, interpolated scenes, an induction, an epilogue, and possibly some new characters. Randolph was dead by Commonwealth times, and almost all the speeches and scenes with Commonwealth allusions lack any counterpart in Aristophanes' original, so that F.J.'s augmentations are fairly easy to isolate.[31]

31. G. E. Bentley, *The Jacobean and Caroline Stage*, Vol. 4 (Oxford, 1956): 980–82. Cyrus L. Day, "Thomas Randolph's Part in the Authorship of *Hey*

The literal palimpset formed by F.J.'s additions makes the play a social palimpset as well. Randolph's original version was probably intended for in-house revels at Trinity College; F.J.'s augmented version, printed during the Puritan prohibition of playacting, turns the play into a closet drama, a piece of political propaganda like Charles Wase's Royalist version of Sophocles' *Electra*. Generically, *Hey for Honesty* is a palimpset, as well. Randolph's original version adapts the play in the spirit of new comedy; F.J.'s additions, filled with allusions to Civil War controversies and to actual personages like Pym, return the play to its old comedy topicality.

Randolph's *Plutophthalmia* shows us the same curious combination of in-house amateurishness and public theater savvy that we find in *The Birth of Hercules*. The production's festive academic context is reflected in the scene where Poverty pleads her case. Randolph casts the whole thing as a formal academic debate and supplies an audience of rustics who keep demolishing the elevated proceedings with their commonsense wisecracks and get all the technical terms hilariously wrong. Says Clodpole: "At Oxford or Cambridge 'twould make a man a-hungry to hear 'um talk of 'gisms and argations, and pretticables and predicaments, and gatur antecedens, and prorums, and postriorums, and probos, and valeris. 'Cha think this logic a hard thing, next to the black art" (2.5, pp. 418–19).

The humor in this scene may be intramural, but Randolph's frame of reference is wide enough to include all the particularities of London life that mark the comedies of Jonson and

---

for Honesty," *PMLA* 46 (1926): 325–34. Randolph's version of *Plutus* is the last recorded production of a classical comedy at Oxford or Cambridge in the seventeenth century. Samuel Brooke's Latin *Adelphi* (Trinity College MS R.10.4) is described in the *Annals of English Drama* as an adaptation of Terence, but it shares with Terence's play only the title and the central importance of twins. Joshua Barnes's "Plautus his Trinummus imitat'd" (Emmanuel College MS III.i.2, dated 1693) makes a very promising start at turning Lesbonicus into a Restoration rake but leaves off after just two scenes, the equivalent of Plautus's Act One. Moore Smith, *College Plays*, pp. 10ff., notes that most Cambridge colleges had ceased to put on plays long before the official prohibition in 1642.

Middleton. Plutus, for example, is given a proud city genealogy: "my father was Pinchback Truepenny, the rich userer of Islington; my mother, Mistress Silverside, an alderman's widow. I was born in Golden Lane, christened at the Mint in the Tower; Banks the conjurer and old Hobson the carrier were my godfathers" (1.2, p. 391). The better to establish his literary genealogy, Randolph's Plutus emerges from Aesculapius's temple quoting Volpone: "Good morrow to the morn[;] next[,] to my gold" (3.3, p. 444). Poverty, too, is thoroughly acclimatized: she introduces herself as "the daughter of Asotus Spend-all, of Brecknockshire" (2.4, p. 415). Plutus and Poverty are typical of the way Randolph fleshes out Aristophanes' characters. In Aristophanes' script, Chremylus's poverty-stricken friends speak as an undifferentiated Chorus; in Randolph's version they have become country bumpkins out of *Henry IV, Part Two*. Clodpole, Lackland, Stiff, Scrape-all splutter away most amusingly in country dialect. Listen to Clodpole greeting Chremylus in his new-found wealth: "Valiant! Why, Mars himself was an arrant coward to me; I have beat him at vootball above twenty times. If you did but zee me once, I warrant you would call me goodman Hector, as long as I lived for't. Did you not zee how I cuffed with Hercules for a twopenny loaf last Curmass? Let Plutus go! No, let me return again to onions and pease-porridge then, and never be acquainted with the happiness of a sirloin of roast-beef." By fleshing out Aristophanes' spare dialogue, Randolph manages to bring the play to life for his seventeenth-century audience as if it were *Volpone* or *A Chaste Maid in Cheapside*.[32]

To bridge the one big lacuna in Aristophanes' text, when Plutus is taken to the temple of Aesculapius and cured of his blindness, Randolph has devised a new scene that provides some funny dialogue and some knockabout stage-business at the same time that it dramatizes the moral message of the play.

---

32. 2.7 in *The Poetical and Dramatic Works of Thomas Randolph*, ed. W. C. Hazlitt (London, 1875), 2: 427–28. All quotations from *Hey for Honesty* are taken from this edition and will be cited in the text by act and scene.

Just what goes on during Aristophanes' missing lines is not quite clear, though Cario's hilarious report of spending the night in Aesculapius's temple suggests that Plutus's de-blinding was not in fact acted out. As an onstage counterpart to this climactic offstage event, Randolph has Poverty assemble a ragtag army, attack Plutus's sympathizers, and retreat in even greater disarray than they assaulted. The Scot, the Welshman, the Irishman, and the Englishman who make up Poverty's recruits bark, lilt, shout, and rhetoricize, respectively, in their own comic dialects.

Randolph's management of the ending serves the same double purpose of playing up the comedy's contemporaneity at the same time it nails down the play's moral program. Compared with Plautus and Terence, Aristophanes is not notable for bringing his plays to stunning conclusions. What happens in the end is less important than how we get there. Plutus's redistribution of wealth serves simply to let Aristophanes bring on a succession of comic pairs whose roles have been reversed: a poor but Just Man and a rich Informer, a Young Man and the Old Woman who has been giving him money and clothes in exchange for sexual services, hard-pressed Hermes and a Priest of Zeus who changes his allegiance from the impecunious old god to Plutus the rich new one. After these pairs have all had their moment at center stage, the play simply ends—a certain disappointment to audiences who expected the revelations and revels of Roman comedy. Randolph manages to satisfy those expectations: he swells the merry party of comic types, turns the Priest of Zeus into none other than the Pope himself, and even contrives an obligatory marriage to round things off. After an Attorney, a Tinker, a Miller, a Tailor, and a Shoemaker have joined the Just Man (Ananias Goggle), the Informer (Never-good), the Old Woman (Anus), the Young Man (Neanias), and Mercury, in comes the Pope, desperate now that only good men are rich and hungry enough to sell his soul for a mess of pottage—or even less:

I am *servus servorum*, your servant's servant.
Sans compliment, like Ham—
O that this leather of thy shoe, this leather,
Could be made flesh by transubstantiation!
I would not only kiss, but eat thy toe.   (5.1, p. 488)

Watching the Pope eat humble pie makes everyone hungry. A choir comes on, and the proceedings end with a madcap macaronic chorus:

POPE. *O fratres nostri ventres sint repleti,*
    For empty maws are never truly *laeti*:
    To feed on meats and drink of *potionibus*,
    Is the only physic for *devotionibus*.
OMNES. *Benedixit Esculapius.*
POPE. Cheese-cakes and custards, and such good *placentas*
    Excel Good Fridays, Ember weeks, and *Lentas*:
    When belly's full, we'll go to the *Cloisteribus*
    To kiss the nuns and all the *Mulieribus*.
OMNES. *Benedixit* &c.   (5.1, p. 489)[33]

And so on for twenty more rolicking lines. When we recall that the performance at Trinity likely ended with actors and audience adjourning to a Christmas or a New Year's feast, this chorus becomes all the jollier.

Two sets of speeches follow the chorus in the printed version of *Hey for Honesty*: the epilogue is full of Commonwealth allusions and is clearly one of F.J.'s additions, but the "SCENE ult[ima]" that immediately precedes it may well be Randolph's.[34] There Plutus meets up with "Mistress Honesty Cleon, an honest scrivener's daughter," woos her, wins her,

33. Since Dull-pate, one of F.J.'s creations from elsewhere in the play, is the Pope's interlocutor, it is possible that this scene has been rewritten by F.J. Dull-pate's observation as the choir comes in, "The Roundheads will not come, 'cause the Pope's here," is certainly suspicious; perhaps, however, it is only a speech that F.J. has added.

34. Day claims this scene as F.J.'s, but, as Hazlitt notes, Plutus's allusion to "this parliament" may refer to the parliament of March 1628 as easily as to the parliament of 1640.

and prepares to wed her, thus supplying the romantic happy
ending and didactic message that Aristophanes' play lacks:

> HONOR. Sir, if I may confess, love's art
>   Not only touch'd my eyes, but heart.
> PLUTUS. Nay, then, the parson straight shall do his part,
>   Let's in: the Gordian knot none can untwist,
>   We'll tie it fast, and as we go, we'll kiss.
>   In any state never will be foul weather,
>   When honesty and riches meet together.   (5.2, p. 491)

Even an audience with a taste for the satiric salt of Donne and
Jonson liked their drama sugared with romance.

Looking back over the first century of productions of
Plautus, Terence, and Aristophanes in England, we discover,
then, a series of attempts to reconcile classical comedy's oppo-
site aspects. Bounded on one side by the harbor, by mystery
and romance, and on the other by the country, by everyday
realities, comedy on the ancient stage brought together two
very different areas of human experience and played them off
against each other. The productions that we have surveyed
here combine those areas of experience in startlingly different
ways. To judge from their prologues, the earliest academic
producers of Plautus and Terence seem to have been deter-
mined to play up comedy's moral satiric side at the expense of
its romantic side. Transported to the court of Henry VIII, the
scripts of Plautus and Terence were framed by mythological
forepieces and afterpieces set up as moves in the game of
courtly love. The romance of these chivalric devices spilled
over into the plays themselves in the productions of Latin
comedy that were mounted before Elizabeth. First performed
as a Christmas entertainment at Gray's Inn, Shakespeare's *The
Comedy of Errors* sets satire and romance in just the delicate
poise that made comedy a vital dramatic genre in the Eliza-
bethan public theater. Finally, in Thomas Randolph's aca-
demic adaptation of Aristophanes' *Plutus*, satire overtakes
romance, just as on the public stage the city comedies of
Jonson and Middleton supplanted plays like *As You Like It*.
Even here, however, seventeenth-century taste demanded a

romantic happy ending. Satire and romance embrace in Randolph's wedding of Mistress Honesty and the god of Wealth.

II

Thoroughly English characterization, contemporary topicality, a distinctly mercenary version of what it means to live happily ever after—all of Randolph's additions to Aristophanes are representative of what happened to classical comedy when it reached the public stage. Not once was a Greek or Roman comedy mounted in London's public theaters under its own name. Classical drama, clearly enough, was seen as coterie entertainment. Not one of the professional playwrights—not even such proudly self-proclaimed classicists as Jonson and Chapman—ever billed any of his public-stage plays as adaptations of particular comedies by Plautus and Terence or by Aristophanes. Jonson "had ane intention to have made a play like Platus Amphitrio," Drummond reports, "but left it of, for that he could never find two so like others that he could persuade the Spectators they were one."[35] In the scripts he saw through to completion Jonson, like Chapman, Middleton, and Brome, uses character types and plot motifs from Roman comedy as ways of satirizing modern mores, but he is content to borrow promising material wherever he happens to find it. Not one of his comedies stands in such close relationship to a single model as *The Comedy of Errors* does to *Menaechmi*.

It took not a self-conscious classicist, but a hard-pressed professional like Thomas Heywood to exploit Roman scripts slavishly enough to let us see what happened when Rome came to Clerkenwell. The author, by his own reckoning, of more than two hundred plays, Heywood ransacked every possible source in his twenty-year search for dramatic ideas. Along with ballads, chronicles, and Italian *novelle*, classical literature served Heywood well. In *The Golden Age, The Silver Age, The Bronze Age*, and *The Iron Age* (1610–1612) he

---

35. Ben Jonson, *Discoveries 1641* and *Conversations with William Drummond of Hawthornden 1619*, ed. G. B. Harrison (Edinburgh, 1930), p. 18.

brought the mythological entertainments of intramural Whitehall to the broad public spaces of the Red Bull Theater: Ovid's *Metamorphoses* became a series of Elizabethan history plays. For dramatizing Jupiter's dalliance with Alcmena in *The Silver Age*, Heywood found an entire act ready-made in Plautus's *Amphitruo*, translated and adapted it, and inserted it, unacknowledged, right into his own script. Heywood's method in adapting Plautus's play was simple: he livened it up by omitting long set pieces like Alcmena's lonely lament and by dramatizing events that are only narrated in Plautus. Thus *The Silver Age* takes the audience inside Amphitrion's house to witness firsthand the birth of the twins.[36] Literally as well as figuratively, Heywood manages to *domesticate* Plautus: the events take on a homely immediacy. Still on the lookout for new material ten years later, Heywood turned to two other comedies of Plautus. In both cases he appropriated plot, characters, even stretches of dialogue; matched the whole thing up with one of the lurid plots that make up Italian *novelle*; and produced a double-plot tragicomedy distantly related to *Cymbeline* and more immediately to Beaumont and Fletcher.

At first glance *The Captives; or, The Lost Recovered*, acted at the Drury Lane Cockpit in 1624, seems to represent a heightening of realism and satire at the expense of romance. Nothing about the thoroughly anglicized characters would make an audience suspect that the play is a modern-dress version of Plautus's *Rudens*, crossed with a *novella* by Masuccio di Salerno, and provided with an original denouement.[37] Nothing, that is, but the extravagantly romantic situation. By setting the play at Marseilles about a century before his own

36. A. H. Gilbert tallies up "Thomas Heywood's Debt to Plautus" in *JEGP* 12 (1913): 593–611. In addition to Heywood's wholesale appropriations of *Amphitruo*, *Rudens*, and *Mostellaria*, Gilbert considers Plautus's more general influence on all of Heywood's plays.

37. The authorship, date, and sources of *The Captives* are discussed by Alexander Corbin Judson in his edition of the play (New Haven, 1921), pp. 9–25. Judson's endnotes, pp. 151–68, provide a scene-by-scene account of Heywood's borrowings and departures from Plautus, including quotations of passages that are translated directly or closely imitated

day, Heywood perhaps faces up to this discrepancy between characters and situation and distances the action just enough to make it believable that a "male bawd" (Labrax in Plautus; Mildew in Heywood) could pretend to sell one of his slave girls (Palaestra/Palestra) to the wealthy young merchant who is in love with her (Plesidippus/Raphael), then try to sail away with her and the fellow slave who is her confidante (Ampelisca/Scribonia) to a more lucrative market, and end up getting shipwrecked in a remote location where a divine (Ptolemocratia/the Abbot), an old merchant who has lost his fortune and is living in exile (Daemones/John Ashburne), the wealthy young man's wily servant (Thrachalio/clown), and a local fisherman (Gripus) together manage to reveal that the object of the young man's desire is not a slave girl at all but none other than the old merchant's long-lost daughter. For all the Englishness he gives to the characters and what they say, however, Heywood has made *The Captives* a far more romantic play than Plautus's original in at least three ways: he has multiplied the incidents and complicated the love interest, he has supplied a subplot that extends the range of emotions that the play asks from an audience, and he has contrived an ending that not only pairs up all the lovers but affirms a romantic ideal specially tailored to suit his audience of merchant Londoners.

Many events that are only narrated in Plautus are dramatized in Heywood: the young man making his deal with the slave trader, the storm and shipwreck, the jealousy of the old merchant's wife when he takes the slave girl in, the wife's tearful reunion with her daughter when her identity is revealed, the matching up of the daughter with the wealthy young man. There are possibilities for big dramatic effects in all these scenes, but they serve also to enhance the romantic attachment between the lovers. Plautus gives us no reason to doubt that Plesidippus has fallen in love with Palaestra as one of her customers. Raphael, however, is enthralled with Palestra precisely because she is triumphantly chaste. His friend Treadway tries to dissuade him from his choice, but handily falls in love at first sight with Palestra's confidante when the time comes and so doubles the amorous interest in the play with one twang of Cupid's bow. It is the young man's servant who asks for the second girl in Plautus, strongly suggesting that she genuinely is a slave and not yet another wellborn damsel in distress as she turns out to be in Heywood.

By crossing Plautus's play with Masuccio's tale of a jealous husband who traps and strangles his faithful wife's would-be lover, Heywood likewise heightens romantic interest in the play. Whatever claims to fame Heywood may have, his tact as a matcher-up of plots is not one of them. Masuccio and the *Rudens* may not be as oddly sorted as *The Four Prentices of London, together with The Conquest of Jerusalem*, but the only thing the two plots share in common is passion as a motive. In *Rudens* the temple where the shipwrecked slave girls first take refuge is dedicated, appropriately enough, to Venus. Heywood takes the hint and makes it a monastery filled with lustful friars. One priest in particular, Friar John, conceives a passion for Lady Averne, the wife of the monastery's patron. He sends a letter asking for an assignation, receives from Lady Averne a feigned invitation dictated by her incensed husband, and ends up dead at the husband's hands. The gruesomeness of this turn of events is made all the ghastlier by the wisecracks of the duke's servant Denis. What shall they do with the friar's body? "Sir, shall we poppe him in som privy?" (3.3.98). What the duke and Denis in fact do is to pop the body back into the monastery, where a priestly rival finds it, takes it to be alive, and strikes it when it won't reply to him. The hapless fellow friar thinks that he has killed his adversary and takes the blame—until the duke owns up in the play's last scene, just in time to receive a pardon from the offstage king, who is never even mentioned in the play until he is needed to tidy up the ending. Shades here of Beaumont and Fletcher. Inescapably, this lurid subplot colors our perception of the main plot. Plautus's slave trader comes to look all the more sinister, passion as a motive operates on more than one level, and the satiric thrust of Plautus's single plot is diffused in the subplot with its distinctively lurid tone. In effect, Plautus's comedy becomes a tragicomedy.

To Heywood's practiced eye it must have seemed shocking that Plautus failed to provide a big pairing-off scene to end the play. Heywood remedies that. Once Palestra's parentage has been revealed, the young man does indeed go off with her father's blessing to claim her in marriage, but Plautus ends the play on a mercenary note. The ruined old merchant gets back not only his daughter but his fortune. When Gripus, the fisherman who serves the old merchant, finds the slave trader's lost chest of gold, the old merchant claims it for his own and strikes a deal with the slave trader to split it between them. Heywood's merchant nobly gives the fortune to the fisherman who found it—a gesture he can well afford, since the storm has washed up not only his long-lost daughter but his long-lost brother from London with the news that the old merchant's creditors are all dead and that he has inherited twenty-five thousand pounds from his uncle. In Plautus the emphasis falls on the merchant's trickiness; in Heywood, on his magnanimity. Here is romance—but with a mercenary side not found at court. The long-lost brother from London turns out to be—who else?—the father of Palestra's confidante and Treadway's ladylove. Financial matters secure all around, Heywood ends *The Captives* with lovers falling into each other's arms. The fact that all this crowd—fathers, daughters, lovers—are exiles from England gives the whole ending a patriotic flourish and dissolves the realism of satire in the wish-fulfillment of romance.

The English Traveler, acted at the Drury Lane Cockpit probably about the same time as *The Captives*, follows Plautus's *Mostellaria* even more closely than *The Captives* follows *Rudens*. Plautus's plot situation provides some of the most uproarious farce in Roman comedy: when the conservative father (Theoproprides/Old Lionel) comes back to town unexpectedly and almost catches his rake of a son (Philolaches/Young Lionel) in the midst of squandering the family fortune, partying with a courtesan (Philematium/Blanda), and wrecking the family house, the tricky servant (Tranio/Reginald) comes to the rescue. He intercepts the father in front of the house, convinces him that the house has been dis-

covered to be haunted and cannot be entered, and persuades
him that the moneylender knocking at the gate has been
financing the son's real-estate speculations, not his debauches.
In the end, of course, the truth comes out, and all is forgiven.
As in *The Silver Age* and *The Captives*, Heywood multiplies
the play's incidents, giving the courtesan two companions and
the son some riotous friends and dramatizing several events
that are only narrated in Plautus's play. Heywood's alteration
in how the whole business ends does more, however, than
liven up the action: it gives the plot a distinctively Renaissance
moral twist. In Plautus it is the son's friend who pleads with
the father and secures his forgiveness; in Heywood the son
himself does the pleading—and reenacts the parable of the
Prodigal Son:

> Y[OUNG] LIO[NEL]. Before you chide, first heere mee,
>   next your Blessing,
>   That on my knees I begge; I have but done
>   Like mis-spent youth, which after wit deere bought,
>   Turnes his Eyes inward, sorrie and ashamed.
>
>   . . .
>
> OLD LIO[NEL]. See what Fathers are,
>   That can three yeeres offences, fowle ones too,
>   Thus in a Minute pardon.

There is one stipulation, however: Young Lionel must give up
"that Wanton," his mistress. "A just Condition," the son
agrees, "and willingly subscrib'd to."[38] No such penance, of
course, is imposed on Plautus's Philolaches. Nowell would
have approved.

The same heavy-handed morality guides the play's other
plot, in fact its main plot, in which the young wife of an old
husband has an affair with a younger man and, like Anne in *A
Woman Killed with Kindness*, dies of grief when her guilt is
exposed. The lusty younger man has a virtuous friend who
loves the wife chastely and determines to leave the country—
hence the play's title—when he finds out about the wife's hid-

---

38. *The English Traveler*, Act Five, in *Dramatic Works*, ed. A. H. Bullen,
Vol. 4 (London, 1885): 82–83. Future quotations are cited in the text.

eous deception with his friend. Only loosely connected in other respects, both plots of *The English Traveler* are thus focused on adultery, and both affirm middle-class morality about such things. As with *The Captives*, this yoking together of classical plot and modern plot has the effect of turning Plautus's original into quite another play. In *The Captives*, the second plot serves to emphasize the tragicomic haps that bring together the well-born slave girl and the young man who loves her; in *The English Traveler* it serves to emphasize the lax morality of the son and his riotous friends.

Heywood's attempts to translate Plautus for the public stage show us, then, the same interplay between satire and romance that we have observed in academic productions of Greek and Roman comedy. The difference lies in what makes up the romantic dream. At the Red Bull, no less than in the great halls of the inns of court, audiences were delighted when obstacles disappeared and lovers were granted their hearts' desires. However, the ruined old merchant of *The Captives* and Lionel the old father in *The English Traveler* show us a different kind of romantic hero, a figure more at home doing business on the Exchange than shipwrecked on a distant seacoast. The fact that Heywood specifies just what the old merchant's new-found fortune is—twenty-five thousand pounds, an astounding sum in the 1620s—lets us know we are witnessing a dream vision that had just as much attraction for city merchants as battles on distant shores had for courtiers accoutered for Queen Elizabeth's Accession Day tilts. The old merchant displays his heroism in his magnanimity; Old Lionel, in his generous forgiveness of his profligate son. From a father's point of view, the Prodigal Son pageant that ends *The English Traveler* is finally part of the play's romance, its wish-fulfilling side rather than its realistic moral side. The same is true of Palestra's highly improbable chastity in *The Captives*. Plautus on the Jacobean public stage shows us the same interplay between satire and romance that we find on the stages of Elizabethan private households, with the same emphasis on morality and romance. What differs is the substance of the romantic and moral ideals. Dreams of chivalric heroism give way to dreams of financial security.

III

Restoration mores—or at least the mores that we see in Res-
toration comedy—would seem closer than Renaissance mores
to the satiric spirit of Plautus and Terence. What could be fur-
ther from the strictures of sixteenth-century schoolmasters
than the protagonists' sensual self-indulgence in such seven-
teenth-century morality plays as *The Man of Mode* and *The
Kind Keeper*? The kept ladies who entice young men to finan-
cial ruin in Plautus and Terence may be an embarrassment in
"The House of Chivalry," but they are perfectly at home in
the environs of St. James' Square. Restoration dramatists are,
moreover, much more historically self-conscious than their
Renaissance counterparts. The neoclassical Quarrel between
Ancients and Moderns is predicated on an awareness of the
historical differences that separate past from present. Nowell
and his peers may have read Terence's comedies as if they were
contemporary morality plays; Restoration playwrights were
far too sophisticated for that. Thomas Heywood may have
disguised the fact that *The Captives* and *The English Traveler*
are reworkings of plays by Plautus and Terence; Sir Charles
Sedley in *Bellamira; or, The Mistress* and John Dryden in
Amphitryon proudly advertise that they are adapting Roman
comedy to English manners. They set up an active dialogue
between ancient models and modern experience.

In his preface to the printed text, Sedley, for example,
explains how he came to write *Bellamira*. The play "was orig-
inally *Maenanders* in the Greek, *Terence's* in the Latin; whose
great names gave me a Curiosity to try how I cou'd make it
run in English: A Friend came to my Chamber as I was upon
the first Act, he seem'd to approve my design: I told him I
found it extream easie to go through with: And what if he
cou'd get it Acted under his own or anothers Name, I wou'd
finish it for him: But for I know not what reasons he cou'd
not do it; and I was oblig'd to own it my self, or my friend
had lost his third day."[39] Though no cast list survives, the play

39. Sir Charles Sedley, *Bellamira, or The Mistress*, in *The Poetical and Dra-*

was probably staged for the first time at Drury Lane on May 12, 1687, when James II was in the audience. To make Terence's *Eunuchus* "run in English," Sedley translated and adapted everything but the denouement of Terence's play, while interspersing among Terence's ten scenes an equal number of new scenes that set in motion two new subplots and give the audience interior views of the major characters, psychologically as well as scenically. All of Terence's scenes take place, of course, on a public street; Sedley takes the audience off to bowers in Kensington and Knightsbridge and inside Bellamira's house, where the audience gets to see her conspire with her friend Thisbe in totally feminine surroundings. The result of Sedley's alterations and additions is a play that is even sharper than Terence's in the satiric view it takes of sexual passion.

In superficial ways Sedley manages quite handily to anglicize Terence's Romans while keeping their Latin distinctiveness. Phaedria, the profligate, becomes Keepwell; his brother Chaerea becomes Lionel; Thraso, the *miles gloriosus*, becomes Dangerfield; Gnatho, the ruined nobleman who makes his way in the world by following Thraso around and flattering him, becomes Smoothly. Place names in the West End and the immediate countryside localize the action. There were no slaves in seventeenth-century London, of course, so Terence's servants all become the friends of their masters. Parmeno, Phaedria's clever servant who stage-manages most of the high jinks, becomes a Falstaffian boon companion named Merrywell. Sedley characteristically tosses his efforts off as the diversion of a few hours, but transferring Terence's *Eunuchus* to seventeenth-century London is not without its problems: plenty of Restoration comedies show us braggadocio Thrasos whose mistresses lead them by the nose, but in how many do we see a suitor use a eunuch's disguise to rape the lady he loves? These events, Sedley admits, "cou'd not be omitted, nor well fitted to our Stage without some expressions or Met-

---

matic Works, ed. V. De Sola Pinto (1928; repr. New York, 1969), 2: 5. Future references are cited in the text.

aphors, which by persons of a ticklish imagination, or over-
quick sense that way, seem'd too lascivious for modest Ears
. . ." (Pref. 19–23). For all his feigned fastidiousness, Sedley
has in fact used Terence's salacious subject as an excuse to fill
the play with salacious speeches that Terence never dreamed
of. Phaedria's love-languishing for Thais was, as we have seen,
a favorite occasion for Renaissance commentators to warn
young men about the follies of passion. Sedley's Keepwell
suffers just as intensely, but he is a great deal more direct in
bragging to Merrywell about his relationship to Bellamira,
the Restoration Thais: "when my *Bell.* frowns I had rather be
in a Sea-Fight for the time, I'll say that for her, tho 'tis soon
over. I gave her but a dozen pair of *Marshal* Gloves, and she
was in the purest Humour all day! We took the Air in the after-
noon, Sup't and went to Bed together" (1.1.28–33). What
would Nowell have made of that! Dangerfield is just as blunt.
When Bellamira has gotten rid of Keepwell so as to entertain
Dangerfield, the lusty soldier tells her, "I long to play my
lower Tire of Guns at thee" (3.1.195). Terence's Thraso is not
clever enough to think of such a line. In Sedley's play, Mer-
rywell gets his own chance to enjoy Bellamira's favors but
flubs his chance because he has, as usual, drunk too much
wine, "that Aeternal Foe to better sport" (4.6.2). No more
overindulgence, he declares. Not to worry, Bellamira replies:
"Your Pennance is too severe, meerly for a sin of Omission"
(4.6.19–20).

The lusty intrigues in Terence's play are heightened by Sed-
ley's two new subplots. In one of them Dangerfield's boasts
are hilariously deflated when Bellamira and Merrywell restage
Gad's Hill by disguising themselves and jumping Dangerfield
in a remote walk in Kensington. Merrywell's own shortcom-
ings with Bellamira are exposed when the two of them go off
afterwards to celebrate the success of their ruse. Sedley's other
subplot follows Merrywell's romantic fortunes with Bella-
mira's friend Thisbe, whose part in the play is much expanded
from Thais's maidservant Pythia. Ostensibly Thisbe's
guardian, Merrywell is in fact Thisbe's lover and ends the play
as her husband—that, despite Bellamira's experienced advice

to Thisbe early in the play: "Get Mony enough and you can never want a Husband. A Husband is a good Bit to Close ones Stomach with, when Love's Feast is over. Who wou'd begin a Meal with Cheese?" (1.3.115–18). Thais's progression from ward to mistress to wife is typical of the deviously satirical course that true love runs in the play.

All ends happily, of course, but Sedley's one big departure from Terence is in how he brings this denouement off. No father figure appears to forgive Chaerea/Lionel for his rape and take Thais/Bellamira into the family's protection so that Phaedria/Keepwell can enjoy her all to himself; Sedley's lovers manage to work things out quite tidily by themselves. Like Phaedria, Keepwell finally beats out Thraso/Dangerfield (not to mention Merrywell and most of the other men in the play) for Bellamira's favor; unlike Phaedria, he makes a big point of reminding the audience that he does *not* plan to marry her:

> My *Bell.* and I will lead a marri'd Life,
> Bating the odious Names of Man and Wife;
> In Chains of Love alone we will be ty'd,
> And every Night I'll use her like a Bride.   (5.1.618–21)

All such cynical protestations to the contrary, Sedley's play is finally far more romantic than Terence's. The perfect foils to Keepwell and Bellamira are Lionel, Keepwell's brother, and Isabella, the nobly born damsel who was stolen as a child by kidnappers, purchased in Jamaica by one of Bellamira's mother's admirers, raised by Bellamira's mother as a lady of quality, lost through debt, bought by Dangerfield in Spain, rescued from Dangerfield by Bellamira, fallen in love with by Lionel—and raped by him in a eunuch's disguise. Not the likeliest beginning for living happily forever after, one has to admit. Terence's Chaerea pulls the eunuch's disguise trick— we have seen already how he boasts about it to Antipho—and does indeed marry the girl when she turns out to be nobly born. A nonspeaking part, Terence's Pamphilia never gets a chance to let the audience know how *she* feels about the whole thing. Sedley's Isabella, by contrast, is a fully rounded character—and she is already in love with Lionel before he beds her. By casting her as an exotic, melancholy "Lady of Spain," a refugee from one of Dryden's heroic dramas, Sedley almost succeeds in turning the misadventures of Terence's Pamphilia, stolen in childhood by pirates and sold as a slave, into a believable seventeenth-century story. The day before she left Spain for England, Isabella just happened to kneel next to Lionel in church. It was love at first sight on both sides. Back in England, neither learns the other's true identity, however, until after the rape, when all is of course forgiven. "I hold her Innocent, as violated Temples," Lionel maintains (5.1.314–15). For her part Isabella declares:

> My heart was your's, when we first met in *Spain*.
> You seiz'd the rest somewhat too rudely here:
> But I am your Wife, and now am all Obedience.   (5.1.552–55)

As so often in Restoration comedy, the audience gets first to eat its wedding cake and then have it, too.

Sedley's additional scenes inside Bellamira's house allow the audience to savor the contrast between Isabella's innocence and Bellamira's worldly experience. When Isabella confesses that she can never love anyone else but the stranger who knelt beside her in Spain, Bellamira's ridicule knows no bounds:

> BELL[AMIRA]. Pretty Innocence! this is a Nation of such men thou talk'st of; every Street affords a dozen of 'em. Come, thou shalt Love, and Love, and Love again, never fear it.
> THIS[BE]. We'l shew her the Park, the Playhouse, and the Drawing-Room.
> BELL[AMIRA]. She needs no Paint, for Complexion, but 'twill not be amiss to use Juniper Water, for good Humour, she is so melancholy, and looks as if she would not be acquainted.
> THIS[BE]. It is fit men make the advance.
> BELL[AMIRA]. Some are such Jades, they must be Spur'd up, with a quick Eye, or wanton Glance.   (2.2.86–98)

Only slightly compromised by rape, Isabella's innocence triumphs in the end—but so, too, does Bellamira's experience. Each gets the man she wants, and each gets him on the terms she wants: Isabella, in marriage; Bellamira, in adulterous passion. The contrast between romance in plot situa-

tion and realism in characterization, so typical of Terence's
plays, is turned by Sedley into a thematic contrast between
innocence and experience, so typical of Restoration comedy.
The irony of it all is that experience, not innocence, is charged
with romantic power. Thus, the satiric impulse in Sedley's
comedy is rather less earnest than it first appears. Like the
witty couples in Etheredge, Dryden, and Congreve, Sedley's
lovers are just as happy to cast an ironic look at themselves as
at society, but they play out a plot that in its own way is just
as romantic as the *Triumph of Love* at the court of Henry
VIII—a plot that ends with adultery rewarded and wit trium-
phant. The result is a blend of romanticism tempered by expe-
rience that is distinctve to Restoration theater. Jack may
indeed get Jill, but not before he has first enjoyed Arabella,
Belinda, and Cecilia, and even then he is unlikely to do any-
thing so déclassé as to *marry* her. Not chivalric heroism, not
financial security, but moral license is the stuff of romantic
dreaming in Restoration comedy.

In Dryden's *Amphitryon*, first acted at Drury Lane in
October 1690, we discover the same interplay between satire
and romance, but set off by a much more sophisticated sense
of how classical models intersect with modern experience.
Where Sedley assumes compatibility, Dryden plays up incon-
gruity. The result, for the playwright, for the audience, and
for the characters themselves, is a sense of self-irony that
stands at the farthest possible remove from the medievalizing
impulses of Nowell and humanist scholars of the sixteenth
century. Betterton as Jupiter and Mrs. Bracegirdle as Alcmena
set Dryden's *Amphitryon* on a course of popularity that
extended well into the eighteenth century, when only *The
Spanish Friar* was revived more often among Dryden's plays.[40]
Incidental music by Purcell and several spectacular set pieces
to show off the Drury Lane's stage machinery also contrib-
uted to the play's spectacular first performance at Drury Lane

40. The play's acting history is discussed by Earl Miner in his edition of
the play in Dryden, *Works*, Vol. 15 (Berkeley, 1976): 460–62; the first per-
formance and subsequent revivals are cataloged in *The London Stage 1660–
1800*, pt. 1, ed. William Van Lennep (Carbondale, Ill., 1965): 389–91.

in October 1690; but more than actors, music, and scenery, it was Dryden's success in acclimatizing Plautus's characters to England that impressed contemporary commentators the most. Ordering a copy of the script from Dryden's publisher, Luke Milbourne passed along his hope that Dryden would go on to "endenizen" all of Plautus's plays.[41] Cultural adjustment was precisely the goal that Dryden had set himself, according to the dedicatory epistle that prefaces the printed script. The play's inspiration—Dryden mentions this with pride—was not only Plautus's Latin original but Molière's French adaptation, first performed in Paris twenty-two years before. "I will not give you the trouble," Dryden writes to Sir William Leveson-Gower, "of acquainting you what I have added, or alter'd in either of them, so much it may be for the worse; but only that the difference of our Stage from the *Roman* and the *French* did so require it. But I am affraid, for my own Interest, the World will too easily discover, that more than half of it is mine; and that the rest is rather a lame Imitation of their Excellencies, than a just Translation."[42] Modesty is always to be suspected in a playwright. The parts of *Amphitryon* taken from Plautus directly and from Plautus via Molière are seldom just translated, but neither are they "imitated," lamely or otherwise. Rather, they are transformed into a remarkably original piece of theater that sets romantic dreaming and satiric laughter in creative opposition.

Often enough the play moves behind the proscenium arch to open up to the audience the world of heroic illusions that lies beyond. The presence of Jupiter, Mercury, Apollo, and Molière's personification of Night allows Dryden to thrill his audience with spectacular set pieces that might have been expected in tragedy or heroic drama but hardly in comedy. At the play's beginning, Mercury and Apollo "descend in several Machines" (s.d., 1.1.1), followed shortly by Jupiter (s.d., 1.1.56) and by Night, who "appears above in her Chariot"

41. Quoted in Miner, ed., *Works*, 15: 461.
42. Ibid., 15: 225. Future references from *Amphitryon* are taken from this edition and are cited in the text.

(S.D., I.1.203). Later Jupiter and Mercury woo their mortal lovers in a pair of interludes that combines song and dance (3.1.583ff. and 4.1.482ff.). Mercury's device is a full-dress pastoral, complete with a song to Iris, "a fantastick Dance," and a sung "Pastoral Dialogue betwixt *Thyrsis* and *Iris*." Finally, to stage-manage the play's happy ending, Jupiter "appears in a Machine," amid thunder (S.D., 5.1.387ff.). It is not the gods' propensity for spectacle that Dryden emphasizes, however. Quite the contrary, it is their petty humanity. Jupiter's mission to earth is "some Petticoat Affair," Mercury surmises in the play's first scene, and the gossip he exchanges there with Apollo makes Olympus sound like Hyde Park:

MERC[URY]. There has been a devillish Quarrel, I can tell you, betwixt *Jupiter* and *Juno*: She threaten'd to sue him in the Spiritual Court, for some Matrimonial Omissions; and he stood upon his Prerogative. Then she hit him on the Teeth of all his Bastards; and your Name and mine were us'd with less reverence than became our Godships. They were both in their Cups; and at the last the matter grew so high, that they were ready to have thrown Stars at one another's Heads.
PHOEB[US]. 'Twas happy for me that I was at my Vocation, driving Daylight about the World; but I had rather stand my Father's Thunderbolts, than my Step-mother's Railing.

(I.1.22–32)

Such homey details could not be further from the neoclassical dignity that the gods maintain in Molière's play. Dryden's confusion of things divine and things domestic, of romance and satire, produces ironies of three kinds: sexual, social, and political.

Like his English predecessor in *The Birth of Hercules*, Dryden plays up the love interest in Plautus's play, but whereas the model for romance in *The Birth of Hercules* was Chrétien de Troyes, here it is *Marriage a la Mode*. Jupiter speaks with the same sensuality and the same disdain for matrimony as a Restoration rake. Taking his leave of Alcmena after his long night of pleasure, Jupiter, in the guise of Amphitryon, has to confess to Alcmena,

> But yet one Scruple pains me at my parting;
> I love so nicely, that I cannot bear
> To owe the Sweets of Love which I have tasted,
> To the submissive Duty of a Wife:
> Tell me: and sooth my Passion e're I go,
> That in the kindest Moments of the Night,
> When you gave up your self to Love and me,
> You thought not of a Husband, but a Lover.

Taking Jupiter as indeed her husband, and uninstructed in Restoration morality, Alcmena is understandably taken aback. Jupiter reassures her:

> The being happy is not half the Joy;
> The manner of the happiness is all!
> In me (my charming Mistris) you behold
> A Lover that disdains a Lawful Title;
> Such as of Monarchs to successive Thrones:
> The Generous Lover holds by force of Arms;
> And claims his Crown by Conquest. (2.2.60–67, 81–87)

Here is not only the sensualist's exquisite boredom and the gourmand-lover's refined taste but the despot's casual tyranny. We shall have occasion to examine Jupiter's politics later.

To complicate the confusion and to widen the play's social range, Dryden adds a new pair to the cast of lovers. We have not only the Amphitruo-Alcmena and the Sosia-Bromia of Plautus's and Molière's plays but a couple who are altogether Dryden's invention: Alcmena's waiting-woman Phaedra and her suitor Gripus, a corrupt judge who has accompanied Amphitryon on his military expedition. A gold digger who never misses a chance to extract a bribe, Phaedra (no doubt pronounced "*Fee*-dra") is a "mercenary Mistress" to match Gripus (surely he "grips" rather than "gripes") as a "mercenary Magistrate" (5.1.10–11). Not only that, but Dryden complicates affairs further by turning Plautus's and Molière's happy pairs into unhappy triangles. In his disguise as Sosia, Mercury falls in love not with Bromia but with Phaedra; when Mercury promises better gifts than Gripus can offer,

Phaedra returns the compliment. Dryden's inspiration was perhaps Plautus's triangle of Jupiter-Juno-Alcmena.

The sexual edge to these intrigues is far sharper in Dryden's *Amphitryon* than it is in Plautus's original. Double-entendre leers in line after line. Mercury first falls in love with Phaedra, as he tells us himself, through his divine power of viewing her naked through her clothes (2.2.36–38). Dressed in lowly servant's garb, he plies his passion to Phaedra even before he has greeted Bromia, his ostensible wife. In disdaining his overtures along with his gifts of war booty, Phaedra sets up a most unladylike pun about his "load" that Mercury gleefully takes up and puts to even more graphic uses:

PHAED[RA]. . . . What *Bromia*, I say, make hast; here's a Vessel of yours, full fraighted, that's going off, without paying Duties.
MERC[URY]. Since thou wilt not let me steal Custom, She shall have all the Cargo I have gotten in the Wars: but thou mightst have lent me a little Creek to smuggle in.   (2.2.157–62)

Jupiter's sexual energy presses for release just as insistently. He tells us so in his own words: "make haste to Bed," he begs Alcmena when she asks to hear about the war,

> There let me tell my story, in thy Arms;
> There in the gentle pauses of our Love,
> Betwixt our dyings, e're we live again,
> Thou shalt be told of the Battel, and success:
> Which I shall oft begin, and then break off;
> For Love will often interrupt my Tale,
> And make sweet confusion in our talk,
> That thou shalt ask, and I shall answer things,
> That are not of a piece: but, patch'd with Kisses,
> And Sighs, and Murmurs, and imperfect Speech;
> And Nonsense shall be Eloquent, in Love.   (1.2.100–111)

Just as important in charging the reunion scene with sexual power are Phaedra's stalling tactics to secure a bribe: she has made Alcmena promise to sleep with *her* that night, so that wife and husband-apparent have to buy her off to get their double bed.

In keeping with the mores of Restoration comedy, the

ending to these intrigues is altogether more cynical than Plautus's celebration of Hercules' birth. Here is nothing so socially discommoding as a birth, only a prophecy of it. Dryden perhaps intends a sentimental touch when he arranges that Alcmena, forced to choose between the real and the false Amphitryons, instinctively goes to her husband, but no sooner has he pushed her away with the cry of adulterer than she swoons contendedly in the imposter's arms. The one event that decisively gives the whole affair its cynical stamp is the business contract that Mercury and Phaedra draw up before indulging their mutual desire:

PHAED[RA]. Begin, begin; Heads of Articles to be made, &c. betwixt *Mercury*, God of Thieves——
MERC[URY]. And *Phaedra*, Queen of Gypsies.——*Imprimis*, I promise to buy and settle upon her an Estate, containing Nine thousand Acres of Land, in any part of *Boeotia*, to her own liking.
PHAED[RA]. Provided always, that no part of the said Nine thousand Acres shall be upon, or adjoyning to Mount *Parnassus*: for I will not be fobb'd off with a Poetical Estate.
MERC[URY]. *Memorandum*, that she be always constant to me; and admit no other Lover.
PHAED[RA]. *Memorandum*, unless it be a Lover that offers more: and that the Constancy shall not exceed the Settlement.   (5.1.343–55)

Substitute English place names for Boeotia and Parnassus, and you have the ending of a typical Restoration comedy: self-interest triumphs, cleverness is rewarded, passion and property pair off.

Mercury and Phaedra's business contract is typical of how Dryden has updated Plautus's play to match the social mores of seventeenth-century London. That is no more than Sedley did for Terence's *Eunuchus*. Sedley may have found it easy to acclimatize Phaedria as Keepwell, Thraso as Dangerfield, and Thais as Bellamira, but Jupiter and Mercury prove rather less at home in West End society. Dryden reminds us of that incongruity constantly. "Why should I love this *Phaedra*?" immortal Mercury asks himself just before he starts to woo this mortal little flirt: "She's Interessed, and a Jilt into the Bargain. Three thousand years hence, there will be a whole

Nation of such Women, in a certain Country that will be call'd
France; and there's a Neighbour Island too, where Men of that
Country will be all Interest. Oh what a precious Generation
will that be, which the Men of the Island shall Propagate out
of the Women of the Continent!" (2.2.103–11). The manners
may be immediate, but Dryden never lets us forget that the
play is taking place three thousand years in the past. Perhaps
that is why the characters several times make their quibbles in
Latin, not in English. When Phaedra teases Sosia that he looks
as if he is "in a brown Study," he admits to being "a little *co-
gitabund*, or so" over all the confusions in identities, his own
included (3.1.347–51). As a judge, Gripus uses Latin as his
stock in trade. When he cannot tell the real Amphitryon from
the false he exclaims, "In sadness I think they are both Jug-
glers: Here's nothing, and here's nothing: and then *hiccius doc-
cius*, and they are both here again" (5.1.210–12). All these
details invite us to play off past against present, but it is the
spectacle of gods cavorting with men that constitutes the big-
gest irony in the play. The effect is double: it scales the gods
down to human size at the same time that it blows up human
passions to preposterous proportions. We have listened
already to Mercury and Apollo gossiping about Juno's threat
to sue Jupiter "in the Spiritual Court, for some Matrimonial
Omissions" (1.1.23–24). Near the end of the play, Phaedra
leaps at Mercury's offer to stellify her as if she were a seven-
teenth-century lady leaping at the offer of a title. Mercury's
promise is as matter of fact as if he were indeed peddling a
peerage:

MERC[URY]. Thou *Gripus*, and you *Bromia*; stay with *Phaedra*:
    Let their affairs alone, and mine we ours:
    Amphitryon's Rival shall appear a God:
    But know before-hand, I am *Mercury*;
    Who want not Heav'n, while *Phaedra* is on Earth.
BROM[IA]. But, and't please your Lordship, is my fellow *Phaedra*
    to be, exalted into the Heav'ns and made a Star?
PHAED[RA]. When that comes to pass, if you look up a-nights, I
    shall remember old kindness, and vouchsafe to twinkle on you.
                                              (5.1.291–99)

If we suspect that what we are hearing here is a satire of aristocratic prerogatives, we are confirmed a few minutes later when Sosia points out that Mercury's contract with Phaedra has no force, since, as Phaedra herself has to agree, "Gods, and great Men, are never to be sued; for they can always plead priviledge of Peerage . . ." (5.1.380–84). It is Phaedra, indeed, who has the last word in the play. In the epilogue she sets heroic past and hypocritical present in sharp juxtaposition, to wonderfully satiric effect:

> I'm thinking, (and it almost makes me mad,)
> How sweet a time, those Heathen Ladies had.
> Idolatry was ev'n their Gods own trade;
> They Worshipt the fine Creatures they had made.
> *Cupid* was chief of all the Deities;
> And Love was all the fashion, in the Skies.

Adultery then could hardly be a sin, when Jupiter himself set such a good example. And with what civility he behaved toward his conquests, keeping his trysts secret unlike the boastful rakes of today, rewarding the cuckolded husbands with honors, turning his bastard sons into stars! The present age, of course, is far more moral. When, after two thousand years of sexual exploits, Jupiter and his priests "grew old,"

> Severity of Life did next begin;
> (And always does, when we no more can Sin.)
> That Doctrine, too, so hard in Practice lyes,
> That, the next Age may see another rise.
> Then, Pagan Gods may, once again, succeed;
> And *Jove*, or *Mars*, be ready, at our need,
> To get young Godlings; and, so, mend our breed.
>   (Epi. 1–6, 23, 26–32)

This intermeddling of mortal failings and immortal foistings-on allows Dryden to set his characters in the same mock-heroic poses he does in his verse satires. The result, in *Amphitryon* as in those poems, is a satire of Restoration manners that is even more searing than in Dryden's straight comedies.

Dryden has more on his mind, however, than fashions and foibles. The prologue to *Amphitryon* begins with what seems to be an allusion to the proscribed prologue, with unflattering reflections on the "Glorious Revolution," that Dryden had provided for Betterton's *The Prophetess; or, The History of Diocletian* a few months before:

> The lab'ring Bee, when his sharp Sting is gone,
> Forgets his Golden Work, and turns a Drone:
> Such is a Satyr, when you take away
> That Rage, in which his Noble Vigour lay.   (Pro., 1–4)

For all his protestations to the contrary, Dryden has not yet turned a drone; he has simply become more careful about which flowers he lands on. As a corrupt judge, Gripus offers a rather generalized caricature of corruption in high places— "He sells Justice as he uses, fleeces the Rich Rebells, and hangs up the Poor," as Mercury observes (2.2.123–24)—but Jupiter represents the kind of arbitrary monarch that William III so conspicuously was not. We have observed already how Jupiter delights to portray himself, not as a lawful husband, but as a ravisher who imposes his will by force: "The Generous Lover holds by force of Arms; / And claims his Crown by Conquest" (2.2.86–87). Mercury sums up Jupiter's Hobbesian politics in one terse phrase to Apollo: "I confess if he had been a Man, he might have been a Tyrant, if his Subjects durst have call'd him to account" (1.1.137–38). The political allegory that Cicero relished in Roman comedy flourished anew when Roman comedy reached the Restoration stage.

Like all the productions of Greek and Latin comedy that we have surveyed, Dryden's *Amphitryon* shows us the dynamic interplay between the two contradictory versions of experience that framed the Roman stage: romance and satire. Other productions may have deflected the audience's attention to satire at the expense of romance or to romance at the expense of satire; Dryden plays them off against each other. In the amorous gods of Plautus's *Amphitruo*, Dryden found heroes who enjoyed the sexual license and the latitude of action that constituted his Restoration audience's own romantic myth; he also found personal jealousies, social snobbery, and political peremptoriness that cried out for satiric redress. Jupiter and

Mercury may show us immortal passions on an epic scale, but we see also their petty humanity. Amphitryon and Alcmena may show us mortal limitations, but we see also their mortal decency. Romantic desire is tempered by satiric detachment. In that ageless antimony lies classical comedy's truth to human experience.

v · *Tragedy*

THE HEROINE stood over the cold mangled body of the man she desired, admitted that her love had caused his death, and prepared to free herself from the sexual passion that consumed her still:

> The innocent boy, charged with inchastity,
> Lies dead, untouched by sin, untouched by shame.
>
> . . .
>
> My guilty breast awaits the avenging sword;
> My blood is shed to pay the dues of death
> For one who never sinned.

And with those words the schoolboy dressed up in a matron's gown feigned to kill himself, falling down to join his classmate, an "innocent boy" in actual fact, as he already lay in semblance of death. To the young scholars and other onlookers gathered in the hall of Westminster School in the mid-1540s the deaths of Phaedra and Hippolytus posed an ethical dilemma. The speeches that Seneca gives Phaedra pointedly mention "sin" (*crimen*), yet the lust that overwhelms Phaedra is a spiteful visitation by Venus, a "monstrous doom" as unwillingly laid upon her as was her mother's lust for the bull-man Minotaur.[1] Guilty or innocent? The situation must have seemed all the more perplexing to an audience who were witnessing the first recorded performance of a classical tragedy in England.

Like Pomponius, when he introduced the same play to a Roman audience sixty years before, Alexander Nowell, headmaster of Westminster School, first sent out a Prologue to set things up. In doing so he was following the example not only of Latin comedy but of native English entertainments, in which poets would recite their own works to assemblies of noble listeners. Seneca's story of Hippolytus and Phaedra, says the Prologue, "plays upon" (*alludit*) the story in Genesis

---

1. Seneca, *Phaedra*, 1195–98, trans. E. F. Watling in Seneca, *Four Tragedies* (Harmondsworth and Baltimore, 1966), p. 146.

of Joseph and Potiphar's wife—and at no great distance, either
(*non procul*).² Genesis 37–43 recounts how Joseph, sold into
slavery by his jealous brothers, has managed to rise to a place
of responsiblity in his master Potiphar's house when Poti-
phar's wife turns a lustful eye upon him and offers him her
bed. Joseph refuses. "Beholde, my master knoweth not what
is in the house, and all that he hath, that hath he put under my
hande. And there is no man so greate in the house as I, and he
hath kepte nothinge fro[m] me, excepte the: for thou art his
wife. How shulde I then do so great evell, and synne agaynst
God?"³ Potiphar's wife takes her revenge: to her husband she
accuses Joseph of making the very proposition he has refused
from her, and Joseph lands in prison.

    However striking the parallel, the Biblical story ends rather
more inspirationally than the pagan myth. Far from meeting
Hippolytus's horrible death, Joseph cleverly manages with
Jehovah's help to turn this temporary setback into yet another
triumph, and by explaining the Pharaoh's dreams he ends up
as the ruler's right-hand man. To a humanist educator's point
of view such an ending, with its ultimate reward for virtue,
made for an even better "tragedy" than Seneca's *Hippolytus*.
One of the first results of serious study of Latin tragedy was a
widespread attempt to Christianize classical tragedy—or,
rather, to classicize Christian drama—by applying Seneca's
florid diction, five-act structure, and sententious choruses to

    2. Transcribed from Bodleian MS Brasenose College 31, fols. 25ff., my
translation: "Senecae tragici poetae hyppolitum, spectatores candidissimi,
apud vos acturi, non formidamus haec praefari, ut inter tragicos omnes latinos
non tantum primus, sed propemodum etiam solus—vel fabii iudicio—dignus
[est] quod legatur est hic Seneca; ita inter omnes huius tragedias longe primas
obtinet, haec quam sumus representaturi hyppolitus fabula, ad eius, tum apud
alios omnes, tum apud vos praecippue, utpote sacrarum literarum Audiosos,
commendationem etiam hoc accedit, quod a iosephi et potipharis uxoris his-
toria in sacris genesios libris prodita haec hyppoliti fabula non procul alludit:
et quod illic citra omnem controversiam revera gestum legitur."
    3. *The Coverdale Bible 1535*, intro. S. L. Greenslade (Folkestone, 1975), fol.
17ᵛ (Genesis 39:8–9 in later translations). The Geneva Bible (1560) provides
this marginal note: "The feare of God preserved him against her continual
temtations" (*The Geneva Bible*, intro. L. E. Berry [Madison, 1969]).

Biblical subjects. Leicester Bradner's checklist of extant neo-
Latin plays from all over Renaissance Europe reveals that
Joseph, so exemplary in turning every trial into stunning suc-
cess, emerged during the course of the sixteenth century as the
single most popular subject for dramatization. The Christian
Hippolytus, Joseph dressed up in the trappings of Seneca, was
the "tragic" counterpart to the Prodigal Son dressed down in
the trappings of Terence.[4] About the rest of Westminster
School's production of Seneca's *Hippolytus* we have no record,
but Nowell's prologue prepares the audience to view Phaedra,
not as Seneca's wretch overwhelmed by a lust she recognizes
as evil yet cannot control, but as a calculating temptress; Hip-
polytus emerges, not as Seneca's austere, fanatical misogynist,
but as a martyr to integrity, trust, and the fear of God. Sen-
eca's *Hippolytus* becomes, in effect, a morality play. Only by
so regarding it could Nowell's audience make sense of what
they were seeing. The 1540s may have witnessed Roger
Ascham's translation of Sophocles' *Philoctetes* and George
Buchanan's Latin versions of Euripides' *Alcestis* and *Medea*,
but more representative of what audiences actually were
seeing at midcentury are John Bale's Protestant resurrection
play (*c.* 1545), Nicholas Grimalde's Biblical play *Archipropheta*
(*c.* 1547), and the polemical moral plays *Impatient Poverty* (*c.*
1547), *Lusty Juventus* (*c.* 1550), and *Nice Wanton* (*c.* 1550).

Nowell's prologue tosses off the comparison casually and
confidently enough, but to see Hippolytus as Joseph and
Phaedra as Potiphar's wife in fact requires an audience's eyes
to be focused on moral contexts larger than the play itself pro-
vides, not to mention some rather selective hearing of Sen-
eca's lines. That adjustment in the audience's perspective is
just what Nowell's prologue sets out to manage. For all the
similarities to Genesis in incidents of the plot, for all the Stoic
sentiments declaimed by Hippolytus and by the Chorus, the
grim universe of Seneca's play is, ethically speaking, worlds

---

4. Leicester Bradner, "The Latin Drama of the Renaissance (1340–1640),"
Studies in the Renaissance 4 (1957): 31–70. On the Christian Terence tradition,
cf. Frederick S. Boas, *University Drama in the Tudor Age* (Oxford, 1914), pp.
19ff.

away from the justly ordered universe assumed in morality plays. If Hippolytus/Joseph chooses wisely, why is he killed? If Phaedra/Potiphar's wife cannot help her passion, why should she be judged guilty? Those are questions—genuinely tragic questions—that Nowell neither asks nor answers. He and his in-house audience simply read their own moral prejudices into Seneca's script.

From the very first English production of classical tragedy, then, we are faced with a polarity between ancient experience and modern, between the awkward ethical questions posed by classical tragedy and the simple answers offered by Christian dogma. In the world of classical tragedy, larger-than-life heroes with an awesome capacity for action, for suffering, and for eloquence are destroyed by external forces—often very unjust forces—over which they nonetheless triumph in the very act of dying. In the world of medieval morality plays, on the other hand, heroes with the life-size homeliness of Everyman are faced with moral choices and are rewarded by a providential God when they choose rightly and are punished when they choose wrongly. Classical tragedies, Seneca's in particular, make no claims for the justice of the universe; morality plays assume a sometimes inscrutable yet always certain providence. It is, perhaps, the interplay between these polarities, pagan and Christian, that defines the imaginative power of modern tragedy. In gauging that interplay we can discern between 1500 and 1700 three separate periods that coincide with three separate configurations of philosophical outlook, physical space, and social circumstance. During most of the sixteenth century, classical tragedy was acted exclusively within the walls of schools, colleges, the inns of court, and the court of the realm, all of which imposed their moral and political certitudes on the plays. Around the turn of the century, however, several adaptations of classical tragedies began to test the ethical verities of these closed societies in the open spaces of Elizabethan and Jacobean public playhouses. At the Restoration, finally, dramatists found in the heroes of classical tragedy neither malefactors nor paragons of virtue but exemplars of epic aspiration—and opened up yet another set of ethical questions. What we discover in these three different attempts to reconcile ancient scripts with modern experience is the vitality of the Elizabethan and Jacobean public theater. Free from dogmatic special interests, tragedy on the public stage could explore character and situation more searchingly than was possible before the academic and courtly in-groups who used drama as a way of affirming their social identity. Only in that open context were the kinds of ethical questions that Seneca poses allowed to remain in the state of unresolved tension that, in Aristotle's view, characterizies the greatest tragedies.

I

The very fact that Nowell should have chosen a play by Seneca is significant. Whatever criterion we use—date of the *editio princeps*, number of translations, number of vernacular imitations, success in production—Seneca's preeminence in the Renaissance is beyond dispute. Seneca's tragedies were first printed by Andrea Gallus at Ferrara just about the time Pomponius Laetus's students were acting his *Hippolytus* in Rome— fully thirty years before the Aldine editions of Sophocles and Euripides appeared in 1502 and 1503, respectively.[5] Seneca's ascendancy over the Greek tragedians is clearly indicated, too, in the number and range of translations into vernacular languages. R. R. Bolgar has cataloged nineteen translations of six different plays by Euripides before 1600, including six of *Hecuba* and four of *Iphigenia in Aulis*. Directly and indirectly, Erasmus's Latin translations of 1506 opened up these two particular plays to a wider audience than the others. In the same period there were, to be sure, eighteen translations of plays by Sophocles, but they were concentrated almost exclusively on only three plays, *Antigone*, *Oedipus Rex*, and *Electra*. By 1600 there was not even one translation of a play by Aeschylus in Italian, French, English, German, or Spanish. Of Seneca, by

5. Thomas F. Dibdin, *An Introduction to the Knowledge of Rare and Valuable Editions of the Greek and Latin Classics*, 2d ed. rev. (London, 1804), pp. 5–6, 137–38, 354, 362–63; Joseph W. Moss, *A Manual of Classical Bibliography*, 2d ed. (London, 1837), 1: 6–7, 414–16; 2: 575–76, 595–96.

contrast, there had been no fewer than thirty-seven translations by 1600, chosen fairly evenly from among all his plays.[6]

As the inspiriation for new "classical" tragedies in the vernacular, Seneca likewise outdistanced the Greeks. Sophocles may have had academic snob appeal; Seneca pleased audiences. The product of scrupulous imitation of Sophocles and painstaking study of Aristotle's *Poetics*, Giangiorgio Trissino's *Sophonisba* earned its author academic praise when it was written in 1515, but it had to wait half a century, until 1562, twelve years after Trissino's death, before it was first performed. In the meantime, Giambattista Cinthio Giraldi had established a more viable precedent for Italian neoclassical tragedy with his Senecan *Orbecche*, an immediate success when it was acted at Ferrara in 1541. In a defense of his play a few years later, Cinthio makes no bones about it: Seneca is in every way superior to Sophocles, and the proof is on the stage.[7] Cinthio's bold assertion and the statistics that back it up need some qualification, however. The three sixteenth-century English productions of tragedies by Seneca that have left some record show us that Seneca as a text for study was not the same thing as Seneca as a script for the stage. In all three cases we can observe subtle and not so subtle changes that make his plays accord with already familiar ways of putting plays onstage and already familiar ways of defining man's place in the universe.

The Westminster School production of *Hippolytus* in the mid-1540s is the first of these three productions. Heavy-handed morality is not the only thing that measures the distance between Rome and Westminster. Seneca's *Hippolytus* may raise large questions about fate and justice, but more immediately it dramatizes a tale of adulterous love—the very stuff of medieval romance. By and large, sexual passion does not figure as a motivating force in Greek and Latin tragedies,

---

6. R. R. Bolgar, *The Classical Heritage and its Beneficiaries* (Cambridge, 1954), provides a complete catalog of translations of the classics into the vernacular. Cf. Appendix II, pp. 512–15, 524–25, 534–37.

7. P. R. Horne, *The Tragedies of Giambattista Cinthio Giraldi* (Oxford, 1962), pp. 23–47.

yet the earliest Renaissance readers, scholars, and producers
sought out the few unrepresentative plays in which love and
jealousy do appear as motives. It is no accident that the four
plays of Euripides printed at the end of the fifteenth century,
five years or so before the first complete edition, all feature
striking female protagonists: Medea, Phaedra, Alcestis,
Andromache. Not surprisingly, then, Euripides' most fre-
quently translated plays in the sixteenth century were *Hecuba*
and *Iphigenia in Aulis*.[8] One of the reasons Nowell chose Sen-
eca's *Hippolytus* was surely the similarity of its plot to medi-
eval romance. Sir Gawain and Sir Galahad are both besieged
by adulterous wives just as Hippolytus is. All told, the sense
of Seneca's *Hippolytus* communicated by Nowell's prologue
seems firmly grounded in medieval dramatic traditions.

The same is true of Alexander Neville's translation of Sen-
eca's *Oedipus*, first printed in 1563 and collected nearly twenty
years later by Thomas Newton in his anthology of *Seneca His
Tenne Tragedies*. Neville was a nineteen-year-old student at
Trinity College, Cambridge, when his translation of *Oedipus*
was printed in 1563. By that time Trinity had a well-estab-
lished tradition of productions of classical tragedy at Christ-
mas: indeed, an "Oedipus" costing the considerable sum of
one pound 13 shillings 4 pence had been acted along with a
"Hecuba" in 1559. In more recent years there had been an
equally expensive staging of a "Medea" and a "Troas."[9] In his
preface young Neville may be more than just politely apolo-
getic when he says that his translation of *Oedipus* was intended
to be acted on the stage, not read in print. His whole reason
for undertaking the translation was, he says, to take the play
and "put it to the very same use, that Seneca himselfe in his

8. The translations are cataloged in Bolgar, *Classical Heritage*, Appendix II.
9. Cf. G. C. Moore Smith, *College Plays Performed in the University of Cam-
bridge* (Cambridge, 1923), pp. 53ff. H. B. Charlton, *The Senecan Tradition in
Renaissance Tragedy* (Manchester, 1946), p. 154, specifies that Neville's college
was Trinity and provides the interesting detail that Neville went to study at
one of the inns of court and became the friend of George Gascoigne. Gas-
coigne and Francis Kinwelmershe's version of Euripides' *Phoenician Women*
was acted at Gray's Inn in 1566.

Invention pretended: Which was by the tragicall and Pompous showe upon Stage, to admonish all men of their fickle Estates, to declare the unconstant head of wavering Fortune, her sodayne interchaunged and soone altered Face: and lyvely to expresse the just revenge, and fearefull punishments of horrible Crimes, wherewith the wretched worlde in these our myserable dayes pyteously swarmeth."[10] Neville apparently sees no logical problem in having it both ways: the universe of tragedy can be a place either of arbitrary shifts of fortune or of ineluctable moral laws. Either way, it is the end of tragedy that counts, and either way that end remains the same: to warn men to put no trust in their own power.

By allying "tragicall" and "Pompous," Neville shows that he thinks of tragedy not just as a certain kind of narrative but as a theatrical experience. Though studiously literal for the most part, his translation includes changes and additions that are designed to enhance the play onstage—in terms of both theatrical effect and moral message. Neville never scruples over amplifying a speech when he can thunder on the audience's ears and emblazon on their minds moral points that Seneca himself may have touched too briefly. Such additions tell us a great deal about how university audiences listened to tragedy. From the speeches they heard declaimed onstage they expected not just revelations of character and emotion but moral wisdom, formulated with epigrammatic precision and, presumably, declaimed with appropriate emphasis. With their sense of the play-as-rhetorical-event, Neville's audience expected great set speeches, and he contrived to provide even more than the copious plenty that Seneca supplies. What must have been heard in the theater is visually apparent on the printed page in many sixteenth-century editions of classical and neoclassical tragedy: running quotation marks in the left-hand margin serve to set off memorable *sententiae* from the rest of the text. In the printed editions of their Englishing of Euripides' *Phoenician Women*, George Gascoigne and Francis

10. *Seneca His Tenne Tragedies*, ed. Thomas Newton, intro. T. S. Eliot (London, 1927), pp. 187–88. Future page references are indicated in the text.

Kinwelmershe even provide such speeches with marginal glosses. Near the beginning of the play, for example, Antigone's tutor hears the approaching rabble attending on Polyneices and advises his pupil to go back inside to "your maiden chamber." Nine lines of what is casual advice—perhaps even comic solicitude—in Euripides become twenty-one lines of moral exhortation in Kinwelmershe, distinguished from the rest of the text with quotation marks and labeled in the margin "A glasse for yong women."[11]

Resolute Stoics that they are, Seneca's characters have plenty of such sententiae in all of Seneca's tragedies: "What king is happy on his throne? False joy, / How many ills thy smiling faces conceals!"[12] These two terse, epigrammatic lines in Latin become four diffuse, hyperbolic lines in Neville's English:

> Doth any man in Princely throne rejoyce? O brittle Joy,
> How many ills? how fayre a Face? and yet how much annoy
> In thee doth lurke, and hidden lies? what heapes of endles strife?
> They judge amisse, that deeme the Prince to have the happy life.
>
> (p. 192)

Accustomed as we are to Shakespeare's heroes, who use soliloquies to reflect, not preach, we are apt to write off such effusions as antidramatic. What to us seem cerebral intrusions that threaten both the dramatic illusion and the emotional continuity of the play-as-object were for Neville and his contemporaries the thrilling highlights of the play-as-rhetorical-event.

Audiences heard such speeches not with their minds only but with their hearts. In his definition of sententiae as a dramatic element, Cinthio, author of *Orbecche*, the first Italian vernacular tragedy to be acted in the Renaissance, and of the novella from which Shakespeare took the plot of *Othello*,

11. George Gascoigne and Francis Kinwelmershe, *Jocasta*, repr. in John W. Cunliffe, *Early English Classical Tragedies* (Oxford, 1912), p. 83.

12. Seneca, *Four Tragedies*, trans. Watling, p. 209. Further translations of Seneca not assigned to Neville are from Watling's version and are indicated in the text by line numbers of the Latin original.

makes it clear that moral apothegms like Oedipus's were among the most powerful devices a dramatist could command. A sententia, explains Cinthio, is "an expression in accordance with the usage of the time, taken from everyday life and from the common opinion of men, which describes with great efficacy and with suitable variety some feature of human life that either has been, or is, or must be. They are very common in tragedies, being unbelievably effective [*credenza attisime*] as a means of presenting actions, passions, and manners, the terrible and the pathetic, to the eyes of the spectators."[13] Efficacious rhetoric, variety, the inescapable necessity of what "has been, or is, or must be"—no other formula could be more powerful in its appeal to Renaissance sensibility. Far from being aural "footnotes" that a spectator's mind would note in passing, sententiae carried an emotional charge that put them at the very heart of tragedy in performance. It was the *combination* of oratorical effect and moral thrust that made sententiae so thrilling. In Cinthio's view the two things are inseparable. The aesthetic here has as much to do with St. Dominic's pulpit as it does with Cicero's rostrum.

Neville's second strategy in producing an actable script is to alter Seneca's choruses. The license that Neville assumes came on good authority. The Latin translations of Euripides' *Hecuba* and *Iphigenia in Aulis* that Erasmus produced during his stay in England from 1501 to 1506 are remarkable for their felicity in rendering Euripides' still exotic and difficult, not to mention corrupt, Greek texts. Erasmus allowed himself a freer hand with the choruses than with the protagonists' speeches. In the whole task of translating, Erasmus writes in the letter dedicating *Iphigenia* to William Warham, Archbishop of Canterbury, he has balanced literal strictness against "failure to do justice to the theme," and in the case of Euripides' choruses that end has meant very free adaptation of the originals. In imitating the Greeks, Horace did not try to reproduce all the metrical experiments of the lyric poets, nor did Seneca those

13. Quoted and translated in Horne, *Cinthio*, p. 30.

of the Greek tragedians. Horace dismisses such things as "melodious trifles." "For it seems to me that nowhere did the ancients write more foolishly than in choruses of this sort, where through excessive striving for novelty of utterance, they destroyed clarity of expression, and in the hunt for marvellous verbal effects their sense of reality suffered."[14] To judge from Neville's alterations, the ancient playwrights' "sense of reality" primarily involved ethical matters.

Seneca's first chorus, for example, is a rehearsal of the miseries of Thebes in the midst of the plague. Part of the horror of Seneca's vision is the utter indifference of the "insatiable gods" to the human suffering that grips the city. Presiding over Neville's Thebes, however, is a wrathful but approachable God, and the Chorus's invocation, with their plea for mercy and their self-righteous call for destruction on the heads of God's enemies, sounds more like a Psalm than the chorus of a classical tragedy. The whole of their prayer has no counterpart in Seneca's text:

O God withold thy fury great, thy Plagues from us remove.
Ceasse of afflicted Soules to scourge, who thee both serve and love.
Powre downe on them diseases fowle, that them deserved have.
A Guerdon just for sinne (Oh God) this this of thee wee crave,
And onely this. We aske no more, the cause and all is thyne,
A thing not usde of Gods it is, from pity to declyne.   (pp. 196–97)

Neville has not considered the gods of Seneca's plays too closely.

From his acting script Neville omits altogether Seneca's second chorus with its praise of Bacchus as Thebes's patron deity and its recital of famous exploits of Theban heroes. The most significant change of all he reserves for the third chorus. Following the example of Sophocles' Theban elders, who at first do not want to believe Teiresias's prophecies any more than Oedipus himself, Seneca's Chorus argue that Oedipus is not the cause of Thebes's sufferings:

14. *The Correspondence of Erasmus*, trans. R.A.B. Mynors and D.F.S. Thomson, *Collected Works of Erasmus*, Vol. 2 (Toronto, 1975): 132–35.

> Not yours, not yours the fault that brought such peril to us.
> Not for that do the Fates bear hard on the house of Labdacus.
> We are assailed by the ancient anger of the gods.   (ll. 709–12)

Unlike Sophocles' elders, Neville's Chorus never get so
involved in the action that they lose their philosophical
detachment, and, unlike Seneca's Chorus, they throw the
emphasis not on "the ancient anger of the gods" but on Oed-
ipus as a mirror for magistrates:

> Thus hee that Princes lives, and base estate together wayes,
> Shall finde the one a very hell, a perfect infelicity:
> The other eke a heaven right, exempted quight from mysery.
> Let Oedipus example bee of this unto you all,
> A Mirrour meete, A Patern playne, of Princes carefull thrall.
> Who late in perfect Joy as seem'de, and everlasting blis,
> Triumphantly his life out led, a Myser now hee is.   (p. 216)

For Seneca's fourth chorus, a celebration of the *via media*,
Neville substitutes a lament over Fortune's power. The senti-
ments there are sounded again at the end of the play. In the
Chorus's final dialogue with Oedipus, "fate" in Seneca
becomes in Neville the "tumbling fatal course of fortunes
wheele" (p. 226).

Thus does Neville medievalize Seneca's sense of fate:
inscrutable fate in the Roman Stoic becomes very scrutable
Fortune in the Christian humanist. In Seneca's Latin, fate is
the inexorable principle that rules all the universe; in Neville's
English, Fortune is the principle that governs this world but
not, by implication, the next. Beyond the shifts of Fortune
stand changeless Christian verities. Neville's interest in Oed-
ipus as a mirror for magistrates is strong enough to alter not
only the audience's view of the hero but the hero's view of
himself. Neville's universe may be a sublunary realm of
chance events ruled over by Fortune, but that does not prevent
him from presenting Oedipus, with a lapse of ethical logic, as
a thoroughly responsible, thoroughly culpable figure unde-
serving of the audience's sympathy.

Oedipus as Seneca originally conceived him voices a sense
of fatedness and impending doom from the beginning of the

play and at the end of the play seems to take almost masoch-
istic delight in having blindly committed even more crimes
than he first imagined. He cries out to Apollo:

> Now hear me,
> Guardian and god of truth, Fate's messenger!
> One death, my father's, did the fates demand;
> But now I have slain twice; I am more guilty
> Than I had feared to be; my crimes have brought
> My mother to her death. Phoebus, you lied!
> I have done more than was set down for me
> By evil destiny.   (ll. 1042–46)

For all his willing acceptance of misery, Seneca's Oedipus still
presents himself as a victim of destiny. In his acting script of
1563, Neville turns this final speech of twenty lines into a ver-
itable litany of fifty lines in which Oedipus scourges himself
as a sinful creature thoroughly deserving of whatever tor-
ments may yet come to him:

> Thou God, thou teller out of Fates. On thee, on thee, I call
> My father onely I did owe, unto the Destinies all.
> Now twise a Paracide, a worse than I did feare to bee:
> . . .
> My Mother I have slayne, (Alas) the fault is all in mee.
> O cursed head: O wicked wight, whom all men deadly hate.
> O Beast, what meanst thou still to live in this unhappy state?
> The skies doe blush and are ashamed, at these thy mischiefes great.
>   (pp. 229–30)

For this recasting of Seneca's hero, Neville has his eye on the
choosing protagonist of morality-play tradition, and in his
direct-address harangues Oedipus confronts the audience not
as Seneca's sublimely isolated sufferer, marked out by fate for
a destiny all his own, but as chastened Mankind who willfully
has worked his own destruction: "(Alas) the fault is all in
mee."

That same moral hard-line we can observe in William Gag-
er's version of Seneca's *Hippolytus*, acted at Christ Church,
Oxford, in 1592. Taking the script that Nowell had produced
at Westminster School nearly fifty years earlier, Gager man-

aged to arrive at an equally rigid but totally opposite moral
interpretation. Backed into a corner by a hostile critic like his
colleague John Rainolds, Gager could marshal splendid argu-
ments about the moral utility of tragedy. He and his students
perform Plautus and Seneca not only "to recreate owre selves"
but "honestly to embolden owre pathe." In addition to exer-
cising their memory and their voices, his students learn
thereby "to conforme them to convenient action."[15] Gager has
heightened the moral program in *Hippolytus* by making a few
strategic additions to the script. Not content with adding new
speeches, as Neville does with Seneca's *Oedipus*, Gager adds
entirely new scenes. Like Nowell introducing the same play
nearly fifty years before, Gager first of all supplies a prologue
in the manner of Roman comedy. In this case, it is not just the
strategy of the comic prologue that Gager has adopted but its
flippant tone, as well. "Another stage presented the story of
chaste Penelope," the Prologue starts out, recalling perform-
ance of a play called *Ulysses Redux* two days before. "Lest
women therby become overweeningly proud, today's play
will tell of chaste Hippolytus, so that men may obtain an equal
reputation for chastity." This time it will be a woman who
solicits a man—indeed, a stepmother her stepson. Who will
believe it? "But if some woman perchance plucks at the coat
of a young man, and desires too eagerly to know what is hap-
pening here, let him ingeniously invent something new, or
shamelessly make it clear that it is a fictitious story. Let the
women be spared, let them not know their own disgrace."[16] Is
there a roguish edge to all these remarks about male chastity
and sparing ladies who must be as innocent of Latin as they
apparently are about life? The presence of women was one of
the very things that Gager's spiteful colleague Dr. John Rain-
olds used to attack lewd theatricals like classical tragedy. Gag-

15. Gager's answer to Rainolds' attack is quoted in Boas, *University Drama*,
pp. 235–36.

16. J. W. Binns, "William Gager's Additions to Seneca's *Hippolytus*,"
Studies in the Renaissance 17 (1970): 153–91, sets out the occasion in detail and
reprints Gager's additions with English translations on facing pages. My quo-
tations are taken from Binns's translation.

er's Prologue positively seems to flirt with them. The pro-
logue's shift to the narrative background of the play in the
next dozen lines sounds serious enough, but the final two lines
may well be as ironic as the beginnng: "I entreat you give your
attention to the troop of actors—at least as much as is given in
the popular theatre."

Gager's second strategy is to heighten the spectacle of Sen-
eca's play onstage. No sooner has the Prologue departed than
Cupid and the fury Megaera rise from the Underworld, fast
on the coattails of Tantalus's ghost in the first scene of Sen-
eca's *Thyestes*. In the Underworld, it seems, Theseus and Pir-
ithous have been attempting to abduct Proserpine, and
Megaera has come to wreak revenge. She will make Phaedra
fall in love with her own stepson. Cupid is horrified. This
incestuous passion, he protests, will give love a bad name. The
whole of Seneca's play, then, is set up as a kind of contest
between the two deities, between the force of Love and the
force of Revenge. This cosmic "overplot" in which gods come
onstage to pull the strings of human actors below had already
been shown to advantage in plays like *The Rare Truimphs of
Love and Fortune*, acted at court by Derby's men in 1582–1583,
and in Gager's own *Dido*.[17]

Finally, Gager underscores the philosophical issues implicit
in Seneca's text. Like Neville's amplifications of sententious
speeches in Seneca's *Oedipus*, Gager's new beginning for Act
Two brings the issues of the play out into the open just as they
would be stated in a morality play. Gager's Hippolytus has to
be almost superhumanly resolute to ward off his tempters.
Not just the Nurse and Phaedra attempt to persuade him to
passion but two new characters as well: a leacherous Pandarus

---

17. To settle a dispute as to which has the greater power over men, Jupiter
directs that Venus and Fortune shall take turns demonstrating their sway. Act
by act, first one and then the other stage-manages the main plot of the play, a
Roman comedy of frustrated lovers, estranged sons, and nobility unwittingly
going about in honest poverty. Finally Mercury calls a draw, and all ends
happily. Cf. *The Rare Triumphs of Love and Fortune* (London, 1930). This is
probably the "Historie of Love and Fortune," which the Earl of Derby's com-
pany was paid for performing before Elizabeth on December 30, 1582.

and a chaste wood-nymph Nais. As with the temptation of
Mankind in morality plays, Gager seems determined to make
Hippolytus's temptation as seductive as possible. Gager
apparently succeeded. Rainolds was especially horrified by
Nais, "a new *Nymph* . . . bringing fewell enough to heate and
melt a heart of yse or snow"—and this response at second-
hand, too. Rainolds had not even accepted Gager's invitation
to attend the performance. In his riposte Gager defends Nais
as a foil to Phaedra: "the devyse was, partly to sett owte the
constant chastetye or rather virginytye of Hippolytus, whoe
neyther with honest love made to hym in the woods, nor with
unhonest attempts in the cyttye could be overcumme; partly
to expresse the affection of honest, lawfull, vertuous marriage
meaninge love; for no other did she profer, and therfor me
thinkes she is not, unharde, to be reproched with the brode
name of bawderye, wherof there is no one syllable in worde
or sense to be founde in all her speches."[18]

In a real morality play the tempters would have urged argu-
ments that we in the audience could see through at once. Pan-
darus and Nais, however, are given arguments out of Phae-
dra's letter to Hippolytus in Ovid's *Heroides*—arguments
rather more luscious than lascivious. Nais's love seems, in
fact, so ingenuous that Gager manages to confuse the moral
issue rather than clarify it. Nais's love, says Gager, is meant as
a positive contrast to Phaedra's. In refusing Nais's chaste love
as well as Phaedra's lecherous love, Hippolytus is made to
appear downright stubborn. He ends up in the position of a
blocking-figure in romantic comedy, a sour Malvolio inca-
pable of feeling anything. Considering the Prologue's coy
remarks about male virginity, Gager's audience might well
have responded to Nais's blandishments with amusement. In
any event, the spurned Nais adds her curses to Megaera's:
"But go on making sport of girls through your pride, O hard,
cruel man, lead your savage triumph. Let every girl seek you,
and none bear you away. Nemesis will requite this conduct,
and let her requite it, I pray. Let her regard the haughty pride

18. Quoted in Binns, "Gager's Additions," p. 161.

of this barbarous man—take vengeance, goddess. May he perish by the worst of deaths. May Hippolytus atone for hating and despising my love. May an avenger of this disgraceful repulse appear in a short time, and may she bring the furies of a woman in love, who has been scorned." Phaedra, of course, figures as this avenger. The Nurse appears at once to plead Phaedra's case even more directly than Pandarus, this time in speeches by Seneca. As far as Nais is concerned, Hippolytus well deserves the punishment of Nemesis. Again, Gager rather confuses things morally. The dying Hippolytus must figure as both the innocent passive victim of Seneca and the culpable, hardhearted lady-killer of Gager's additions. The moment-to-moment battle lines of debate, it appears, are never carried to their logical conclusions.

Why does Gager, like Nowell and Neville, never sense such discrepancies? One suspects that these academics simply delight in speechmaking and debate for their own sake. What the characters' elegant disputations solve or do not solve seems almost beside the point. The dramatic vehicle best designed to satisfy such love for debate is the morality play, and Gager has simply added to Seneca's text two scenes of temptation and argumentation inspired by the polemical plays that he and his academic audience already knew and liked. The only difficulty is that Seneca's ethical assumptions and Gager's polemical program work at cross-purposes. Gager evinces the same easy moral self-assurance as Nowell and Neville, the same assumption that one can make a simple moral judgment about the tragic protagonists and the complicated situations in which those characters find themselves. Settled snugly within the walls of school or college, Seneca's sixteenth-century English audiences were unprepared to acknowledge ethical ambiguities, unwilling to question the values that defined themselves as households.

Like these three productions of Seneca, the three sixteenth-century English productions of Greek tragedy that we know something about all seem to have been heavy-handed attempts to hammer out ethical irregularities into dogmatic certainties. Stagings of Sophocles' *Ajax* at King's College, Cambridge, in

1564, of Euripides' *Phoenician Women* at Gray's Inn in 1566, and of Sophocles' *Antigone* probably at St. John's College, Cambridge, in the early 1580s show us a variety of attempts to turn ancient tragedies into medieval morality plays.

For Queen Elizabeth's reception at Cambridge during her summer progress of 1564, masters and students planned a production of Sophocles' *Ajax*. Weariness prevented the queen from actually seeing the play, but one of the disappointed dons wrote an account that tells us what the producers had hoped for. For displaying Ajax in his fury "the masters of the entertainments had adorned the entire stage tragically, and had prepared the most select actors, sparing no expense, and no attention. For they had brought the warlike arms, the costumes, the illustrious splendors, and all the other equipment from London and other quite remote places, and had chosen orators from the numerous academy and had found a place sufficiently apt and spacious." But the queen failed to come, cheating Robinson and his colleagues of "whip-bearing Ajax, whom we wished to see in his rage."[19] Whatever else *Ajax* was to have been, it was to have been visually splendid and aurally exciting. Ajax in his fury would have been a supreme example of the *amplitude* that Renaissance audiences expected from tragic heroes.

When he printed an authorized edition of his pirated tragedy *Roxana* in 1632, William Alabaster carefully specified how the Latin text should be declaimed. Presumably Alabaster had his eye on the first performance of his tragedy at Trinity College, Cambridge, about 1592 when he directs actors to speak the lines "with a foaming sound, just as poets are accustomed in their tragedies, since things read in a bombastic voice [*cum ampulla oris*] are somehow made even more sublime [*in grandius quodammodo excoluntur*]."[20] *Granditas* is the

---

19. Translated by Carter Anderson Daniel, "Patterns and Traditions of the Elizabethan Court Play to 1590" (Ph.D. diss., University of Virginia, 1965), p. 79, from the Latin original repr. in John Nichols, *The Progresses and Public Processions of Queen Elizabeth*, 1st ed. (London, 1807), 3: 129.

20. Quoted in J. W. Binns, "Seneca and Neo-Latin Tragedy in England,"

level of style and emotion to which Alabaster and the Cambridge producers of *Ajax* both aspired. As Nicholas Robinson describes it, the effect of *Ajax* would, then, have been something rather different from katharsis as Aristotle analyzes it. What was looked for was not a "spending" of emotion or even a "purifying" of emotion but a *heightening* of emotion. Cinthio defines this exhilarating effect: "I believe that the whole aim of the tragedian is to arouse terror and compassion, and to fill the audience with wonder [*meraviglia*]."[21] Whatever Aristotle means by katharsis, he does not mean "wonder" at lavish stage effects or at bombastic speeches or at the strange ways events can turn out. "Terror," "compassion," "wonder"—these are the grand emotions one feels in the presence of passion, violence, splendid rhetoric, dazzling spectacle—and stern moral truth.

It is just such a combination of sensation and sententiousness that we find in *Jocasta*, the verbally and visually sumptuous version of Euripides' *Phoenician Women* that George Gascoigne and Francis Kinwelmershe provided for the Gray's Inn Christmas revels of 1566–1567. Far as it may be from the Acropolis to Clerkenwell, it is even farther via Italy. Though the British Library manuscript labels the play *Jocasta: A Tragedie written in Greeke by* Euripides, *translated and digested into Acte[s] by George Gascoigne, and Francis Kinwelmershe,* the collaborators in fact worked from Ludovico Dolce's Italian version *Giocasta* (1549), which in turn was based on a Latin translation of Euripides' original. After such perils, the version of Euripides that the gentlemen of Gray's Inn saw that night in 1566 had suffered the richest and strangest of sea changes. Thanks to Gascoigne's irrepressible habit of self-advertisement, *Jocasta* was printed in his self-collected works, complete with elaborate stage directions that allow us to reconstruct the performance in some detail.

Jocasta's grand first entry with a chorus of four and no

in *Seneca,* ed. C.D.N. Costa (London and Boston, 1974), p. 210. I offer a closer translation of the relevant phrases than Binns provides.

21. *Giuditio sopra la tragedia de Canace e Macareo* (1550), attributed to Cinthio, quoted in Horne, *Tragedies of Giraldi,* p. 149.

fewer than sixteen supernumeraries (in Euripides she comes on alone) is typical of how Gascoigne and Kinwelmershe have played up the occasions for "wonder" in Euripides' play. Another instance is the big scene of divination in Act Three. Not content with Euripides' Teiresias, who merely comes right out and tells Creon that his son Menoeceus must be sacrificed if Thebes is to be saved from Polyneices' Argive invaders, Dolce, and Gascoigne after him, interpolate a scene inspired by Seneca's *Oedipus*, in which a priest carries out a sacrifice onstage and reads its frightful auguries as they come. In Seneca the whole business is only narrated, but Gascoigne plays it for all the spectacle it is worth. "Accompanyed with xvi. Bacchanales and all his rytes and ceremonies," the Priest officiates in language that sounds curiously like the Book of Common Prayer:

> . . . with hart devoute and humble cheere,
> Whiles I breake up the bowels of this beast,
> (That oft thy veneyarde Bacchus hath destroyed,)
> Let every wight crave pardon for his faults,
> With bending knee about his aultars here.[22]

"[M]ake your humble confession to almighty God before this congregation here gathered together in his holy name, meekly kneeling upon your knees"—there is nothing in Seneca or Euripides quite like this.[23]

The "wonder" in *Jocasta* resides not only in such spectacular stage effects but in the sure swift justice that governs the universe of the play. This is just the combination of theatrical effect and moral truth that Cinthio commends in *sententiae* as a dramatic device. Nothing could be further from the spirit of Euripides. In the *Phoenician Women*, as in most of Euripides'

---

22. George Gascoigne and Francis Kinwelmershe, *Jocasta*, 3.1.76–80, repr. in Cunliffe, *Early English Classical Tragedies*, pp. 65–159. Further quotations from this edition will be indicated in the text by act, scene, and line number. My quotations from the *Phoenician Women*, indicated in the text with line numbers, are taken from the translation by Elizabeth Wyckoff, repr. in *Euripides V* (Chicago, 1968), pp. 67–140.

23. *The Book of Common Prayer 1559*, ed. J. E. Booty (Charlottesville, 1976), p. 259.

tragedies, what we see is not the moral *justice* of the situation
but the *irony* of the situation, the incongruity between human
suffering and the ineluctable plan of the gods. Euripides
makes the historical events fall into place as neatly as we
would expect from received tradition, but the human suf-
fering those events entail seems altogether less tidy. Out of
these disturbing confusions Gascoigne and Kinwelmershe
arrange reassuring symmetries by pairing the protagonists,
simplifying their characters, and setting them in opposition as
positive and negative examples.

Menoeceus, for example, emerges in Dolce and Gascoigne
as a martyr to selflessness and self-control, Creon as a cow-
ardly, conniving tyrant. In Euripides, Creon is offstage when
he gets the unexpected news that Menoeceus has killed him-
self. We find out about it when Jocasta does (ll. 1090ff.). In the
Renaissance versions, on the other hand, Creon finds out
about his son's death right onstage. Dolce and his English imi-
tators have made the change not so much to heighten Creon's
sense of grief and loss (he has already told us at 4.2.1–14 that
he has had a premonition of Menoeceus's death) as to give
Creon a clear-cut motive for seizing power in Thebes. Eurip-
ides' Creon reenters the play grief-stricken and helpless but
quietly proud:

> What shall I do? And do my tears lament
> myself, or this poor city, held in gloom
> as if it traveled over Acheron?
> My child has perished, dying for the land.
> The name he leaves is noble, but sad for me.   (ll. 1310–14)

Dolce and Kinwelmershe's Creon knows only too well what
he will do. He will get revenge any way he can:

> Well, since the bloud of my beloved sonne,
> Must serve to slake the wrath of angrie *Jove*,
> And since his onely death must bring to *Thebes*
> A quiete end of hir unquiet state,
> Me thinkes good reason would, that I henceforth
> Of *Thebane* soyle should beare the kingly swaye:
> Yea sure, and so I will ere it be long,
> Either by right, or else by force of armes.   (4.2.53–60)

Such ruthless rancor would have come as no surprise to the gentlemen of Gray's Inn, since Gascoigne and Kinwelmershe, following Dolce's lead, had already seized every chance to vilify Creon. Antigone arouses the audience's suspicions in the play's second scene, long before Creon enters. All Creon needs is a little supernatural encouragement and the excuse of Menoeceus's death, and he emerges as the very type of the tyrant. The supernatural encouragement he gets from Teiresias. During the scene in which he announces that Menoeceus must be sacrified, Teiresias entices Creon with a prophecy that sounds like that of Macbeth's witches. Pointing to the carcass of the sacrificed beast, the prophet volunteers,

> But in thy woe to yeelde thee some reliefe,
> I tell thee once, thou shalt be Lorde of *Thebes*,
> Which happe of thine this string did well declare,
> Which from the heart doth out alonely growe.   (3.1.200–203)

In Euripides the deaths of Eteocles and Polyneices leave Creon with glory thrust upon him; in Dolce and in Gascoigne and Kinwelmershe he seeks that glory greedily.

Balancing Creon/Menoeceus as moral opposites are Eteocles/Polyneices. From the opening scenes of *Jocasta* Eteocles is cast as a heartless villain who wrongly keeps the throne from his brother Polyneices. Antigone sets the brothers' conflict straight in the same scene when she voices her suspicions about Creon. "As both my brethren be," she declares to her tutor,

> so to both I bear
> As much good will as any sister may,
> But yet the wrong that unto *Polynice*
> This trothlesse tyrant hath unjustlie shewd,
> Doth leade me more, to wishe the prosperous life
> Of *Polynice*, than of the cruell wretch.   (1.2.88–93)

And, besides, Polyneices always loved her better than Eteocles has. Antigone's judgment we never forget. When Eteocles enters the play with ".xx. gentlemen in armour"—a virtual army on an indoor stage—the Chorus of Theban women speak aside to Jocasta, denouncing him as the tyrant Antigone has led us to expect. Nor does Eteocles disappoint us in his own person. His death is made to appear just what he deserves. Polyneices, foreign invader though he be, dies unjustly. Dolce and his English imitators are determined to turn both Eteocles and Creon into morally culpable figures— the very thing that Euripides assiduously avoids. In Euripides' play, Menoeceus's suicide seems in the last event utterly wasteful: he saves Thebes, just as the received myth says he did, but his self-sacrifice does nothing to stop the self-slaughter of Eteocles, Polyneices, and Jocasta. In the Renaissance versions of the play, on the other hand, Menoeceus figures as a martyr to his country, a positive example to be set against selfish, power-hungry Eteocles and Creon.

As Euripides handles it, the conflict between Eteocles and Polyneices admits of no easy solution: both brothers present rightful claims, and the conflict between them spells disaster for everyone. A struggle of such ironic cast, so utterly unlike the struggle of Satan against God in the great cycle plays or of evil counselors against good counselors in morality plays, was beyond the ken—or at least the dramatic interest—of Dolce and Gascoigne and Kinwelmershe. It takes them surprisingly few additions of lines and scenes to upset the delicately balanced irony of Euripides' play and offer us instead a dramatic universe where good and evil are clearly demarcated. One big question, however, confronted Gascoigne and Kinwelmershe at the end of the play: what to do with the monster they have created in Creon. The tyrant marches off the stage fully in control and totally unrepentant. Fortunately, Euripides had pulled in the business of Oedipus's exile to end the play. Oedipus can then become the positive example needed to offset Creon. It takes only a few amplifications of Euripides' text to turn Oedipus into a victim of Fortune, a veritable "mirrour for Magistrates," as the marginal gloss labels him opposite this final speech:

> Deare citizens, beholde your Lord and King
> That Thebes set in quiet government,
> Now as you see, neglected of you all,

And in these ragged ruthfull weedes bewrapt,
Ychased from his native countrey soyle,
Betakes himself (for so this tirant will)
To everlasting banishment: but why
Do I lament my lucklesse lot in vaine?
"Since every man must beare with quiet minde,
"The fate that heavens have earst to him assignde.   (5.5.240–49)

The moral frame that surrounds *Jocasta* is not just meta-
phorical. Following a precedent first set in England by Sack-
ville and Norton's *Gorboduc* at the Inner Temple five years ear-
lier, Gascoigne and Kinwelmershe quite literally frame each of
the five acts of their version of Euripides with a spectacular
dumb-show at the beginning and a choral homily at the end.
Before Jocasta first enters from her palace, for example, we
hear the mournful sounds of stringed instruments and are con-
fronted with a lavishly costumed king in procession: "Firste,
before the beginning of the first Acte, did sounde a dolefull &
straunge noyse of violles, Cythren, Bandurion, and such like,
during the whiche, there came in uppon the Stage a king with
an Imperial crown uppon his head, very richely apparelled: a
Scepter in his righte hande, a Mounde with a Crosse in his
lefte hande, sitting in a Chariote very richely furnished,
drawne in by foure Kinges in their Dublettes and Hosen, with
crownes also upon their heades." In their stage directions Gas-
coigne and Kinwelmershe explain who this triumphant figure
is: Sesostres king of Egypt, who "to content his unbrideled
ambitious desire" yoked captive kings to draw his chariot. In
watching the play onstage, however, the spectators would
have to wait for the chorus at the end of Act One to make the
meaning of what they had seen explicit:

> If greedie lust of mans ambitious eye
> (That thirsteth so for swaye of earthly things)
> Would eke foresee, what mischefes growe therby,
> What carefull toyle to quiet state it brings,
> What endlesse griefe from such a fountaine springs:
> Then should he swimme in seas of sweete delight,
> That nowe complaines of fortunes cruell spight.

By that time, of course, the meaning of the dumb-show should have become clear already from what they had witnessed in Act One, especially from Antigone's references to the ambitions of Creon and Eteocles.

What Gascoigne and Kinwelmershe give us in each act of *Jocasta* is a dramatic emblem, a translation into space and time of the combination of picture and poem that not only satisfied the Renaissance critical principle *ut pictura poesis* but made good profits for publishers of emblem books. An emblem's strategy on the reader-viewer falls into three parts: first the reader takes in a bizarre picture that cries out for explanation; then he reads a narration of what is going on in that picture; finally he reads the moral of the whole. Gascoigne and Kinwelmershe dramatize this three-step process. Their image of Sesostres as the type of ambition later appeared, in fact, in at least three continental emblem books.[24]

The collaborators' full repertory of emblems provides a kind of moral gloss on the events of Euripides' play—and a remarkable record of the stage effects the gentlemen of Gray's Inn could manage:

1. Sesostres king of Egypt figures the "greedie lust of mans ambitious eye" before Act One;
2. two coffins buried together that burn with separate flames signify discord between brothers before Act Two;
3. a gaping gulf that finally closes over a knight with sword drawn, though not over the doublets and hose, baskets of earth, or ladies' jewels that others have thrown in, symbolized the sacrifice of self for country before Act Three;
4. the battle of the Horatius brothers with the Curiatius brothers signifies brotherly concord before Act Four;
5. Fortune in a chariot drawn by ruined kings prepares us for Creon's rise to power and Oedipus's exile before Act Five.

Here, in the most vivid terms possible, is the combination of theatrical effect and moral truth that inspires meraviglia.

24. Florentius Schoonhovius, *Emblemata* (Gouda, 1618); Dirck Pers, *Bellerophon* (Amsterdam, 1633); Peter Iselburg, *Emblemata Politica* (Nuremburg, 1640). Cf. Arthur Henkel, ed., *Emblemata: Handbuch zur Sinnbildkunst des XVI and XVII Jahrhunderts* (Stuttgart, 1967), cols. 1142–43.

The Englishmen were not alone in decking their tragedy with music and spectacle. Every edition of *Orbecche* printed in the sixteenth century, for example, carries not only Cinthio's name but the name of Alessandro da Viola, who composed entr'acte music for the first performances. At the third performance of his play, Cinthio notes, he experimented by having the play performed continuously "in the Greek manner," without these musical interludes. The effect proved tedious. Interludes are necessary, he concludes, to give the audience relief from the tension of the drama and to renew their attention for the events to come.[25] Gascoigne and Kinwelmershe's interludes do rather more than that: they do not simply renew the audience's attention; they refocus it. The dumb-show before each act of *Jocasta* gives the audience a particular angle of vision for viewing the events they are about to see in the upcoming act; the chorus at the end of each act rewards them for having put the right moral interpretation on what they have seen. The effect of these frames is to divide the play into a series of episodes, a gallery of discrete *exempla*— the very opposite of what Aristotle admired in Greek tragedies as they were performed originally. It is the unity and concentration of tragedy, Aristotle says, that makes it "better" than epic (*Poetics* 1462.a.1–b.1). But Aristotle could hardly have foreseen the Renaissance lust for variety. Dumb-shows seem a particularly successful way of satisfying that lust while honoring the Renaissance aesthetic of unity-in-variety. Variety in this case is supplied by spectacle, music, and the Chorus's speechmaking, unity by the play's continuous storyline. The most important effect of these devices of Renaissance showmanship, however, is the way they transform the moral universe of Euripides' play.

An even more startling instance of how production values can change moral values is Thomas Watson's Latin translation of *Antigone*. Unlike Dolce's free handling of Euripides, Watson's translation of Sophocles keeps scrupulously close to the

25. Horne, *Tragedies of Giraldi*, p. 39.

Greek text. There are no added lines, no extra speeches, no
interpolated scenes; not even the choruses are altered. At the
end of the play, however, Watson prints texts for four allegor-
ical *pompae* and four homiletic *themae* that completely
destroy—to the twentieth-century view, at least—the
meaning of Sophocles' play.

The printed text of Watson's translation makes no mention
of performance. Some years after the play's appearance in
1581, however, Gabriel Harvey was moved to comment on
Watson's version in a marginal note to Gascoigne and Kin-
welmershe's *Jocasta*, as reprinted in his copy of Gascoigne's
collected works, and the terms he uses there strongly suggest
that Watson's translation was in fact performed: "Omne genus
scripti, gravitate Tragoedia vincit. Huc Vatsoni Antigone,
magnifice acta solenni ritu, et vere tragico apparatu: cum pul-
cherrimis etiam pompis, et accuratissimis thematibus."[26]
G. C. Moore Smith, editor of both Harvey's marginalia and
the Cambridge dramatic records, supposes that the play must
have been performed during Harvey's years at St. John's Col-
lege, Cambridge, possibly in 1583.[27] If Mark Eccles is right in
identifying the translator as the Thomas Watson of Worcester-
shire who entered the Middle Temple at age twenty in 1581—
the same year *Antigone* was printed—Watson would have been
well settled in inns-of-court circles by the time Harvey saw his
play at Cambridge two years later. Watson himself had been
an undergraduate at Oxford.[28] Although it is almost unheard
of in the English Renaissance for a play to have been first pub-
lished and then acted, it is not impossible that the accessibility

26. *Gabriel Harvey's Marginalia*, ed. G. C. Moore Smith (Stratford, 1913),
p. 166.
27. Smith, *College Plays*, p. 63. Smith's suggestion is accepted in Alfred
Harbage, *Annals of English Drama, 975–1700*, rev. S. Schoenbaum (London,
1964).
28. Sir Sidney Lee's article on Watson in the DNB has been considerably
added to by Mark Eccles, *Christopher Marlowe in London* (Cambridge, Mass.,
1934), pp. 128–44, 158–60. From about 1573 to 1577 Watson traveled in
France and Italy and studied for a time in the English College at Douai.

of Watson's printed translation, with its pompae and themae, could have inspired a production, especially in a place with as rich a tradition of productions of classical tragedy as Cambridge.

Looking back near the end of the century, Francis Meres could rank Watson with Peele, Marlowe, and Shakespeare as "among our best for tragedie," but only Watson's *Antigone* remains to sustain Meres's claim. Nothing in the printed text indicates when in the play Watson's four pompae are to be performed—or, indeed, whether they are to be performed at all—but it accords well not only with the plot of the play but what we know about Cinthio's *Orbecche* and Gascoigne and Kinwelmershe's *Jocasta* to imagine these allegorical pageants between the acts. Harvey's adjective for the pompae, *pulcherrimis*, perhaps indicates that he was thinking visually of the speeches being declaimed, and two lines printed after the fourth *pompa* are explicitly labeled "Ista dicuntur pro Epilogo."[29]

Watson's prologue to the play prepares us not only for the catastrophic events we are about to see but for the stern moral judgments we must make as we witness them. As befits a play about a city where a son has married his own mother and where brothers have killed each other in combat, Nature is Watson's spokesman:

I am the column of impartiality and the base of justice and law.
Do you want to be happy? Live with Nature as a guide.
Enormous is my power. But I am rejected nonetheless,
and evil-doers break my laws.
The sanctified honor of human law perishes:
Piety, purity, faith itself are banished from the world.

Men of Thebes have often denied her power; men of Thebes have often paid. Nature proceeds then to outline the background of the play, sparing us no salacious detail, no sententious aside. Her final words define a standard of judgment we

29. *Sophoclis Antigone. Interprete T. Watsono. Huci adduntur pompae quaedam ex singulis tragoediae actis derivatae* (London, 1581), p. 63.

must keep in mind when we turn to hear Antigone argue her case to Ismene in the play's opening scene:

> Therefore, learn out of all these evil things
> how healthful it is to follow Nature's rule.
> If I am unwilling, in due course nothing prospers.[30]

So far, it seems, so good: Creon is clearly violating natural law by refusing Polyneices burial. Certainly the pompa after the first act would confirm such a judgment. Just before Creon makes his magisterial first entry in the play at the beginning of Watson's second act we hear out a debate among seven disputants: Justice, carrying a scepter; Equity, a woman with scales; Rigor, a man with a sword; Obstinacy, a man with a cuirass; Impiety, a man with a lance; Scourge, a man with a whip; and Late Repentance, a man whose countenance and delivery presumably need no hand-held icon. They discuss Creon's decision. Each personage has his say, but Late Repentance gets in the last word: a decision that started out as "just" and "equitable" comes quickly to appear first "rigorous" then "obstinate," "impious," and punishable. The exchanges among these seven figures, like those in the later pompae proper to Antigone, Haemon, and Ismene, figure as a kind of *psychomachia* that bodies forth two things: the debate that must be going on in each protagonist's mind and the moral judgment we the audience must make about what each protagonist has decided. Each of the pompae thus adds depth to Sophocles' rigid, rather two-dimensional figures by showing us at least some of the vacillation that even the crudest morality play could manage; at the same time, each of the pompae underscores the themes of the play—at least as Watson reads them—with some of the emphasis that, again,

---

30. This and other translations from Watson's Latin are my own. "Sum, Aequi columna, iuris & legum basis: / Vis esse foelix? vive Natura duce. / Tanta est potestas nostra. Sed spernor tamen, / Measque leges plurimi frangunt mali: / Periit sacratum iuris humani decus, / Pietas, pudorque, ac exulat mundo fides. /. . . . / Vos ergo famuli discite ex tantis malis, / Quam sit salubre iura Naturae sequi. / Invita si sim, rite procedet nihil" (*Sophoclis Antigone*, pp. 12–14).

any morality play would supply. Sophocles himself disappointingly shows us neither vacillation nor clear moral judgment. The purpose of poetry, says Watson's stage manager Poet before the first pompa, is to impress on the mind of man a speaking picture of virtue. With persuasive rhetoric and with the visual impressiveness that prompted Harvey's description "passingly beautiful," Watson's four pompae are calculated to provide just that.

Granted that Creon is stubborn and unfair, but when Antigone emerges in the second pompa as a headstrong fanatic who should give up her private grief for the public good, we begin to realize how far our twentieth-century perspective on the play misses that of Watson and his university audience. The logic with which Watson accomplishes this reversal is astounding. We would see this allegorical display just after Creon has had Antigone and Ismene both arrested and just before Haemon accuses his father of rigidity and injustice. Marshaled onstage by The Poet, a female figure called Greatness-of-Heart stands in for Antigone, articulates her predicament, and hears the conflicting arguments of Country, an old woman, and Bloodtie, a man in mourning. Blood-tie, not Country, finally wins her allegiance. The four figures who next step forward leave no doubt that Greatness-of-Heart, alias Antigone, has made the wrong choice:

TRANSGRESSION, *a man*:
  Transgression of Equity is my name: I follow
  Wherever Inclination leads me. I knock down the boundaries of
    fields;
  I leap across walls; I destroy boundary paths.
  Some sort of barrier always enkindles the breast:
  nothing can constrain, when public laws are broken.
  If something has the appearance of virtue, I don't care about it at
    all.

STUBBORNNESS, *a man*:
  Here I stand up, rebellious to the end—Stubbornness.
  I carry around a shameless face, go around in a great huff.
  The face of a judge doesn't faze me to do anything wrong.

A crime done—I defend it, toss it off, glory in it!
Eager for fame, I'll gladly carry out what the Fates have ordained.

OPPROBRIUM, *a man*:
I, Opprobrium, chase after guilty folks.
Behind perverse people I press up close
With a heavy push. Nobody holds me back.
After this, I'd shun even good friends.
Good deeds and former concerns drop out of my mind
altogether.
No harm admonishes me, obstinate as I am:
every snapping accusation I bark back at like a dog.

PUNISHMENT, *with an ax*:
With a booming loud voice, Punishment I'm called.
I wait upon the issue from judges' mouths.
With my right hand I carry out exile, death, imprisonment.
I prosecute royal decrees. I bring back heads that have been
chopped off.
No man who's answerable can avoid this cruel ax.[31]

What we have here, clearly enough, is a little morality play. In
their direct addresses to the audience the speakers display both
an interior and an exterior aspect: Blood-tie on the one hand
and Country on the other articulate the debate that must be
going on in Antigone's mind—or would be going on if she
were the vacillating protagonist of a morality play—at the

31. "TRANSGRESSIO, *vir.* / Transgressio aequi nomen est mihi: sequor /
Quo fert voluntas: Laedo vicinos agros, / Transilio septa, limites demolior; /
Admotus & obex pectus inflammat magis: / Nihil coercet iura frango publica.
/ Species honesti si qua, nil quicquam moror. /
"CONTUMACIA, *vir.* / Istuc rebellis asto Contumacia, / vultum impu-
dentem, spiritus magnos gero: / Nec me timere iudicis vultus facit. / Peccasse
quicquam non pudet, factum scelus / Defendo, iacto, glorior. Famae quasi /
Studens, libenter fata quod statuunt feram. /
"ODIUM, *vir.* / Odium scelestos prosequor: pravos premo / Vi ponderosa,
nemo me bene sustinet: / charos amicos ante hac tandem horreo, / Merita &
priora prorsus ex animo cadunt. / Me partinacem nullius damnum monet: /
Cuiusque mordax crimen allatro ut canis. /
"SUPPLICIUM, *cum securi.* / Immane recta voce supplicium vocor; / Ex ore
semper iudicantis pendeo. / Exilia, mortem, carcerem hac dextra fero. /
Perago imperata, reffero abscissum caput. / Saevam hanc securim nemo
declimat reus" (*Sophoclis Antigone*, pp. 57–59).

same time that Transgression, Stubbornness, Opprobrium, and Punishment make absolutely clear which of Antigone's alternatives is the right one. After such a display, who could feel any sympathy for Antigone when she stalks off to her cave, selfishly absorbed in her private grief, neglectful of her public duty?

Watson's third pompa is focused on Haemon. Predictably, Creon's rebellious son figures as a demonstration, as Watson puts it, that "scarcely anybody can love and be wise at the same time." Watson's poetic handling of this commonplace in the fourth thema was forceful enough to be anthologized several times in the next fifty years. Watson's translation of part of his fourth thema from *Antigone* is included in his *EKA-TOMPATHIA, or Passionate Century of Love* (1582) and was reprinted in all editions of *A Poetical Rhapsody* (1602 et seq.) as well as in *England's Parnassus* (1606):

> Where heate of love doth once possesse the heart,
> There *cares* oppresse the minde with wondrous ill,
> *Wit* runns awrye not fearing future smarte,
> And fond *desire* doth overmaster will:
>   The *belly* neither cares for meate nor drinke,
>   Nor over watched *eyes* desire to winke:
> *Footesteps* are false, and wavr'ing too and froe;
> The brightsome *flow'r of beauty* fades away:
> *Reason* retyres, and *pleasure* brings in woe:
> And *wisedome* yeldeth place to black *decay*:
>   *Counsell*, and *fame*, and *friendship* are contem'nd:
>   And bashfull *shame*, and Gods them selves condem'nd:
> Watchfull *suspect* is linked with *despaire*:
> Inconstant *hope* is often drown'd in *feares*:
> What *folly* hurtes not *fortune* can repayre;
> And *misery* doth swimme in Seas of *teares*:
>   Long use of *life* is but a lingring foe.
>   And gentle *death* is only end of woe.[32]

32. Thomas Watson, *EKATOMPATHIA*, ed. C. G. Cecioni (Catania, 1964), p. 99. In *A Poetical Rhapsody* Watson's verses appear as no. 226; in *England's Parnassus*, as no. 1045.

The only difficulty with Nature's severe judgments on
Creon, Antigone, and Haemon is that she apparently leaves
no one to stand as a positive example. The fourth and final
pompa gives us the figure we need to set against the others.
Even though she has made her final exit from the play nearly
six hundred lines before, never to reenter, Ismene is the char-
acter who, in the words of Watson's stage manager Poet,
"teaches the course our lives ought to follow." Reason and its
attendant virtues, Piety and Obedience, prepare the way for
Safety and Happiness with a crown. Watson's third thema
summarizes Ismene's virtues precisely: "what we cannot cor-
rect we should not bother ourselves about—this Ismene
teaches, leading the pattern of a quiet life."[33] Brave Antigone
a selfish wretch to be eschewed? Cowardly Ismene a model to
be emulated? There could be no clearer proof that sixteenth-
century academic audiences listened to speeches and followed
the unfolding plot exactly as Cicero instructed them to: as if
they were the jury at a trial. The litigants pled their cases; the
audience passed judgment. As the protagonists had to be
either right or wrong, so the audience had to feel either sym-
pathy or disdain. As there was no room for moral ambiguity,
so was there no room for the kind of divided response, the
tension between eleos and phobos, that Aristotle proposes as
tragedy's essential effect.

A decisive end to this academic tradition of staging classical
tragedies is marked by *The Tragedy of Orestes*, written by
Thomas Goffe most likely while he was an undergraduate at
Christ Church, Oxford, and acted in-house sometime
between 1613 and 1618. Not only is *Orestes* the last university
production of a classical tragedy cataloged in the *Annals of
English Drama*, but it displays the overwhelming influence of
a dramatic tradition totally unknown to Sulpicius, Erasmus,
and Nowell: the popular tragedies of London's public thea-
ters. In this respect Goffe's *Orestes* is the tragic counterpart of

33. *Sophoclis Antigone*, p. 66: "Quae corrigere non possumus, ea attentare
ne velimus docet Ismene, vitae quietae formam tradens."

The Birth of Hercules and Thomas Randolph's *Hey for Honesty,
Down with Knavery.*
   The prologue, spoken by the author himself, announces,

> We heere present for to revive a tale,
> Which once in Athens great Eurypedes
> In better phrase at such a meeting told
> The learn'd Athenians with much applause:
> The same we will retell unto your eares,
> Whose Atticke judgement is no lesse then theirs.[34]

Athens's civic Dionysia was hardly "such a meeting" as Christ
Church's Christmas revels, but Goffe in any case has his eyes
and ears trained on a metropolis far closer at hand: Southwark.
Goffe's *Tragedy of Orestes* has less to do with Euripides' *Orestes*
than it does with the likes of *The Spanish Tragedy, Hamlet, The
Revenger's Tragedy,* and *Antonio's Revenge.* Euripides' play pre-
sents the same part of Orestes' story as Aeschylus's *Eumenides*:
Agamemnon has already returned from Troy, Aegisthus and
Clytemnestra have already murdered him, Orestes has already
taken his bloody revenge and now faces not only the private
torment of the Furies but the public scrutiny of a trial. Goffe's
play crams all these prior events into four sensational acts,
turning to the more limited subject of Euripides' play only in
Act Five. Even more striking than the difference in subject is
the difference in tone. *Orestes* is one of Euripides' most ironic
plays: the enormous gap that separates Apollo's neat ordina-
tion of events from the altogether less neat reality of the
humans who have to *live* those events seems a matter for
laughter as much as tears. Goffe's play, with its gruesome
murders and forensic *copia,* shows us, by contrast, how Seneca
would have written the play if he had taken the subject in
hand—or rather how Kyd, Marston, or Tourneur would have
written the play remembering their Seneca from school. For
Goffe's *Orestes* is nothing else but a Jacobean revenger: he
feigns death to find out the truth of Aegisthus and Clytem-
nestra's guilt, he receives confirmation from his father's

---

34. Thomas Goffe, *The Tragedy of Orestes* (London, 1633). Quotations will
be cited in the text.

ghost, he poses as a physician in order to catch the couple alone and torture them before he kills them. In drawing Orestes' character, Goffe seems to have had his eye on Hamlet in particular: it is his mother's guilt as much as his father's death that disturbs Orestes; Pylades' reasonableness—so like Horatio's—offsets Orestes' passion, Aegisthus tries to use ever-dutiful Electra to pry into Orestes' secrets as Claudius uses Ophelia; Agamemnon's exhumed skull gives Orestes occasion for a long speech on human vanity, confirmation of Aegisthus and Clytemnestra's guilt comes in a dumb-show. It is not just the characters and incidents of *Hamlet* that Goffe has copied but the play's very language: Pylades and Orestes show, for example, a curious fondness for theatrical meta-phors. Perhaps because the Trojan War has only just con-cluded, Pylades seems to be remembering "What's Hecuba to him or he to Hecuba?" when he consoles Orestes:

> PYLADES. If actors on the stage having no cause,
>   But for to winne an hearers hands applause,
>   Can let fall teares, wee'll thinke wee Actors be,
>   And onely doe but play griefes Tragedie.
> ORESTES. O, but deare friend, should we but act a part,
>   The play being ended, passion left the heart,
>   And we should share of joy, but my whole age
>   Must never move from off this wofull Stage. (2.3. sig. c4)

It may be to the London stage that Goffe looks for striking characters and startling incidents, but when he has to decide how to end things, he turns to the book presses of the college library. In Euripides' play, as in Aeschylus's *Eumenides*, Orestes' act of vengeance poses a difficult ethical question: is Orestes guilty of murder, or does the prior guilt of Clytem-nestra and Aegisthus exonerate him? As spokesmen for the letter of the law, Menelaus and Clytemnestra's father Tynda-reus step forward in Euripides' play and condemn Orestes to exile. Too stern, the audience is likely to conclude—until Orestes and Pylades respond with a series of attempted revenges so violent and arbitrary as to alienate the sympathy they have earned by their suffering. In Aeschylus's play it was

Athena who decided the issue by breaking the divided jury
and casting her vote in favor of Orestes; in Euripides' play
Apollo descends just in time to order Orestes to drop his
sword from the neck of Helen's daughter and to marry his
intended victim instead. Menelaus gets a new wife, and all live
happily ever after. No such ethical ambiguity perplexes Goffe;
he simply ends the play as Seneca would, with Orestes and
Pylades committing Stoic suicide:

> PYLADES. . . . come *Tyndareus*, see,
>   We scorne to live when all our friends are dead,
>   Nor shall thy Fury make base famine be
>   The executioner to my dearest friend,
>   Whilst I can kill him, therefore spight of thee,
>   Wee'll free our selves, past all calamity.
> ORESTES. Yes *Pylades*, we will beguile our time,
>   And make him search through every nooke a' th['] world,
>   If he in all his race can ever spie,
>   Two that like us did live, like us did die.   (5.7. sig. 12ᵛ)

But, on second thought, Orestes *has* committed murder.
Goffe cancels the heroic effect of this exemplary suicide by
bringing on Tyndareus to speak the epilogue. Law has the last
word, after all:

> 'Tis vile to hate a Father, but such love,
> As breeds hate to' th['] mother, worse doth prove:
> Our life consists of ayre, our state of winde,
> All things we leave behind us which wee find,
> Saving our faults; witnesse *Orestes* here,
> Who was his owne tormentor, his owne feare.
> Who flying all, yet could not fly himselfe,
> But needs must shipwrack upon murders selfe;
> And so his brest made hard with miserie,
> He grew himselfe to be his enemy.   (5.8. sig. 13ᵛ)

And for good measure Tyndareus goes on to warn about the
sway of fickle Fortune. Stoic hero, moral criminal, victim of
Fortune: Goffe's philosophical views of Orestes are as much a
grab bag of clichés as his characters and incidents are. Less
important than which of the three views really applies is the

very fact that Goffe assumes that one of them, singly, will. Here is the academic hard-line we have heard so often before. To Goffe, no less than to Nowell, Neville, Gascoigne, Watson, and Gager, the ethical issues in classical tragedy are always reducible to a simple, indeed simplistic, moral argument.

When we survey the first century of productions of classical tragedy in England, we might logically expect to see a pattern of slow development, in which increasing awareness of the true nature of classical tragedy gradually replaced the medieval nearsightedness of the first generation of humanists. If the seven English productions that we know about are at all representative, nothing could be further from the case. The same defenses voiced in Sulpicius's prologue for Seneca's *Hippolytus* in 1485 are voiced in Gager's defense of university drama more than a century later; the same attempt to bend ethical complexities into straight moral lines that is implicit in Alexander Nowell's draft prologue for Seneca's *Hippolytus* in 1546 informs the pompae that Thomas Watson provided for *Antigone* in 1581; the same delight in spectacular stage effects that governed plans for "whip-bearing Ajax" in 1564 explains Cupid and Megaera's rise from the Underworld in 1592; the same fascination with romantic passion as a motive that made *Hippolytus* Pomponius's first choice in 1485 and prompted Nowell to rank it foremost among Seneca's tragedies inspired Gager to heighten the love interest when he directed that play near the end of the century. The academic perspective on classical tragedy was an astonishingly sure and fixed perspective, and it suggests several general conclusions about how in-house English audiences experienced tragic plays in performance.

The seven productions that we have surveyed make it clear that academic audiences in England had arrived at that crucial poise of responses that seems essential to tragedy, a balance between a visceral emotional response to the sufferings of an individual hero, immediately before us, and a cerebral sense of the larger issues his suffering touches. Academic and courtly audiences may have felt a *poise* of responses, but it is equally certain that they had not yet arrived at the *tension* between responses that figures for Aristotle as the central fact of tragedy in the theater. Guided by the morality-play tradition, the Englishmen who watched productions of Seneca in schools, colleges, the inns of court, and the court of the realm preferred those larger issues a great deal more immediate, a great deal more clearly stated—and a great deal simpler than we do. Drawing on Aristotle, Hegel distinguishes the kind of simplified emotions we feel in these academic productions from the more complicated emotions that the ancient scripts in fact engage. There are two kinds of pity, Hegel insists:

The first is just the ordinary sensibility—in other words, a sympathy with the misfortunes and sufferings of another, and one which is experienced as something finite and negative. Your countrified cousin is ready enough with compassion of this order. The man of nobility and greatness, however, has no wish to be smothered with this sort of pity. For just to the extent that it is merely the nugatory aspect, the negative of misfortune which is asserted, a real depreciation of misfortune is implied. True sympathy, on the contrary, is an accordant feeling with the ethical claim at the same time associated with the sufferer—that is, with what is necessarily implied in his condition as affirmative and substantive.[35]

True tragic pity, in Hegel's view, is a synthesis of our compassion for the hero as an individual with our awareness of the universal, morally justified principle that the hero has embraced.

The greatest Greek tragedies, Hegel proposes, show us the clash of two such heroes, the irreconcilable conflict of two such universal rights. With its warring demands of divine law against human law, of individual conscience against public responsibility, Sophocles' *Antigone* figures as Hegel's "model" tragedy, just as *Oedipus Rex* figures as Aristotle's. Though we might not put it in such dogmatic terms as Hegel, we must

35. Friedrich Hegel, *The Philosophy of Fine Art* (collected and published posthumously, 1835), trans. F.P.B. Osmaston (1920), excerpts repr. in *Tragedy: Vision and Form*, ed. Robert W. Corrigan (San Francisco, 1965), p. 431. Hegel's theory is analyzed in Walter J. Kaufmann, *Tragedy and Philosophy* (New York, 1968), pp. 200–212.

concede that tragedy does seem to focus on human will *in extremis*: if not a deadlock of one willful character against another as in *Antigone*, we witness the clash of human will with external forces: with circumstance, with society, with "fate," with God. Hegel contends, with some justice for Greek tragedy at least, that in such clashes neither side is wrong. In this view the very essence of tragedy is contradiction. The business of tragedy, Jean-Pierre Vernant proposes, is to set up and to work through the contradictory elements in a culture's experience, particularly the conflict between the will of the individual and the strictures of society. Seen in its fifth-century social context, *Oedipus*, for example, presents the clash of two opposed systems of justice, an archaic code in which the individual is responsible for justice himself and a new code in which justice is determined by democratic vote. The same conflict governs Aeschylus's *Oresteia*.[36] It is these contradictions, this tension between competing systems of value, that explain the complex emotions, the tension between eleos and phobos, that Aristotle sees as tragedy's characteristic effect.

From such a double perspective on the tragic hero and his situation the academic producers of the sixteenth century could hardly be farther removed. Pomponius, Cinthio, Gager, and the others may seem an unlikely group to act the country cousin, but in their prologues, entr'acte devices, and critical apologies, all of them are quite clearly thinking of Hegel's "ordinary sensibility" whenever they speak of "pity." They submit the tragic hero to moral scrutiny and judge him as one thing or the other: either a victim or a malefactor. The result is a simple ethical situation that calls for an equally simple response: either pity for the victim's undeserved sufferings or horror at the deeds of the malefactor. As we have seen, Aristotle's insistence that the tragic hero should err, but

36. Jean-Pierre Vernant, "Greek Tragedy: Problems of Interpretation," in *The Structuralist Controversy*, ed. Richard Macksey and Eugenio Donato (Baltimore, 1972), pp. 273–95, and "Ambiguity and Reversal: On the Enigmatic Structure of *Oedipus Rex*," repr. in *Greek Tragedy: Modern Essays in Criticism*, ed. Erich Segal (New York, 1983), pp. 189–209.

err *unwittingly*, was one of the hardest parts of the *Poetics* to reconcile with Christian accountability. Morality plays show heroes who err altogether wittingly. However funny and engaging they may have been along the way, they leave the play with the audience's moral condemnation heaped upon them. The seven productions we have reconstructed make it clear enough that academic producers looked to the immediate example of morality plays, not to the distant prescriptions of the *Poetics*, for guidance in how to present the protagonists of Sophocles, Seneca, and Euripides. Behind Watson's allegorical pompae, behind Neville's amplified speeches in Seneca's *Oedipus*, behind Gascoigne and Kinwelmershe's dumb-shows and extended debates stand the time-tested devices of plays like *Mankind* and *The Castle of Perseverance*. By casting their heroes as martyrs or malefactors, Nowell, Gascoigne and Kinwelmershe, Watson, Gager, and Goffe seek a much simpler emotional response to tragic drama than either Aristotle or Hegel describes. Watson's impulse to find a moral flaw in the hero was strong enough, as we have see, to turn Antigone—"the most glorious figure ever to have appeared on earth," Hegel hailed her—into a blind and obstinate creature who shirks her public duty to the state and fully deserves to be sealed off from society in a cave—and this without Watson's mistranslating a single speech of Sophocles' text. Nowell and Gager could take the same hero, Hippolytus, and read him in absolutely contradictory ways: Nowell, as a victim who suffers innocently; Gager, as a proud snob who thoroughly deserves his punishment.

The *agon* that gives shape to a play like *Mankind* and brings its characters to life is a conflict not of right against right but of right against wrong. Cast as an antagonist who chooses wrong, Antigone demanded a protagonist who chooses right: with more than a little stretching of Sophocles' point, Watson found his positive example in Ismene. Euripides suffered the same moral revision. In the clash of Eteocles and Polyneices in the *Phoenician Women*, Euripides seems determined to deny us, as he usually does, any moral rope to catch hold of amid the sinking fortunes of Thebes. What we witness is not so much right against right as wrong against wrong. Dolce and Gascoigne and Kinwelmershe manage to steady the ship of state. Their Eteocles emerges as a tyrant to be despised; their Polyneices, as a martyr to be admired.

For all its fiery poetry, for all its fierce portrayal of social disaster and intense human suffering, classical tragedy was produced so as to confirm, not challenge, the values of the closed societies, the private sixteenth- and seventeenth-century households, who watched it. Seneca's Phaedra and Oedipus, Euripides' Creon and Eteocles, Sophocles' Antigone, Euripides' Orestes—the insistent individuality of these heroes was seen as a threat to established social values of moderation, obedience, and rationality and thus was not allowed to engage an audience's sympathy for long. In the hands of the earliest English producers, performance of Greek and Roman tragedy became a ritual in which indomitable individuals were ceremonially exorcised from the social order.

II

The open space of the public stage left more room for contumacious characters to press their case. When Nowell, Neville, Gager, Gascoigne, Watson, and Goffe brought together classical texts and English dramatic traditions, they set up an encounter of actors and audience that the conventions of neither ancient theater nor medieval theater could accommodate alone. In range of motives, in depth of character, in intensity of emotion, in rhetorical force of language, above all in different ethical assumptions, classical tragedy opened up new dramatic territory in which Renaissance playwrights, actors, and audiences had to find their bearings. Existing dramatic traditions could guide them only so far. In the morality plays of William Wager, in the diverse experiments of Christopher Marlowe, and in the history plays of William Shakespeare we can feel an ever tighter tension between observed experience and the dramatic devices available for bringing that experience to the stage. The heroes of classical tragedy posed a potent challenge to existing dramatic conventions.[37] It was a chal-

37. Most attempts to demonstrate the influence of classical tragedy have

lenge that academic producers by and large ignored. The arena
in which past and present met most creatively was not in the
great halls of schools, colleges, and the inns of court but in the
public playhouses of Elizabethan and Jacobean London. With
tragedy as with comedy, Shakespeare and his fellow play-
wrights for the public theater were able to bring together
present experience and past experience in sometimes explosive
ways. Out of those contradictions emerged modern tragedy.

Many superficial features mark *Titus Andronicus* as a "clas-
sical" play: its Roman subject matter (this, despite Shake-
speare's unhistorical, thoroughly romantic sources), its bor-
rowing of plot motifs like Thyestes' banquet, its several Latin
sententiae (including one quotation from Seneca's *Hippolytus*),
its numerous parallels between the protagonists and myth-
ological characters, its characterization of Titus as a hero who
suffers with the Stoic patience of Seneca's Oedipus—until he
turns into an implacable avenger like Seneca's Tantalus.
Lavinia's similarity to Philomel, raped and then silenced by
having her tongue cut out, is pointed out several times, most
strikingly by Lavinia herself when she uses her handless stubs
to turn the leaves of a volume of Ovid and show Philomel's
story to her father and uncle (4.1.47–53). In her barbaric cru-
elty, Tamora figures as Semiramis (2.3.118). More than once,
Saturninus is called Tarquin; the raped Lavinia becomes a
modern Lucrece; Titus, a modern Lucius Junius Brutus
(3.1.296–98, 4.1.88–94). The function of all these myth-
ological parallels is indicated by Titus just before he throws
off the guise of Stoic endurance and takes the decisive action
of killing his daughter and slaying her tormentors:

been concerned with matters of structure and style: John W. Cunliffe, *The
Influence of Seneca on Elizabethan Tragedy* (London, 1893); H. B. Charlton, *The
Senecan Tradition in Renaissance Tragedy* (1921; repr. Manchester, 1946); F. L.
Lucas, *Seneca and Elizabethan Tragedy* (Cambridge, 1922); and T. S. Eliot,
Introduction to *Seneca His Tenne Tragedies* (London, 1927) and "Shakespeare
and the Stoicism of Seneca" (1927), repr. in *Selected Essays* (London, 1950),
pp. 107–20. Important qualifications to these traditional views are voiced by
G. K. Hunter in "Seneca and the Elizabethans: A Case-Study in 'Influence,' "
Shakespeare Survey 20 (1967): 17–26, and "Seneca and Elizabethan Tragedy,"
in Costa, *Seneca*, pp. 166–204.

TITUS. My lord the emperor, resolve me this:
  Was it well done of rash Virginius
  To slay his daughter with his own right hand,
  Because she was enforced, stained, and deflower'd?
SATURNINUS. It was, Andronicus.
TITUS. Your reason, mighty lord?
SATURNINUS. Because the girl should not survive
    her shame.
  And by her presence still renew his sorrows.
TITUS. A reason mighty, strong, and effectual;
  A pattern, precedent, and lively warrant
  For me, most wretched, to perform the like.
  Die, die, Lavinia, and thy shame with thee,
  And with thy shame thy father's sorrow die![38]

And so he ends Lavinia's sufferings. Such patterns, prece-
dents, and warrants produce a curiously flattening effect: in
these crucial moments at least, they deprive the characters of
their individuality and fix them as heroic types. As if it were
not already distant enough from sixteenth-century London,
Rome itself becomes such a type in the play's last scene.
"Speak," Marcus commands Titus's son Lucius, just returned
from mustering the invading Goths.

Tell us what Sinon hath bewitched our ears,
Or who hath brought the fatal engine in
That gives our Troy, our Rome, the civil wound.   (5.3.80, 85–87)

Already Titus has been called "the Roman Hector" (4.1.88).
  Beyond these obvious "classical" details, however, *Titus
Andronicus* incorporates several specific features that derive
from the traditional ways in which Seneca and other classical
tragedians were brought to the stage in the sixteenth century.
At least in the play's first scenes *Titus Andronicus* is marked,
first of all, by a more solid sense of place than is the rule in
Shakespeare's early history plays. "*Enter the Tribunes and Sen-
ators aloft,*" say the opening stage directions. Saturninus and

---

38. *The Most Lamentable Romaine Tragedie of Titus Andronicus*, 5.3.35–47,
ed. Gustav Cross in *The Complete Works*, gen. ed. Alfred Harbage, Pelican
Text Revised (Baltimore, 1969). Future quotations are cited in the text.

Bassianus, competing for the tribunes' and senators' choice as emperor, enter at opposite doors below. When Saturninus asks the assembly above to "Open the gates and let me in" (1.1.65), the ensuing stage directions give the stage's back wall a fixed identity as "*the Senate House*." One of the openings in the wall, presumably the space "within," becomes a practicable tomb when moments later Titus makes his triumphant entry and inters the coffins of his slain sons. Following the narrative of Shakespeare's romantic source, most of the play, however, moves with very unclassical license from Rome to the dark valley where Lavinia is raped to the camp where Lucius musters the Goths and back again to Rome. A rather more certain reflection of how classical tragedies were staged is Tamora's strategem of appearing to Titus in the guise of Revenge with her two sons arrayed as Rape and Murder. Pageants with just such allegorical personages, we recall, served to demarcate the five acts of Gascogine and Kinwelmershe's *Jocasta* and Watson's *Antigone* and to body forth the philosophical program of the play.

The philosophical program of Shakespeare's *Titus* is, indeed, just the sort of program we have encountered in the great halls of Oxford and Cambridge colleges and the inns of court. The human drama of Titus's suffering is framed by a political lesson. That ideological frame is quite literal, since it is primarily in the first and last scenes of the play that Shakespeare borrows episodes and ideas from Plutarch's *Lives* and applies them to Titus's Rome and, by implication, to Elizabeth's London. In the first scene the rival claims of Saturninus and Bassianus touch on the great political theme of Shakespeare's history plays, while the note sounded by Lucius in the play's closing lines is clearly admonitory:

> See justice done on Aaron, that damned Moor
> By whom our heavy haps had their beginning.
> Then, afterwards, to order well the state,
> That like events may ne'er it ruinate. (5.3.201–204)

Amid the ruins, Titus shines as a mirror of Roman virtue: refusing to capitalize on his own popularity and stand as candidate himself, he agrees to mediate between the rival claims of Saturninus and Bassianus. As the rule of primogeniture demands, he chooses Saturninus—and from that legitimate choice proceed all the horrors of the play. In *Titus*, as in Renaissance productions of ancient tragedy, sexual passion plays its modern romantic part in these horrors, but the last scene of the play does not let us forget that passion and politics are darkly allied.

Does Titus err in following precedent, not policy, in his choice of Saturninus? That possibility is never raised, for *Titus*, like the academic productions of Seneca, presents characters who have already stood up for moral judgment and are cast against each other as polar opposites. Thus, ever-virtuous Titus is contrasted with peremptory Saturninus; chaste Lavinia, with libidinous Tamora. Yet the tragic situation in *Titus Andronicus* is not quite so simple as it is in the productions of Seneca mounted by Nowell, Neville, and Gager. The world of Shakespeare's play corresponds to neither of the worlds usually set in place by academic producers: neither a moral universe ruled over by a providential God nor the domain of blind Fortune, the world of *Titus Andronicus* is positively inimical to any display of virtue. When Stoic patience has seemingly driven Titus mad, his brother Marcus cries out in despair:

> O heavens, can you hear a good man groan
> And not relent, or not compassion him?
> Marcus, attend him in his ecstacy,
> That hath more scars of sorrows in his heart
> Than foemen's marks upon his batt'red shield,
> But yet so just that he will not revenge.
> Revenge the heavens for old Andronicus! (4.1.123–29)

The gods, in this play at least, turn a deaf ear to such pleas. Titus must pursue his own revenge. Still "in his ecstacy," the beleaguered general contrives a bizarre scene that delineates quite literally the bleak universe in which he acts out the ensuing tragedy. First he orders Publius to search the Underworld for justice. Finding no help there, and seeing none about him on earth, Titus directs his kinsmen to take arrows that are tipped with appeals to the gods and shoot them toward heaven. In Shakespeare's source this is a gesture of mad defiance; in *Titus* it is a quixotic gesture of desperation:[39]

> sith there's no justice in earth or hell,
> We will solicit heaven, and move the gods
> To send down Justice for to wreak our wrongs.   (4.3.49–51)

But justice is not forthcoming. Titus must take a stand for justice himself, and the price of that stand is death. In the source Titus's death is a full-scale Senecan suicide; in Shakespeare's play it is the more perfunctory matter of being stabbed by Saturninus, who is executed in turn by Lucius. There is not even time for a death speech.[40] Among the many lapses in Shakespeare's first attempt at tragedy this strange silence is the most crucial. Shakespeare has chosen not to articulate the ethical dilemma here, but the dilemma stands: Titus does a right deed, yet he dies for it. That tragic ambiguity is not to be found in the simpler, more optimistic worlds of academic drama.

From a philosophical viewpoint at least, an inimical universe like that in *Titus Andronicus* is Seneca's most important contribution to Elizabethan tragedy.[41] Most academic produc-

---

39. Compare *The Tragical History of Titus Andronicus* (London, n.d. [mid-eighteenth century], derived from a now lost sixteenth-century original): "Andronicus, upon these Calamities, feigned himself distracted, and went raving about the City, shooting his Arrows towards Heaven, as in Defiance, calling to Hell for Vengeance, which mainly pleased the Empress and her Sons, who thought themselves now secure; and through his Friends required Justice of the Emperor against the Ravishers, yet they could have not Redress, he rather threatening them, if they insisted on it . . ." (repr. Geoffrey Bullough, ed., *Narrative and Dramatic Sources of Shakespeare*, Vol. 6 [New York, 1966]: 43).

40. Compare *The Tragical History*: "After this, to prevent the Torments he expected, when these Things came to be known, at his Daughter's Request, he killed her; and so, rejoicing he had revenged himself on his Enemies to the full, fell on his own Sword and died" (Bullough, *Narrative and Dramatic Sources*, 6: 44).

41. J.M.R. Margeson, *The Origins of English Tragedy* (Oxford, 1967), pp. 82–84.

tions, as we have seen, falsify Seneca's universe by taking the characters and setting them down in the providential universe of medieval morality plays. Shakespeare, braver than the schoolmasters, looks unflinchingly into the surrounding blackness. It is, perhaps, just this friction between Christian ethics and Stoic pessimism that sparks Shakespeare's tragedies to blazing life. As full of miscalculations as it is, *Titus Andronicus* nonetheless shares with Shakespeare's great tragedies a refusal to take the complex matter of man's relationship to the universe and reduce it to a simple formula. Only in the public theater was Seneca's dark world opened up for exploration. Only in that open social context was there no moral argument to be demonstrated, no in-group orthodoxy to be confirmed. To say that is not to turn *Titus Andronicus* into an existential statement. On the contrary, Shakespeare's first tragedy affirms certain clear, indeed conservative moral values—patriotism, courage, chastity—but unlike academic productions of classical tragedy, *Titus* also shows the impossibly high price those values can exact.

The complexities of Titus's situation philosophically demand a corresponding complexity of response emotionally. Like academic productions of Seneca, *Titus Andronicus* provides plenty of occasions for simple pity and simple fear. Indeed, Shakespeare describes in the play a perfect instance of the kind of unreflective fear that Hegel would attribute to country cousins. Lucius's young son tells his uncle how his aunt has read to him about the fall of Troy:

> . . . I have heard my grandsire say full oft,
> Extremity of griefs would make men mad;
> And I have read that Hecuba of Troy
> Ran mad for sorrow; that made me to fear,
> Although, my lord, I know my noble aunt
> Loves me as dear as e'er my mother did,
> And would not, but in fury, fright my youth;
> Which made me down to throw my books, and fly,
> Causeless, perhaps. (4.1.18–26)

Simple fear because an event is terrible, simple pity because someone suffers—*Titus* offers plenty of opportunities for both. But it also attaches ethical values to those emotions. The moral ambiguity of Titus's dilemma, guilty yet not guilty, takes those two separate and simple emotions of pity and fear and sets them in the state of tension that Aristotle describes as the mark of the greatest tragedies.

Unlike Shakespeare's casual borrowings, Ben Jonson's debt to classical tragedy is conscious and carefully considered. Setting out to acclimatize ancient tragedy to the London stage in 1603, eight years before his mentor Heinsius published his systemization of Aristotle, Jonson was tutored in tragedy primarily by Cicero and Horace. Thus, the play's five acts are set apart by choruses of musicians, most of the interesting events (including Tiberius's homosexual debauches as well as the usual acts of violence) happen offstage, the play abounds in *sententiae* awaiting declamation. Though there is nothing in *Sejanus* quite like the whole speech from Cicero that is dropped into *Catiline*, Jonson brings to tragedy a thorough-going sense of the play-as-rhetorical-event. In his preface Jonson apologizes for "the want of a proper chorus, whose habit and moods are such and so difficult as not any whom I have seen since the ancients—no, not they who have most presently affected laws—have yet come in the way of."[42] And yet most of his characters function just as a Chorus would: in satiric asides virtuous observers comment on wicked strategists, and two onstage meetings of the Senate give opportunity for full-scale stand-up speechmaking. In the contrasted trials of Silius in Act Three and of Sejanus in Act Five the tragedy becomes a rhetorical event quite literally. The four elements of tragedy outlined in the preface reveal just how closely Jonson's view of tragedy is allied to academic dogma: neglecting some of Horace's prescriptions in the interest of "popular delight," Jonson has nonetheless aimed at "truth of argument, dignity of persons, gravity and height of elocution, fullness and frequency of sentence." Just as his sprawling historical "argument" has none of the concentration of classical

42. *Sejanus His Fall*, "To the Readers," 17–20, ed. Jonas A. Barish (New Haven, 1965), pp. 26–27. Future quotations are cited in the text.

tragedy, so too is the universe he creates a far more moral place than the worlds of Seneca, Sophocles, and Euripides. There are, to be sure, no Christian anachronisms. Jonson is too much the scholar for that. And yet the pagan gods so often invoked in *Sejanus* are forces of moral justice. The downward-turning point in Sejanus's career occurs when he interrupts the sacrifice to the goddess Fortune, challenges the bad omens, and blasphemes the goddess by declaring his own divinity:

> . . . I, the slave
> And mock of fools? Scorn on my worthy head!
> Yea, sacrificed unto myself, in Rome,
> No less than Jove—and I be brought to do
> A peevish giglot rites? Perhaps the thought
> And shame of that made Fortune turn her face,
> Knowing herself the lesser deity,
> And but my servant. (5.202–209)

Lest we interpret Fortune as only an allegorical stand-in for happenstance, Terentius draws a providential moral in the play's last speech:

> Let this example move th'insolent man
> Not to grow proud and careless of the gods.
> It is an odious wisdom to blaspheme,
> Much more to slighten or deny their powers.
> For whom the morning saw so great and high,
> Thus low and little, 'fore the'even doth lie.

Sejanus falls, not by chance, but in punishment for his proud presumption.

Like the academic producers of Seneca, Sophocles, and Euripides, Jonson provides a moral foil for his protagonist. In their contrasted trials and contrasted deaths, Silius and Sejanus stand as opposite types of civic virtue and self-serving tyranny. A thoroughly self-aware Machiavellian manipulator, Sejanus has none of the moral ambiguity that marks Titus Andronicus. The emotions that Jonson's play engages are thus simple. Pity for the undeserved suffering of Silius, fear at the sheer power of a tyrant like Sejanus—Jonson's play invokes these simple emotions and keeps them separate. With no ethical claim on the audience's sympathies, Sejanus as a tragic hero asks for one thing only: moral condemnation. Jonson intended his public audience to leave the Globe just as private audiences left the great halls of Oxford and Cambridge and the inns of court, with a political lesson learned and their ethical values intact. Jonson's audience apparently left the theater also by tearing the play apart with all the violence that the Romans wreaked on Sejanus's body. The failure of *Sejanus* at the box office confirms how crucially important social context was in shaping tragedy as well as comedy. Moral dogma and forensic display may have been enough to carry a tragedy in schools, colleges, and the inns of court, but on the South Bank they could not compensate for one-dimensional characters and a dearth of incident—in a word, for the complexities of life.

III

When Charles II restored both monarchy and stage drama to England, classical tragedy finally achieved the popular success for which Renaissance humanists like Pomponius Laetus had hoped—but hardly in the guise they had imagined. Throughout the seventeenth century, academic interest in Greek and Latin drama continued, of course. Schools and colleges continued to mount adaptations of Greek and Latin plays, but for Oxford and Cambridge at least the records are scantier than in the sixteenth century.[43] Perhaps because drama disappeared from the public stage, the Interregnum press produced a small shelf-full of elegant verse translations: Seneca's *Medea* by Edward Sherburne (1648), Sophocles' *Electra* by Christopher Wase (1649–1650) with allegorical apparatus comparing the exiled Princess Elizabeth to Sophocles' heroine, Seneca's *Hippolytus* by Edmund Prestwich (1651), Seneca's *Troades* by Samuel Pordage (1660). Nor did the spate of published translations stop with the Restoration: John

43. Moore Smith, *College Plays*, pp. 10ff., notes that most Cambridge colleges had ceased to give plays even before the Puritan prohibition of 1642. The Restoration brought "but a flickering revival."

Wright's version of Seneca's *Thyestes* appeared in 1674, Sir Edward Sherburne's translation of Seneca's *Troades* in 1679, John Talbot's rendering of the same play in 1686, Sherburne's translation of Seneca's *Hippolytus* in 1700 (reissued in a collected edition with Sherburne's *Hippolytus* and *Medea* in 1702). A new name among these seventeenth-century translations is Aeschylus. Thomas Stanley's Latin translation of the seven extant plays, printed in 1673, reflects the increasing sophistication of classical scholarship in the seventeenth century, but it failed to redress Aeschylus's critical misfortunes. The number of translations alone leaves no room for doubt: even after the Restoration, Seneca retained his overwhelming popularity. The fact that most of these seventeenth-century English translations of Seneca are cast not in blank verse but in "heroic" couplets indicates, however, that the polished, eloquent Seneca encountered by Restoration readers was altogether different from the rough, ranting Seneca of Alexander Neville. Seneca submitted to a change in dress to keep up with neoclassical taste. Gathered in the geometric spaces of Drury Lane and the Dorset Garden, Restoration audiences looked upon tragedy as a species of epic. They did so partly because public theater and court theater were no longer the two separate places they had been in the Renaissance: the "epic" aspirations of the restored monarchy left a decisive mark on tragedy on the public stage. The two occasions when the heroes of classical tragedy joined onstage such personages as Aureng-Zebe and the Empress of Morocco reflect these physical, social, and philosophical structures.

From its first appearance at the Dorset Garden Theater in late 1678 or early 1679, when Betterton and his wife took the roles of Oedipus and Jocasta, John Dryden and Nathaniel Lee's *Oedipus: A Tragedy* held the London stage for seventy-five years.[44] Just as Gascoigne and Kinwelmershe approached

---

44. On the theatrical history of Dryden and Lee's *Oedipus*, see John Dryden, *The Dramatic Works*, ed. Montague Summers, Vol. 4 (1932; repr. New York, 1968): 346–50. My quotations from the play come from Summers's edition and are cited in the text. Performances before 1700 are calen-

Euripides' *Phoenician Women* indirectly, via Dolce's *Giocasta*, so Dryden and Lee were inspired in the first instance not by Sophocles or Seneca directly but by Corneille's *Oedipe*, first acted at Paris twenty years earlier and published in 1659. In both cases the English reinterpretation of a continental interpretation of a classical original tells us even more about English theatrical experience than a direct imitation of the classical original would. Dryden and Lee brought to Seneca, Sophocles, and Corneille the sense of historical relativity that touched off the Battle of Ancients and Moderns, but they brought also two practiced playwrights' sharp sense of their London audience. That awareness of audience, as we have noted already, is one of the ways in which Cicero's idea of the play-as-rhetorical-event shaped neoclassical drama even more decisively than Aristotle's idea of the play-as-aesthetic-object. The Ancients may have inspired Dryden and Lee's choice of subject; it was Moderns who would or would not pay money to see their play. "*Sophocles* indeed is admirable every where," says Dryden in his preface to *Oedipus*: "And therefore we have follow'd him as close as possibly we cou'd: But the *Athenian* Theater (whether more perfect than ours is not now disputed) had a perfection differing from ours." For example, in ancient tragedy the Chorus takes as much time singing as the protagonists do speaking. Given their overriding interest in character, modern audiences are not going to be satisfied with secondary characters who appear once and then are heard from no more. Modern audiences expect a subplot. "Custom likewise has obtain'd, that we must form an under-plot of second Persons, which must be depending on the first, and their by-walks must be like those in a Labyrinth, which all of 'em lead into the great Parterre: or like so many several lodging Chambers, which have their outlets into the same Gallery. Perhaps after all, if we cou'd think so, the ancient method, as 'tis the easiest, is also the most Natural, and the best" (p. 352).

But modern custom is modern custom, and Dryden and

Lee accordingly have made two big additions to Sophocles' play, both of them noted in the preface. First, from Seneca's *Oedipus* they have appropriated the scene of Tiresias's raising the ghost of Laius onstage. What was an occasion for brilliant rhetorical display in Seneca becomes in Dryden and Lee an occasion for a spectacular stage set piece. Second, from Corneille's *Oedipe* they have taken over the romantic subplot of Euridice in love with Adrastus but pursued by Creon. What was a sentimental love story with a happy ending in Corneille becomes in Dryden and Lee a dark, forbidding "bi-walk" that converges on "the great Parterre" of Oedipus's tragedy. Other smaller additions enhance the theatricality of the play—Creon is cast as a hunchback Richard III, Oedipus has a sleepwalking soliloquy right out of *Macbeth*, Laius's offstage ghost speaks as a shade from *Hamlet* when Jocasta enters in her nightgown to take Oedipus back to bed—but it is the two larger additions that measure the distance from the Theater of Dionysius to the Dorset Garden. The effects of Dryden and Lee's changes are three.

They serve first of all to enhance the political and romantic interest of the play. Love and politics, the very soul of Restoration tragedy, are both peripheral to Sophocles' sharp focus on Oedipus as a heroically isolated figure. In Sophocles' original, Oedipus only supposes that Creon has designs on the throne; in Dryden and Lee's version Creon actively plots to overthrow his brother-in-law. The play opens not with Oedipus receiving suppliants (that is postponed until halfway through the first act), but with Creon looking, speaking, and acting like an Athenian Richard III. Hunchbacked and bow-legged, his face to Euridice's view "Half minted with the Royal stamp of man; / And half o'recome with beast" (Act One, p. 359), Creon poses as the arch-manipulator and gleefully takes the audience into his confidence about his two passions—seizing the crown and winning Euridice:

> My body opens inward to my soul,
> And lets in day to make my Vices seen
> By all discerning eyes, but the blind vulgar.

I must make haste er'e *Oedipus* return,
To snatch the Crown and her; for I still love;
But love with malice; as an angry Cur
Snarls while he feeds, so will I seize and stanch
The hunger of my love on this proud beauty,
And leave the scraps for Slaves.   (Act One, p. 360)

Creon's grotesque attempts to woo Euridice recall Richard's assault on recently widowed Anne—with a salacious touch of *A King and No King*, since, as Oedipus himself points out, Creon and Euridice are uncle and niece: "'Tis too like Incest: 'tis offence to Kind" (Act One, p. 369). The romantic interest so conspicuously absent from ancient tragedy in general and from Sophocles in particular is supplied not only by the sub-plot perils of Euridice and Adrastus but by the conjugal devotion that Oedipus and Jocasta demonstrate for one another.

Heightening of characterization is, indeed, the second effect of Dryden and Lee's additions. By reducing the role of the Chorus to a few crowd scenes at the beginning and ending of the play, Dryden and Lee turn the tragedy of Oedipus into a much more *private* affair than it is in Sophocles. Several key events that Sophocles stages in public or relays by messenger happen to Dryden and Lee's protagonists while they are alone. Oedipus begins seriously to doubt his identity, for example, not by publicly questioning a messenger but by talking privately with Jocasta (Act Three, pp. 394–98), and in the play's most emotionally harrowing scene we do not just hear about his self-blinding and his confrontation of Jocasta—we actually see them together (Act Five, pp. 418–21). Their exchanges in that final scene together are inspired by a romantic ardor for which Sophocles supplies no precedent:

> JOCASTA. In spight of all those Crimes the cruel Gods
>   Can charge me with, I know my Innocence;
>   Know yours: 'tis Fate alone that makes us wretched,
>   For you are still my Husband.
> OEDIPUS.   Swear I am,
>   And I'll believe thee; steal into thy Arms,
>   Renew endearments, think 'em no pollutions,
>   But chaste as Spirits joys: gently I'll come,

Thus weeping blind, like dewy Night, upon thee,
And fold thee softly in my Arms to slumber.
                                (Act Five, p. 420)

The effect of such intensely private moments is to diminish
the world of the play, to focus the tragedy more sharply on
individual character.

As Jocasta testifies in the speech just quoted, Dryden and
Lee's protagonists are ever insistent about their innocence.
The Restoration Oedipus stands proudly at the farthest pos-
sible remove from Seneca's guilt-ridden Stoic. Oedipus's self-
doubts in Act Three burst forth in some of the play's few
heroic couplets:

> To you, good Gods, I make my last appeal;
> Or clear my Vertues or my Crime reveal:
> If wandring in the maze of Fate I run,
> And backward trod the paths I sought to shun,
> Impute my Errours to your own Decree;
> My hands are guilty, but my heart is free.
>   (Act Three, pp. 397–98)

Here, to all appearances, is just the tragic hero that Aristotle
envisions: Oedipus errs but errs unwittingly. Dryden's
preface, however, indicates a hero of a higher order than Aris-
totle's "man who is neither a paragon of virtue and justice nor
undergoes the change to misfortune through any real badness
or wickedness." Corneille may claim to have copied Sopho-
cles, Dryden says. "The truth is, he miserably fail'd in the
Character of his Hero: if he desir'd that *Oedipus* should be
pitied, he shou'd have made him a better man. He forgot that
Sophocles had taken care to shew him in his first entrance, a
just, a merciful, a successful, a Religious Prince; and, in short,
a Father of his Country: instead of these he has drawn him
suspicious, designing, more anxious of keeping the *Theban*
Crown, than solicitous for the safety of his People . . ." (p.
351). All such blemishes have been removed from Dryden and
Lee's Oedipus, who enters the play "in *Triumph*" (Act One,
p. 364), the perfect foil to Creon, whose political plots and
lusty devices have opened the play.

Oedipus leaves the play, not by going into exile, but by committing suicide in a theatrical gesture of "triumph" equally as grand as his entrance. Appearing at a window in an unspecified place "above," Oedipus hurls himself to earth in a sweep of celestial images:

> *Jocasta!* lo, I come,
> O *Laius, Labdacus,* and all you Spirits
> Of the *Cadmean* Race, prepare to meet me,
> All weeping rang'd along the gloomy Shore:
> Extend your Arms t'embrace me; for I come;
> May all the Gods too from their Battlements
> Behold, and wonder at a Mortal's daring
> And, when I knock the Goal of dreadful Death,
> Shout and applaud me with a clap of Thunder:
> Once more, thus wing'd by horrid Fate, I come
> Swift as a falling Meteor; lo, I flye,
> And thus go downwards, to the darker Sky.
>
> (Act Five, p. 426)

This mortal who dares the gods, this knight who jousts with Death, belongs more among the demigods of epic poetry than among the mortals of tragic drama. The hero of tragedy ought, in Dryden's view, to be a Hero: "it is necessary that the hero of the play be not a villain," Dryden maintains. "As for a perfect character of virtue, it never was in nature, and therefore there can be no imitation of it; but there are allays of frailty to be allowed for the chief persons, yet so that the good which is in them shall outweigh the bad, and consequently leave room for punishment on the one side, and pity on the other."[45] Aristotle had in mind a mixture of good and evil close to the circumstances of actual men; Dryden wants just enough evil to set the good off to histrionic advantage.

In addition to these changes in theme and characterization Dryden and Lee produce a third change: an alteration in the moral universe of Sophocles' play. The fate that leads Oedipus

45. Dryden, "The Grounds of Criticism in Tragedy," preface to *Troilus and Cressida* (1679), in *Of Dramatic Poesy and Other Critical Essays*, ed. George Watson (London, 1962), 1: 245.

Tyrannos into exile is as inexplicable as it is inexorable. The
fate that rules Dryden and Lee's play, cruel and arbitrary as it
may appear, is nonetheless an instance of Providence, a deci-
sion handed down by Heavenly Justice. Tiresias explains the
situation just before he conjures the ghost of Laius:

> The Gods are just.————
> But how can Finite measure Infinite?
> Reason! alas, it does not know it self!
> Yet Man, vain Man, wou'd with this short-lin'd Plummet,
> Fathom the vast Abysse of Heav'nly justice.
> What ever is, is in it's causes just;
> Since all things are by Fate. But pur-blind Man
> Sees but a part o' th' Chain; the nearest links;
> His eyes not carrying to that equal Beam
> That poizes all above.   (Act Three, p. 388)

In this Deistic universe, to embrace one's fate as an innocent
victim is to accept God's providence; to cast off one's mor-
tality, as Oedipus does, is to fathom the abyss of divine justice.
Fate in Dryden and Lee's *Oedipus* is realized in conventional
celestial images like those Oedipus uses in his death speech, in
images of "higher" powers. Those powers become a dazzling
physical fact in two spectacular set pieces. Accompanied by
effects of lightning and thunder, flats are drawn aside in Act
Two to reveal "prodigies" in the sky. Blood eclipses the
moon. Clouds that veil the heads of two figures in the sky are
suddenly drawn aside to reveal two crowns and the embla-
zoned names of Oedipus and Jocasta. Even more splendid dis-
play attends the scene borrowed from Seneca in which Tiresias
conjures and interrogates the ghost of Laius (Act Three, pp.
389–91). Unlike the self-righteous ghosts of Elizabethan and
Jacobean revenge tragedy, who point out malefactors yet alive
and demand punishment, Laius acknowledges his own guilt
in fathering Oedipus and attempting to thwart fate. Oedipus
is innocent yet guilty: "For Fate, that sent him hood-winckt
to the world, / Perform'd its work by his mistaking hands"
(Act Three, p. 391).

  In contrast with most of the play's action, which took place

on the thrust stage in front of the proscenium arch, these spec-
tacular set pieces were mounted in the illusionistic space
behind the arch. The effect would have been to create two dis-
tinct imaginative realms in the play: a distant world of fate and
an immediate world of human suffering. As we have seen, the
two different physical spaces that are assigned to these two
different imaginative realms are the physical expression of two
different ideas about drama in general: to the forestage
belongs the play-as-rhetorical-event; to the framed space
beyond the proscenium arch belongs the play-as-object.
These two contrasted conceptions of drama, we recall, explain
two different kinds of physical space in which Renaissance
productions were mounted: in the play-as-rhetorical-event
speakers and listeners share the same organic space; in the
play-as-object the spectators are set at a geometric perspective
distance from what they see. Dryden and Lee's *Oedipus* illus-
trates the tendency for the action in Restoration drama to shift
from foreground to background, from the play-as-rhetorical-
event to the play-as-object, in moments of great thematic
importance. The prodigies in Act Two and the conjuring of
Laius's ghost in Act Three are occasions for showing off spe-
cial effects, to be sure; they also help define the moral universe
of the play.

In which imaginative realm does Oedipus's suicide take
place? The stage direction says only "*Enter* Oedipus *above*,"
and in his first speech in the scene Oedipus says,

> I've found a Window, and I thank the Gods,
> 'Tis quite unbarr'd: sure, by the distant noise,
> The height will fit my Fatal purpose well.
> (Act Five, p. 425)

Is this window "above" simply one of the openings above the
side doors at each side of the forestage? Or is it part of some
kind of structure beyond the proscenium arch? If he appears
above one of the side doors, Oedipus would be barely visible,
if at all, to spectators seated in the boxes on the same side of
the theater. If he appears beyond the proscenium arch, Oed-
ipus would be nicely echoing the celestial special effects of the

two earlier set pieces in using a meteor image just before he *"flings himself from the Window"* (Act Five, p. 426). If these practical and thematic considerations do indeed suggest action beyond the arch, the play ends by conjoining the two separate imaginative realms that have been set in tragic opposition from the start: the "foreground" of the suffering hero and the "background" of his fate. "Terrour and pity this whole Poem sway; / The mightiest Machines that can mount a Play" proclaims Dryden's epilogue (p. 427). Until the final scene the two different imaginative realms of the play have laid separate claims on those two Aristotelian emotions: the two great set pieces inspire "terrour" at the enormity of Oedipus's fate, the intimate scenes between Oedipus and Jocasta on the forestage invite "pity" for his undeserved suffering. Thus divided between "foreground" and "background," phobos and eleos figure not as the poised opposites that Aristotle describes, but as separate emotions felt for separate objects in the play. Altogether admirable in his status as an epic hero, Dryden and Lee's Oedipus abrogates no universal law and hence provokes none of the fear with which we regard such laws. As an epic hero, Oedipus may inspire the learned neoclassicist's admiration, but in his circumstantial downfall he engages one emotion only: the country cousin's simple-minded pity.

From Dryden and Lee's epic notions of tragedy few traditional subjects could be more remote than Thyestes eating his sons. Only in the third generation, with Agamemnon and Menelaus, did the House of Pelops pass from primitive myth to characters and situations recognizably human. Yet it was this "first-generation" myth that John Crowne brought to the stage of the Drury Lane Theater in 1680. No cast list survives, nor does any diary entry describe the production, but Crowne had a sure eye and ear for what would attract audiences. His comedy *The Country Wit* (1675) was a favorite of Charles II, and his heroic play *The Destruction of Jerusalem*, in two parts, scored a phenomenal success three seasons before he brought Thyestes' gruesome feast to the London stage. Fragments from Sophocles' play on the subject survive (would his

Thyestes have summoned Oedipus's self-possessed dignity, or would he have suffered the physical anguish of Philoctetes?), but it was to Seneca's *Thyestes* that Crowne looked for the general disposition of his plot and for a third of his play's speeches. The one great liability of Seneca's text for modern staging—there are no women's parts at all—Crowne overcame by inventing the role of Aerope, Atreus's long-suffering wife, and by adding a subplot that brings together Atreus's daughter Antigone and Thyestes' son Philisthenes in an ill-fated romance.[46]

Crowne found in Seneca's *Thyestes* numerous opportunities for the grand set pieces that had carried *The Destruction of Jerusalem* to its success. Every act has at least one spectacular moment. Seneca's opening scene, in which a Fury summons the ghost of Tantalus from the Underworld, positively demands a display of special effects. Crowne compresses the dialogue and casts the scene as a dream vision that torments Atreus, who is discovered lying asleep when the scene draws. Act Two brings to the stage an event only described in Seneca, the fetching of the golden ram that is the "Antient Signe of Soveraign Power" in Argos. In Act Three the scene draws to reveal Aerope decoratively manacled in prison; later Thyestes makes his first entry from a practicable cave in a desert. Act Four treats the audience to a temple location first for the sumptuous wedding of Antigone and Philisthenes, complete with music, and moments later for Philisthenes' arrest and equally sumptuous murder. Nor does Crowne disappoint the audience's expectations about Thyestes' banquet. Events that are only described by a messenger in Seneca are shown onstage in Crowne, accompanied by special effects of a collapsing table and lightning and thunder.

The events in Seneca's *Thyestes* may be spectacularly horrible, but the text is even more improbable, even more beset with unstageable action and narrative gaps, than most of Seneca's other plays. After taking advantage of all the play's occa-

46. John Crowne, *Thyestes / A Tragedy* (London, 1681). Citations for quotations are given in the text. The play's only known performance is calendared in *The London Stage*, 1: 285–86.

sions for special effects, Crowne had to face the problem of making ethical and aesthetic sense of some rather boringly wicked characters and some decidedly bizarre events. Crowne improved on Seneca in exactly the same three ways that Dryden and Lee improved on Sophocles: by playing up the romantic interest, by heightening the heroic character of the protagonists, and by restructuring the moral universe of the play.

Totally absent from Seneca's original, love becomes a formidable force in Crowne's adaptation. Most obviously that force enters the play in the romance of Antigone and Philisthenes, who attempt unsuccessfully to flee the kingdom and the family enmity that blocks their marriage. "Our warring Fathers never ventur'd more / For bitter hate, than we for innocent love," says Antigone just before the young lovers are captured (Act Two, p. 14). In addition to the contrast it provides to the malevolence of Atreus and Thyestes, the romantic subplot also helps make more probable Thyestes' decision to return from exile. In Seneca, Atreus sends his own two sons to persuade Thyestes to come home; in Crowne, Atreus captures Philisthenes, easily dupes the naive young lover with a show of reconciliation, and sends the son off with the added prospect of marrying Antigone if he persuades his father to return. With Philisthenes goes Atreus' wise counselor Peneus, who secretly has been aiding the exiled Thyestes and thus also has the exiled brother's trust.

The rule of romantic passion in Crowne's *Thyestes* extends far beyond Antigone and Philisthenes, however. In Seneca, Thyestes' motives seem to have been primarily political. He ravished Aerope, so Atreus implies, mainly to gain her aid in stealing the golden ram, the token of rule in the House of Pelops. "What's on a Brother Villany to act, / On him Justice is," complains Seneca's Atreus in John Wright's translation of 1674.

> What hellish Fact
> Hath he not try'd? what scapes him? he his own
> By Whoredom made my Wife, by Theft my Throne.

By such base frauds he gain'd the Antient Signe
Of Soveraign Power, and next this house of mine.
. . .
This bold attempting Trayter, having made
My Wife a Party, hence that beast convey'd.

"From this," Atreus concludes, "springs all our mutual
strife."[47] The cause of Atreus's anger in Crowne, on the other
hand, is less political than sexual. Crowne provides a scene in
which Antigone seeks to soften Atreus's wrath by bringing in
the infants Agamemnon and Menelaus, sons whose parentage
he now doubts. "I was not always thus," he tells Antigone as
he orders her to take the children away,

> this hellish mind
> Was the Creation of that cursed woman;
> Whom yet I love, so rank a Fool am I,
> And for her sake, her sin-begotten brood,
> For which loathe my self; away with 'em.
>   (Act One, pp. 6–7)

The mental anguish that Aerope suffers in prison also takes
a sexual form. While Antigone is visiting her there, the queen
suddenly lapses into madness, seizing her daughter and imag-
ining Antigone to be "a Whore / That comes to get my Hus-
band from my Arms": "Some Water there! I'm burnt out o'
my Bed, / My Husbands Arms, by a hot flaming whore" (Act
Three, p. 25). Even the romance of Antigone and Philisthenes
becomes tainted with brute sexuality. The chorus sung by the
priests at the young couple's wedding is filled with images of
tender innocence; but the musical offering at the wedding
banquet, Crowne's grimly ironic occasion for Thyestes' feast,
is as smutty as anything in Restoration comedy. Summon
Philisthenes to join in the revelry, asks Thyestes, unaware that
he is drinking his son's blood. Philisthenes "waits upon the
Bride," Atreus explains, just before we hear a song detailing,
stanza by stanza, blow by blow, a bride and groom's first

---

47. Seneca, *Thyestes*, 220–24, 234–36, trans. John Wright (London, 1674),
pp. 22–23.

gamesome and prematurely ejaculatory attempts at making
love:

> To deeper Play, they now begin,
> The happy young man's hand is in,
> Both have stak'd down all their joys,
> But she loses, for she cryes:
> See! she cryes! oh! see she cryes!
> But now the Bride, oh! tempting sight!
> Has won her lapful of delight,
> To deeper Play, she urges on;
> But, alas! his stakes are gone,
> But, alas! his stakes are gone.   (fol. A1)

It is on this note that Atreus reveals just what Thyestes has
been drinking, and the scene draws to reveal Philisthenes'
mangled body in the temple.

Sexual passion, not political ambition, is what Thyestes
himself sees as the cause of his treachery. Seneca's first act,
with Tantalus and the Fury, leaves no doubt that the horrible
events to come are part of the ancestral curse that hangs over
the House of Pelops, the sins of mythic fathers being visited
upon mortal children. In Crowne's play, as we have seen, Tan-
talus and the Fury serve the much smaller purpose of adding
to Atreus's sexual torment. Thyestes, too, acts in his own
capacity, not as a cipher in an ancestral plot but, by his own
account, primarily out of sexual desire. When he first enters
the play in Act Three, Thyestes muses in soliloquy over the
events that have brought him to exile in a desert cave: "Aston-
ishment! Confusion! how came I / To be the horrid Villain
that I was?" It was not Nature, else his evil would have erupted
sooner. Perhaps, then, it was Custom, the fact that he lived in
the very "Element of sin, my Brother's Court."

> No. 'twas not that; I was the first that brought
> Incest and Treason to my Brother's Court.
> From my own self came all my Villany;
> Had I not been a Dunghill, Beauty might
> Have shin'd as wholesomely on me, as others.
> I loath, detest my self, and flye mankind,

Counting the worst of men too good for me.
(Act Three, p. 30)

Significantly, Thyestes refers to his villainy in past tense, for he enters Crowne's play already repentant. His lonely exile figures as the religious penance of a hermit. Seneca's Thyestes, by contrast, confesses his guilt not in the confidentiality of a soliloquy but only in the presence of Atreus—and then probably for the political advantage that reconciliation will give him.

Crowne has effected, then, major changes in Seneca's characterizations of the two brothers. Seneca makes them equally guilty, partners in a pattern of corruption that spans three generations; Crowne draws a contrast between them. Thyestes repents; Atreus remains thoroughly duplicitous and unrepentant to the end. Crowne, however, adds color to this simple black-and-white picture by giving Atreus very good reasons for acting as he does. In Seneca, Atreus is evil by nature; in Crowne he is a once-loving brother who has been corrupted by Thyestes' villainy. If Thyestes plays one of the heroes who so conveniently undergo a change of heart in the tragicomedies of Beaumont and Fletcher, Atreus plays Hamlet, a wronged idealist whose revenge destroys his moral integrity. Like Hamlet and the other heroes of Jacobean revenge tragedy, Crowne's Atreus arranges his revenge as part of a court festival, in this case the wedding feast for Antigone and Philisthenes. He even shares the Jacobean revengers' melancholy view of mankind. Crowne's Atreus walks off the stage uttering an atheistic manifesto worthy of Tourneur:

> Man is a vagabond both poor and proud,
> He treads on beasts who give him Cloaths and Food.
> But the Gods catch him wheresoe're he lurks,
> Whip him, and set him to all painful works.
> And yet he brags he shall be crown'd when dead,
> Were ever Princes in a Bridewell bred?
> Nothing is sinfully begot but he;
> Can baseborn Bastards lawful Soverains be?
> That Tyrant then does best, who uses worst,
> A mutinous Impostour, so accurst:

I'le breed with care these Boys for mischiefs born,
That men may feel new Rods when th'old is worn.
(Act Five, pp. 55–56)

Whatever sympathy Atreus has been able to garner as a
potential Hamlet, this speech, the very last words in Crowne's
play, is surely enough to discredit his claims as an innocent
victim. Moments before, Aerope has articulated a rather more
appealing worldview. Walking into the wedding feast to dis-
cover the body of Antigone, who has stabbed herself amid an
eloquent speech and joined her husband in death, Aerope finds
a dagger and follows her daughter's example, both in taking
her own life and affirming her faith in an ultimately just uni-
verse:

> . . . if I undeserv'd have born all this,
> Then build a Heaven fit for my reward,
> And I will lay the final Foundation Stone.
> Thus, thus, thus. . . .   (Act Five, p. 55)

And with that she proceeds to stab Thyestes. Aerope's murder
of Thyestes and her own suicide moments later thus become
a gesture of confidence in final justice, in hell for the guilty
and heaven for the innocent. Such a view of the universe,
needless to say, has no spokesman in Seneca's play, which ends
with Thyestes and Atreus both alive, vowing yet further
revenge on one another. There is not even a final chorus to
point a moral and round things off.

Thyestes may deserve punishment, but he confesses his
guilt in terms contrite enough to forestall judgment. Thyestes
may indeed deserve to die, but he hardly deserves so atrocious
a punishment as drinking his own son's blood. We end up
feeling sorry for him. Atreus, on the other hand, may deserve
sympathy as a wronged idealist, but he achieves his revenge
only by sacrificing Philisthenes, the altogether innocent hero
of the romantic subplot. Shouldering this guilt, spouting a
blasphemous view of the universe, he leaves the play a thor-
oughly contemptible villain. Crowne's moral polarization of
the play's heroes effects an emotional polarization of the audi-
ence's feelings: we feel pity for Thyestes, terror at the enor-

mity of Atreus's revenge. As with Dryden and Lee's *Oedipus*, the two emotions work, not as the poised opposites that Aristotle describes, but as separate emotions attached to separate objects in the play. Standing before the larger-than-life tragic heroes of the Restoration stage, whose unbounded passion commands an audience's awe, we are a world away from from the morally culpable heroes of Seneca, Sophocles, and Euripides in the great halls of the colleges of Oxford and Cambridge and the London inns of court. In every instance the translators and adaptors have felt impelled to decide moral and political issues one way or the other. Neville's Oedipus and Dryden and Lee's Oedipus represent two opposite ways of simplifying the issues and thus avoiding conflict: Neville castigates Oedipus as a parricide who breaches the restraints that make social life possible; Dryden and Lee laud him as an epic hero who transcends human limitations. Oedipus's timeless fascination lies somewhere in between.

In Aristotle's view, the power of tragedy resides in the way it sets up the conflicting emotions of eleos and phobos and holds them in a state of tension. We feel this conflict, Hegel says, because tragedy presents the conflict between two opposed systems of value, both of them with claims on our allegience. In particular, we recognize a conflict between the autonomy of individuals and the rule of law. Sixteenth- and seventeenth-century productions of classical tragedy show us a series of attempts to deny any such contradiction. Restoration audiences, no less than sixteenth-century academic audiences, were unwilling to tolerate ambiguities, either in the tragic protagonist's situation or in the emotions they would entertain about him. Only in the Elizabethan and Jacobean public theater, with its freedom from the dogmatic interests of any particular social group, could the tensions inherent in tragedy be explored and exploited. Despite its stylistic crudities, *Titus Andronicus* comes closer to the essence of classical tragedy than any sixteenth- or seventeenth-century English production of an ancient script.

EPILOGUE

IF SULPICIUS wrote an epilogue for the papal performance of Seneca's *Hippolytus* in the 1480s, it has not survived. But that's all one: the revolution in dramatic imagination touched off by Pomponius's schoolboys has not come to an end. Critics like George Steiner may have announced the "death" of tragedy, the bleak world we have made for ourselves politically, intellectually, and spiritually may seem to preclude comedy, but "tragic" and "comic" remain reference points that we look to still for mapping the world of human experience. We use those terms both to ally ourselves with the past and to distinguish ourselves from it. The nihilistic plays of Genet are, we say, "*black* comedy." "Tragic" remains a dust-jacket buzzword, the highest accolade that critics can bestow on a new work of fiction that manages to combine emotional sympathy with intellectual rigor. We persist in defining ourselves in terms first articulated by a culture that flourished more than two thousand years ago. To take the drama of the past and to use it in such a way is a distinctively Renaissance idea. In this respect we are the direct heirs of Pomponius, Alexander Nowell, Shakespeare, Jonson, Heywood, Dryden, and all the other producers and adaptors of ancient playscripts in the sixteenth and seventeenth centuries.

More than any other era in recorded history, ours is an age of cultural relativism. In music, in painting, in literature, in drama more works of art from more past eras are alive with us than they have been with any other civilization in history, not excluding Hellenistic Greece, which codified and recorded the scripts of Sophocles and Euripides so that they could be rediscovered by Renaissance scholars. Unlike Hellenistic Greece, unlike Renaissance Europe, we grant each past era its own identity, its own values. Tom Stoppard shares the active repertory with Sophocles and Shakespeare. We would never dress Terence's Gnatho in a Spanish cloak nor Thraso in a coat with St. Andrew's crosses before and behind. Or if we did, we would be making a historically self-conscious point in doing so. We take each era's art on its own terms.

Or so we fancy. The productions of ancient drama reconstructed in this book teach us nothing more forcefully than how self-deceiving it is to think that there is one right way of understanding the art of the past. From 1500 to 1700, productions of Sophocles and Seneca, of Aristophanes and Terence changed radically, reflecting the changing imaginative needs of the people who acted and the people who watched. The fine balance that Roman comedy strikes between satire and romance seems particularly vulnerable to the deconstructions of sixteenth- and seventeenth-century actors and audiences. To judge from the social context, it was the romantic side of Plautus's and Terence's comedies that dominated productions at the Tudor court. Extravagant moves in the game of courtly love, Henry VIII's masked entry as an amorous shepherd and a "Triumph of Venus," framed the production of Plautus's *Menaechmi* that Cardinal Wolsey sponsored in 1526–1527. In the very different social context of Westminster School, the same plays were produced to enhance the scripts' satiric side, as Alexander Nowell's prologues for Terence's *Adelphi* and *Eunuchus* testify. A restored balance between romance and satire in Shakespeare's *The Comedy of Errors* gave way to a bourgeois redefinition of romance in Heywood's *The Captives* and *The English Traveler*. In Sedley's Terence and Dryden's Plautus romance was redefined once again. The very audacity and sexual license satirized by Nowell's schoolboys became the romantic myth of the Restoration rake.

Productions of Sophocles, Euripides, and Seneca show us the same capacity of ancient scripts to reflect the values and concerns of modern viewers. Whatever else tragedy may or may not do, it forces a dramatist and his audience to examine their assumptions about the relationship between individual action and the world in which the individual acts. Which defines which? Is the hero a victim of external forces? Or a defiant individual who does his best to remake the world in his own image? Or something between the two? One crucial passage in *Oedipus* can help us sort out the markedly different

ways in which Renaissance humanists, Restoration drama-
tists, modern translators, and Sophocles himself have
answered these questions.

Surely one of the greatest moments in all of Western drama
is contained in the three lines Oedipus speaks when he first
accepts his fate. Blinded in rage by his own hands, Oedipus
returns to the stage to face the Chorus of Theban elders, who
both tell him of their pity and shrink from him in horror. It is
not just his gory visage that repels them but their fear that
touching him will quite literally "pollute" them, that his curse
can be communicated like a disease. "Do not fear to touch
me," Oedipus assures them, "for no mortal but myself can
bear my own evils" (1414–15).[1] The precise word Sophocles
chooses here, *kaka*, "evils," is just ambiguous enough to
define a listener's or a translator's ethical prejudice. The evils
I have done? Or the evils I must bear? Advisedly perhaps,
Sophocles does not say, though the context with its homeo-
pathic sense of evil as pollution and with the strategic verb
pherein (cf. Latin *ferre*), "to bear up," rather suggests passive
acceptance than active cause.

How a translator renders the passage is bound to reflect his
view of the hero's fate. Thus Dudley Fitts and Robert Fitz-
gerald (1939) suggest a humbled, culpable Oedipus who sup-
plicates the Chorus rather than commands them: "Come, *lead*
me. You need not fear to touch me. / Of all men, I alone can
bear this *guilt*."[2] Yeats's Oedipus (1928), on the other hand,
seems much more a passive victim: "Come near, *condescend* to
lay your hands upon *a wretched man*; listen, do not fear. My
plague can touch no man but me."[3] Yeats's choice of "plague"

---

1. *Sophocles*, trans. and ed. F. Storr, Loeb Library, Vol. 2 (Cambridge,
Mass., and London, 1962): "tama gar kaka / oudeis hoios te plen emou
pherein broton" (1414–15). Storr himself renders *kaka* as "guilt." On crime as
pollution, cf. Brian Vickers, *Toward Greek Tragedy: Drama, Myth, Society*
(London, 1973), pp. 138–56.

2. Reprinted in *The Oedipus Cycle*, trans. D. Fitts and R. Fitzgerald (New
York, 1969), p. 72. In this and other quotations the emphasis given key
phrases is my own.

3. Reprinted in *Sophocles' King Oedipus*, trans. W. B. Yeats, ed. B. Rajan
(New York, 1969), pp. 96–97.

EPILOGUE

for "kaka" nicely catches the sense of evil as pollution while it reminds the listener that Oedipus has been the cause of the plague that has decimated the city. "Condescend" and "wretched" emphasize the hero's passive resignation. David Grene (1942), by contrast, allows Oedipus at least some of the proud and defiant acceptance that we find in *Oedipus at Colonus*, while deftly avoiding the issue of personal guilt or innocence: "Approach and deign to touch me / for all my wretchedness, and do not fear. / No man but I can bear *my evil doom*."[4] "Approach" instead of "come," "deign to touch me" instead of Fitts and Fitzgerald's "you need not fear to touch me" or Yeats's "condescend to lay your hands upon a wretched man"—in Grene's choices we hear the commanding voice of the earlier Oedipus, perhaps even some of the proud sarcasm of the Oedipus who ends his wanderings in the grove at Colonus. Robert Fagles's translation (1982) daringly if obliquely alludes to a sacrificial victim more immediately significant to modern audiences than Oedipus is:

> Closer,
> it's all right. Touch the man of sorrow.
> Do. Don't be afraid. My troubles are mine
> and I am the only man alive who can sustain them.[5]

"He is despised and rejected of men, a man of sorrows, and acquainted with grief" (Isaiah 54:3): Fagles's Oedipus fills the mythic role of Messiah. The Athenian citizens, fearing to touch the man who is saving them from disease and death, become doubting Thomases. Which is the "correct" Oedipus? To the extent that drama is an event, an interaction among actors and audience at a particular historical moment, all of them are. That, indeed, is a measure of Sophocles' timeless stature.

Compared to contemporary translators, sixteenth- and seventeenth-century producers were simply more obvious in

4. Reprinted in *Greek Tragedies*, ed. D. Grene and R. Lattimore (Chicago, 1968), 1: 171.

5. Sophocles, *The Three Theban Plays*, trans. Robert Fagles, Penguin Edition (New York, 1984), p. 244.

acting on their prejudices. Seneca's Oedipus, as we have seen, voices anxiety about his fate from the opening lines of the play; at the end he accepts the double guilt of not only murdering his father but causing his mother's suicide:

> But now I have slain twice; I am more guilty
> Than I had feared to be; my crimes have brought
> My mother to her death. Phoebus, you lied!
> I have done more than was set down for me
> By evil destiny.[6]

Guilty and yet a victim of fate: this is an ethical ambiguity that Alexander Neville cannot accept. In his acting script of 1563, Neville elaborates Oedipus's final speech into a morality-play villain's confession:

> O cursed head: O wicked wight, whom all men deadly hate.
> O Beast, what meanst thou still to live in this unhappy state?
> . . .
> The skies doe blush and are ashamed, at these thy mischiefes great:
> So maist thou yet in tract of time due paynes and vengeaunce have
> For thy mischevous lyfe. Thus, thus, the Gods themselves decree.[7]

The kind of Oedipus we might expect from Burckhardt's romantic view of the Renaissance—an awesomely proud, sublimely self-possessed individual toppled by the petty forces of fate—we find, certainly not in the condemned murderer that Renaissance humanists actually saw in Oedipus, but in the neoclassical epic hero of Dryden and Lee. When Oedipus leaps to his death at the end of their play, we are meant to feel, not righteous satisfaction that a malefactor has been punished, but elegiac regret that the world cannot accommodate such intransigent greatness: "May all the Gods too from their Battlements / Behold, and wonder at a Mortal's daring."[8] The variety of ways in which translators and adaptors have handled

6. Seneca, *Oedipus*, 1044–46, trans. E. F. Watling in Seneca, *Four Tragedies* (Harmondsworth and Baltimore, 1966), p. 251.
7. Trans. Alexander Neville in *Seneca His Tenne Tragedies*, ed. Thomas Newton, intro. T. S. Eliot (London, 1927), p. 230.
8. John Dryden, *The Dramatic Works*, ed. Montague Summers, Vol. 4 (1932; repr. New York, 1968): 426.

Oedipus's final speech reveals how very difficult it has been even to recognize an ethical ambiguity in his situation, much less to accept it.

The larger lesson that these productions teach us is simple: drama is most vital when most susceptive to the ambiguities that beset us. Since the sixteenth century, comedy and tragedy have kept such a hold on Western imagination not because they somehow fix experience in permanent form but because they help us to come to terms with *changing* experience. Tragedy and comedy were rediscovered in the Renaissance because it was just then that they *needed* to be rediscovered: they developed as ways of coping with contradictions at a time when contradictions were rife. There was, to start with, basic disagreement about what a play is, about how audiences are related to actors in physical space, about how the audience defines its collective identity and agrees on a code of values. Onstage those contradictions about practical matters took the form of contradictions about the nature of man. Sixteenth- and seventeenth-century productions of classical comedy show us a variety of attempts to reconcile two conflicting impulses toward the incongruities we see about us: the impulse to wish them away in romance and the impulse to stand back and laugh at them in satire. Productions of classical tragedy show us a variety of attempts to reconcile two different views of ourselves as social creatures: an inside view of ourselves as autonomous individuals and an outside view of ourselves as subjects of all the forces that constrict human will—law, society, fate, God. Most of the sixteenth- and seventeenth-century productions of Greek and Roman drama that we have reconstructed in this book try to pose simple answers to these difficult, ultimately unanswerable, questions. But Aristophanes, Plautus, and Terence, Sophocles, Euripides, and Seneca could not be acclimatized to the modern world quite so easily. They challenged Christian assumptions about human experience, just as certainly as they challenged the staging conventions of medieval drama. Out of that dynamic between ancient scripts and modern experience emerged plays that fascinate still, plays like Shakespeare's *The Comedy of Errors* and *Titus Andronicus*. Pomponius's dream of restoring classical drama to its original importance has indeed been realized, but in ways that a humanist could hardly have imagined in the 1480s.

INDEX

In addition to providing cross references to particular people, plays, and places, this index offers alternative ways of analyzing the productions discussed in the book. Thus, under the heading *issues* are gathered all references to chastity, justice, will, and fifteen other concerns, enabling a reader to compare how particular issues are presented differently earlier in the historical period than they are later, and how they are handled in comedy as opposed to tragedy. Similar large headings catalog *characters, emotions,* and *motives.*

LIBRARY OF CONGRESS CATALOGING-IN-PUBLICATION DATA

SMITH, BRUCE R., 1946–
ANCIENT SCRIPTS & MODERN EXPERIENCE ON THE ENGLISH STAGE,
1500–1700 / BY BRUCE R. SMITH.
P. CM.
INCLUDES INDEX.
ISBN 0-691-06739-2 (ALK. PAPER)
1. CLASSICAL DRAMA—APPRECIATION—GREAT BRITAIN.
2. THEATER—GREAT BRITAIN—HISTORY—16TH CENTURY.
3. THEATER—GREAT BRITAIN—HISTORY—17TH CENTURY. 4. TRAGEDY.
5. COMEDY. 6. GREAT BRITAIN—CIVILIZATION—CLASSICAL
INFLUENCES. I. TITLE. II. TITLE: ANCIENT SCRIPTS AND MODERN
EXPERIENCE ON THE ENGLISH STAGE, 1500–1700.
PA3238.S55   1988
792'.0941—DC19   87-37408
                                                                CIP

BRUCE R. SMITH IS PROFESSOR OF ENGLISH, GEORGETOWN
UNIVERSITY.